WHY WE FIGHT

Dedication

To the ancestors of my native Charente and Poitou, indomitable old Gauls.

To Gilles Soulas and Georges Hupin.

To Lisa-Isabella, *primavera di bellezza*, daughter of the Roman Louve, and to all those of my dear Italy.

In memory of the Countess Hella von Westarp, high representative of Europe's true aristocracy, who resisted the barbarians and was martyred, sacrificing her blood to save that of her people.

To everyone, from Brittany's Aber Wrac'h to the Bering Straits, from Norway's Nordkapp to Greece's Xhora Sphakion, who keeps the flame of resistance alive.

Ac eis quos Imperium imperat, quibus honoris nomen fides dicitur.

GUILLAUME FAYE

WHY WE FIGHT

MANIFESTO OF THE EUROPEAN RESISTANCE

ARKTOS
LONDON 2025

ARKTOS
⊕ Arktos.com   fb.com/Arktos   arktosmedia   arktosjournal

Copyright © 2025 by Arktos Media Ltd.

Original title: *Pourquoi nous combattons: Manifeste de la Résistance européenne* (Éditions de L'Æncre, Paris, 2001).

German edition, *Wofür wir Kämpfen*, published in 2006 by Ahnenrad der Moderne.

First English edition published in 2011 by Arktos Media Ltd.

All rights reserved. No part of this book may be reproduced or utilised in any form or by any means (whether electronic or mechanical), including photocopying, recording or by any information storage and retrieval system, without permission in writing from the publisher.

ISBN
978-1-917646-47-5 (Paperback)
978-1-917646-48-2 (Hardback)
978-1-917646-49-9 (Ebook)

Editing
John Morgan, Matthew Peters, and Constantin von Hoffmeister

Layout
Tor Westman

CONTENTS

Forewords

Prophet of the Fourth Age vii
It's About the Primordial Fire xxi
A Note from the Editor. xxix

1. Preface and Precaution

Unite on the Basis of Clear Ideas Against the Common Enemy 1
Beware of False Friends 4

2. Preliminary Elements

The Logic of Decline 14
    Ethnic Colonisation 15
    The Blocked Society 20
France or Europe? 24
Economic Principles 30
    For Nuclear, Not Petroleum Energy 30
    The Imposture of the 'New Economy' 38
    Toward a Planetary Economic Crisis? 40

3. Strategic Principles

America and Islam Against Europe .45
The Dangers of European 'Disarmament' 48
Notions of the 'Menace from the South' and the 'Domestic Front' 49
Toward a Eurosiberian Strategic Doctrine: The 'Giant Hedgehog' 51

4. Metapolitical Dictionary

From *Aesthetics* to *Xenophilia* 55

5. Conclusion

Why Are We Fighting? 261
Index 271

'For some, I'm a dream, for others a nightmare.'

— Merlin the Magician

'A beautiful night summons a night of wolves.'

— Pierre Vial

'We're going to prevail because we're already dead.'

— Olivier Carré

'So I've been told: I must avenge myself.
With that, deep in the woods,
The wolf carried it off and ate it,
Without further ado.'

— Jean de La Fontaine

TRANSLATOR'S FOREWORD

PROPHET OF THE FOURTH AGE

'History is the realisation of unrealisable ideas.'

— GUILLAUME FAYE[1]

Are these the last days of Europe?

There's no hyperbole here.[2] If major changes are not soon forthcoming, her peoples face the extinction of their civilisation and their kind. Already she is overrun by millions of alien, mainly Islamic colonisers from the Global South, who have begun to replace her native peoples and supplant her order; she is subject to an American overlord whose world system requires her de-Europeanisation and 'globalisation'; she is misgoverned by technocrats, career politicians, and plutocratic elites indifferent to her blood and spirit. And to all this (to which much could be added), her defenders — those who sense the danger and strive to resist it — are disunited, at times even unaware of who or what exactly they are fighting. Within a generation, 'Europe' may go the way of ancient Sumer or the Incas.

---

1 Guillaume Faye, *Nouvelle discours à la nation européenne* (Paris: L'Æncre, 1999), p. 213.
2 Walter Laqueur, *The Last Days of Europe: Epitaph for an Old Continent* (New York: St. Martin's Griffin, 2009).

Guillaume Faye — the one-time *enfant terrible* of France's Nouvelle Droite — believes 'the European Resistance' has the resources and energies to defeat the Continent's enemies, *if* its various elements and tendencies should form a united front around clear ideas and a common ideology. That is, if her defenders would agree to concentrate their forces. His manifesto, and especially its metapolitical dictionary, aspire to lay the metapolitical foundations for such a unification — by designating and defining the key ideas and ideology that will make it possible.

*

Why We Fight (as *Pourquoi nous combattons*) appeared a decade ago, in 2001.

In a few places it shows its age, but much of it seems prescient in its understanding of the challenges confronting Europe's defenders and the ideas that might overcome them. These 'defenders', whom Faye collectively labels the 'resistance', include in their ranks *néo-droitiers*, regionalists, identitarians, traditionalists, and certain other anti-system tendencies upholding the primacy of their particular ethnic distillation of the larger European heritage. A decade after *Why We Fight*, these oppositional elements (the 'resistance') have finally begun to emerge from their political ghetto, as they hesitantly mobilise in the streets and, more confidently, merge with the national-populist formations affecting the present fate of parliamentary coalitions.[3] It's fitting, perhaps, that the English translation of Faye's manifesto should appear in this period of rising anti-system agitation.

---

3   See Fondation Robert Schuman, 'L'Union européenne face aux défies de l'extrémisme identitaire' (12 July 2010), available at *Fondation Robert Schuman* (www.robert-schuman.eu/questions-d-europe/0177-l-union-europeenne-face-aux-defis-de-l-extremisme-identitaire). Also Stéphane François, 'Réflexions sur le mouvement "identitaire"' (3 March 2009), available at Fragments sur les Temps Présents (tempspresents.wordpress.com/2009/03/03/reflexions-sur-le-mouvement-identitaire-12/).

Influenced by the cultural/ideological forces animating the mounting opposition, *Why We Fight* followed a series of works that had earlier lit up the resistance's imagination. These were the essays collected in *L'Archéofuturisme* (1998)[4]; the second, augmented edition of *Nouveau discours à la nation européenne* (1999); and *La Colonisation de l'Europe* (2000)[5] (whose characterisation of Europe's Islamisation, in anticipating '9/11' and other Muslim assaults, earned Faye and his publisher a 300,000-franc fine and a year's suspended sentence).

Why We Fight would be followed by a series of similarly topical and prophetic works: *Avant-guerre*[6] (2003), *La Convergence des catastrophes* (2004),[7] and *Le Coup d'État mondial* (2004).[8] But then, in 2007, the release of Faye's most controversial book, *La Nouvelle question juive*[9] (in which the Jews' place in European life was reconceived in light of the Islamic invasion), set off a heated debate in identitarian and nationalist ranks — eventually bringing his role as the resistance's leading advocate to an end.[10]

If Faye's decision in the period leading up to 2007 — to affiliate with the Zionist bloc in its 'struggle' against Islam — discredited him with certain identitarians,[11] it took away nothing from his earlier contribution to the 'resistance' — which seems especially the case with *Why*

---

4   Translated as *Archeofuturism: European Visions of the Post-Catastrophic Age* (London: Arktos, 2010).
5   Translated as *The Colonisation of Europe* (London: Arktos, 2016). — Ed.
6   'Pre-War'. — Ed.
7   Translated as *Convergence of Catastrophes* (London Arktos, 2012). — Ed.
8   Translated as *A Global Coup* (London: Arktos, 2017). — Ed.
9   'The New Jewish Question'. — Ed.
10 On the links between the Zionist Right and the European, especially French, nationalist Right, see Pierre Vial, 'Grandes manoeuvres juives de séduction à l'égard de l'extrême droite européenne', in *Terre et Peuple* 44 (Summer 2010).
11 See Michael O'Meara, 'Guillaume Faye and the Jews' (31 July 2006), available at *The Occidental Quarterly Online* (www.toqonline.com/blog/guillaume-faye-and-the-jews/); and Michael O'Meara, 'The New Jewish Question of Guillaume Faye', in *The Occidental Quarterly* vol. 7, no. 3 (Fall 2007), also

We Fight, arguably the single best synthesis of the ideas and sensibilities animating the diverse parties and tendencies presently resisting Europe's decline.

*

The reception of Faye's 2007 book epitomises much of what has stifled and stunted the post-war history of European anti-liberalism.

Following V-E Day, the Right, like the rest of Europe, was ordered to Americanise. Joseph Stalin (whose Red Army won the all-important ground war) may have foiled U.S. efforts after 1945 to create a 'new world order' (forcing globalists to wait until 1989),[12] but the American conquerors nevertheless imposed their liberal-modernist system on Western and Central Europe (the system which has since evolved into the basis for the present global market order).

Traditional Right-wing formations critical of the creedal, market-centric dictates of Europe's new masters would henceforth be identified with the 'allegedly' barbaric Germans,[13] escorted offstage, and compelled to abandon whatever anti-liberal or anti-modern sentiment

---

available at *The Occidental Quarterly Online* (www.toqonline.com/archives/v7n3/7310OMearaFaye.pdf).

12 See K. R. Bolton, 'Origins of the Cold War: How Stalin Foiled a "New World Order"' (31 May 2010), available at Foreign Policy Journal (www.foreignpolicyjournal.com/2010/05/31/origins-of-the-cold-war-how-stalin-foild-a-new-world-order/).

13 'Alleged' in the sense that the Americans, Russians, and British, unlike the Germans, waged the war as altar boys — i.e., in a sense that goes beyond all reference to National Socialism. For in the spirit of liberalism's self-righteous, de-spiritualised Protestant suppositions, it inevitably treats every form of anti-liberal ideology as an inhuman malignity, whose only remedy is extermination.' See Carl L. Becker, *The Heavenly City of the Eighteenth-Century Philosophers* (New Haven: Yale University Press, 1932); Joseph de Maistre, 'Reflections on Protestantism in Its Relations to Sovereignty', in Christopher Olaf Blum (ed.), *Critics of the Enlightenment* (Wilmington: ISI Books, 2004), pp. 133–156; and Carl Schmitt, *The Concept of the Political* (Chicago: University of Chicago Press, 1996), pp. 53–58.

still influenced them — as was the case in Eastern Europe, though there the model was Russian, rather than American.

By the time the first post-war baby boomers came of age in the late '60s, it was evident that the Right (this now 'moderate' appendage of the liberal Left) was a losing proposition, having failed not only to halt the ongoing erosion of European civilisation, but having, more shamefully, joined the American system de-Europeanising Europe — betraying, in this way, the purpose of the 'political' — by failing to defend Europe's identity, legitimacy, and sovereignty.

Across the Continent in the '60s and '70s, but especially in France, there emerged tendencies endeavouring to rethink the Right project as an alternative to the prevailing U.S. system (which made the circulation of capital superior to everything, including the sacred). The most successful of these alternatives was the Groupement de Recherches et d'Études pour la Civilisation Européenne (GRECE). Its project, of which Faye was an early advocate, was 'metapolitical': i.e., conceived as a cultural/ideological struggle against the reigning liberal values and beliefs. By means of this 'Gramscianism of the Right', *Grécistes* were to create a 'counter-hegemony' to undermine the legitimacy of the subversive forces — and thus to create a climate receptive to an anti-liberal politics of reconquest.

Effective at first in arousing public debate and reviving aspects of the repressed cultural heritage, the GRECE by the mid-1980s had evolved into just another marginalised tendency. In his recently translated *Archeofuturism*,[4] Faye attributes this to its proclivity, especially pronounced in its leader, Alain de Benoist, to privilege the 'meta' in metapolitics at the expense of 'the political', which had the effect of

---

14 See Guillaume Faye. *Archeofuturism*, pp. 23–51. Also Robert Steuckers, 'Les pistes manquées de la "nouvelle droite": Pour une critique constructive' (2009), available at *Euro-Synergies* (euro-synergies.hautetfort.com/archive/2009/08/28/les-pistes-manquees-de-la-nouvelle-droite-pour-une-critique.html).

making cultural/ideological engagement a substitute for, rather than an active facet of politics.[15]

At one level, Faye's *Why We Fight* is a blistering critique of de Benoist's leadership of the GRECE. Its many negative references to 'the Right' or to 'certain Right-wing intellectuals', etc., are aimed, almost exclusively, at him and the type of politically irrelevant, often system-friendly dilettantism he has come to represent for Faye.

The book's numerous references to Pierre Vial and Robert Steuckers, on the other hand, point to what Faye considers a more viable metapolitics. A university historian and former president of the GRECE, Vial left the group in the late 1980s to join the National Front, where he organised its Terre et Peuple (Land and People) faction,[16] which helped shift the NF away from its earlier Jacobin-Reaganite nationalism and toward the socially-conscious, identitarian populism that has since made it the leading party of the French working class.[17] Steuckers, a Flemish linguist and arguably the most formidable intellectual talent to emerge from the Nouvelle Droite, is the organiser of Euro-Synergies — which synthesises and diffuses much of the most significant thought influencing European anti-liberalism.[18]

*

---

15 See Alain de Benoist, 'Les causes culturelles du changement politique' (1981) in *La Ligue de mire, 1975–1987* (Paris: La Labyrinthe, 1995); and Georges Gondinet, 'Les ambiguités du "gramscianisme du droite"' in *Totalité: Révolution et Tradition* 10 (November 1979).

16 Pierre Vial, *Une terre, un people* (Paris: Éds. Terre et Peuple, 2000). The *Terre et Peuple* website is at terreetpeuple.com.

17 Sylvain Crépon, 'Le tournant anti-capitaliste du Front National' (2006), available at Fragments sur les Temps Présents (tempspresents.wordpress.com/2010/04/25/sylvain-crepon-tournant-anti-capitaliste-du-front-national). Accessed 7 March 2011.

18 Steuckers' two websites are *Euro-Synergies*, at euro-synergies.hautetfort.com/, and *Vouloir*, at vouloir.hautetfort.com/.

'Today, as always, the cornerstone of society is a tombstone.'[19]

In assuming the inextricability of culture and politics, Faye's notion of metapolitics stems from his 'archeofuturist' philosophy, which holds that the European tradition is pre-eminently a 'revolutionary' one — constantly revolving back to the archaic sources of its form of life in order to revolve forward, toward other, original expressions of it. In Italian terms, his archeofuturism combines the revolutionary traditionalism of Julius Evola and the radical Futurism of F. T. Marinetti. Less simply said, it marries the perennial attributes of, say, the Hellenic classical heritage[20] to the most pioneering forms of European thinking and endeavour.[21] Like the primordial and the perennial, the archaic here refers not to some ancient, fossilised canon, but to the original assertion of European being, which, as an origin (an outburst or birth of being), functions as another original opening to the future — in the structuring, civilising sense distinct to Europe's *Hochkultur*.[22] It's not, as such, a traditionalism, an antiquarianism, or a reactionism — but rather a primordialism that constantly renews Europe's rooted life forms by adapting them to face the challenges that come from the future.

Opposing modernity's dysgenic values for the sake of those instincts and refinements that have historically guided Europe's destiny, Faye's archeofuturism strives — in its conception of the world — to revive the Continent's threatened identity, to pull her back from the

---

19   Guglielmo Ferrero, *Words to the Deaf: A Historian Contemplates his Age* (New York: Putnam, 1926), p. 116.

20   Faye did ten years of Graeco-Latin studies with the Jesuits, who educated the children of the high Parisian bourgeoisie.

21   A literary example of this can be found in Joyce's modernist master work, *Ulysses*, which retells the founding story of European man, utilising 'mythopoeic imagery, structural features, formal principles, and linguistic resources' taken from the earliest Greek and Irish myths. See Maria Tymoczko, *The Irish Ulysses* (Berkeley: University of California Press, 1994), p. 1.

22   German: 'high culture'. — Ed.

abyss into which she presently gazes, but, above all, to make certain she gets another chance, a fourth chance, to begin again.

*

The present counter-civilisation, whose reality-denying entertainments, obsessive consumerism, and nihilistic miscegenation have drained all meaning from our world — this liberal-modernist system that succeeded Europe's ancient and medieval civilisations — is not the 'enemy', however, for (in any political, especially Schmittian, sense) the enemy has to be someone or something ('a fighting collectivity of people') threatening imminent death.[23]

Faye also refuses a certain tendency to blame America for the Continent's vassalage and her capitulation to the North African Arabs and Sub-Saharan Blacks (the 'Beur-Blacks') colonising her native lands and exploiting her permissive society.[24]

Europe for him has no one, ultimately, but herself to blame for the policies and social practices now destroying who she is (i.e., her identity).

At the same time, and with greater conviction, Faye believes a very real flesh-and-blood enemy — *un corps étranger et parasitaire*[25] — mortally imperils Europe: the replacement populations gathered under the Prophet's banner.

America may collude with the forces of Islam to divide and weaken Europe for the sake of her global empire,[26] and liberal modernist illusions may lead European elites to believe the Islamic colonisers can

---

23 Schmitt, *The Concept of the Political*, p. 28.

24 See Michael O'Meara, 'Europe's Enemy: Islam or America?', in *The Occidental Quarterly* vol. 5, no. 3 (Fall 2005). Available at *The Occidental Quarterly Online* (toqonline.com/archives/v5n3/53-mo-faye.pdf).

25 French: 'a foreign and parasitic body'. — Ed.

26 Alexandre Del Valle, *Islam et États-Unis: Une alliance contre Europe* (Lausanne: L'Age d'Homme, 1997).

be integrated without destroying her historic family of nations — but neither of these things quite makes them an 'enemy'.

Europe's liberal-modernist elites and America's world empire, Faye argues, are 'adversaries' of Europe — they exploit and manipulate her, but pose no direct threat to her physical existence. Islam and the peoples of the Global South, in contrast, constitute precisely such a threat, for these alien forces have explicitly designated her as the enemy they intend to destroy.[27] In colonising European lands and replacing her native peoples, they have, in fact, already begun turning Europe into a *Dar-al-Islam*[28] — which is eventually going to make her into an anti-Europe.

The question of Islam also affects the sectarian divides running through the 'resistance'. Some, like *Grécistes*, look on tradition-minded Islam as a possible ally in the struggle against the destructuring forces of America's anti-European world order.[29] Allied with Muslim anti-modernists opposing Americanisation, global capitalism, and the prevailing liberal-managerial system, these *néo-droitistes*[30] assume

---

27 See Bat Ye'or, *Eurabia: The Euro-Arab Axis* (Madison: Fairleigh Dickinson University Press, 2005); also Guillaume Faye, *The Colonisation of Europe* (London: Arktos, 2016). — Ed.

28 Serge Trifkovic, *The Sword of the Prophet* (Salisbury: Regina Orthodox Press, 2007).

29 See Alain de Benoist, *Europe, Tiers monde, même combat* (Paris: Robert Laffont, 1986); more recently, 'Interview mit Alain de Benoist' in *Hier & Jetzt* 15 (14 July 2010). Cf. Martin Lichtmesz, 'Alain de Benoist unter Muslimen und Mauretaniern' (27 July 2010), available at *Sezession im Netz* (www.sezession. de/17988/alain-de-benoist-unter-muslimen-und-mauretaniern.html).

30 Bereft of a historical project and nostalgic for the good old days of the Popular Front, the Left (it still calls itself this!) continues to see Adolf Hitler lurking in the GRECE's shadow, but the establishment (which has realised much of the Left's historic project) is increasingly less critical of it. Jean-Yves Camus, in 'La Nouvelle droite: Bilan provisoire d'une école de pensée', *La Pensée* 345 (January-March 2006), now certifies it as 'system friendly'.

a stance almost antipodal to Faye's[31] — with much of the 'resistance' occupying places somewhere between their respective polarities.

Faye's argument is especially convincing in emphasising that the Barbarians crashing the City's gates pose an immediate danger of the highest priority. His view of this danger is, perhaps, more insistent than that of any other commentator. His argument is a good deal less persuasive, though, when minimising the danger that comes from within the City — i.e., the danger that comes from the European elites who have opened the City's gates to the Barbarians. It's as if the 'enemy' for him — the one who creates a state of emergency threatening everything — can only be an external (non-European) rather than an internal (European) one (though he fully acknowledges the self-destructive character of late modern society). For this reason, he sees these elites as an accessory (i.e., something secondary) to the real danger — the gate-keepers being thus less of a threat than the gate-crashers. But here again his critics have trouble distinguishing between the danger posed by the gate-keepers, who make the invasion possible by opening the City gates, and the more obvious danger posed by the menacing gate-crashers already within the City's walls.

However consequential and often unpleasant these differing anti-system orientations have been in fostering sectarian rifts within the 'resistance', they detract not in the least from the quality of Faye's *Manifesto* or the 177 key terms he develops to conceptualise and articulate its metapolitical project.

*

---

31 On Benoist's ethnopluralist rejection of identitarianism, see Michael O'Meara, 'The Faye-Benoist Debate on Multiculturalism' (11 May 2004), available at *La Nueva Derecha* (foster.20megsfree.com/468.htm); Michael O'Meara, 'Benoist's *Pluriversum*: An Ethnonationalist Critique' in *The Occidental Quarterly* vol. 5, no. 3 (Fall 2005), available at *The Occidental Quarterly Online* (www.toqonline.com/archives/v5n3/53-mo-pluriversum.pdf); and Michael O'Meara, 'Community of Destiny or Community of Tribes?' in *Ab Aeterno* 2 (March 2010), available at *Counter-Currents* (www.counter-currents.com/2010/08/community-of-destiny-or-community-of-tribes/).

To appreciate something of its foresight, the reader might recall the historical context in which *Why We Fight* appeared.

For the identitarian, anti-system Right, it was a period ideologically re-armed with the rediscovered heritage of the Conservative Revolution, the great, philosophically unassailable anti-liberal achievement of the German 1920s, but it was also no less important as a period whose postmodernist stirrings seemed to pose the possibility of another Conservative Revolution.[32]

For the system, never more triumphant, it was the everything-is-going-right period before the Islamic terrorist attack of '9/11' and the ensuing production known as the Global War on Terrorism — the period before the hubristic violence of George Bush's 'shock and awe' over-extended the American empire, preparing its present breakdown — before September 2008, when the supposedly irreversible progression of the global market came to a sudden, economy-wrecking standstill (as 'the dream of global free-market capitalism died')[33] — and before October 2010, when the German Chancellor, model of the post-war, American-centric sense of propriety, declared that multiculturalism had 'totally failed' and that immigrants had better start assimilating.

Along with anticipating the devastations accompanying globalism's 'end of history', Faye's *Why We Fight* caught a glimpse of the larger metahistorical logic that was then, and is still, leading the American-centric world system to disorder and possible collapse — the logic he calls the 'convergence of catastrophes' (the same system-destroying

---

32 See Javier Esparza, 'Le pari de la post-modernité' (1986); Claudio Risé, 'La post-modernité est une revolution conservatrice!' (1997); and Robert Steuckers, 'La genèse de la postmodernité' (1989), all available at *Vouloir* (vouloir.hautetfort.com/archive/2011/02/10/pm.html).

33 Martin Wolf, 'The Rescue of Bear Stearns Marks Liberalisation's Limit', *Financial Times*, 26 March 2008 (available at www.ft.com/content/8ced5202-fa54-11dc-aa46-000077b07658).

logic that some label the 'Long Descent', the 'Long Emergency', the 'End of Oil', the 'Coming Anarchy', etc.).

When the *Manifesto* appeared in 2001, unregulated global market practices were considered as 'inevitable' as the 'end of history' that came with Communism's fall; 'hi tech' and the digitisation of financial capitalism were similarly heralded as the economic equivalent of the Second Coming. But most emblematic of the period, Bill Clinton ('America's first Black President') assumed the leadership of what was to be a post-European, post-ideological, and post-historical stage in human development, in which the United States — drunk on its unipolar ideal of power and believing its virtual ideals (the 'end of history' pre-eminently) were somehow immune to reality — sanctimoniously assumed heaven's mandate to safeguard its 'new order of the ages'. This mandate, as the world's sole superpower, successor of Rome, would lead it to wage 'humanitarian wars' (Serbia, Kosovo, Iraq, etc.) in the name of its disordering global *nomos;* to enthrone abstract, disembodied 'human rights' everywhere at the expense of historic and customary rights; to prevent all regulation of High Finance or Wall Street, and to use its vast powers to uphold the claim that the U.S. economy (and, by implication, the U.S. itself) had evolved, as Greenspan put it in 1998, 'beyond history'[34] (i.e., beyond the realities that once conditioned economic/political behaviour); etc.

Against the Philistines of the Marxist Left (who betrayed the European working class for the detritus of an overpopulated Third World) and against the Babbitts of the so-called Right (whose one and only God is Mammon), Faye saw that the anti-European, multicultural, reality-denying forces of America's global economic order would experience (within a decade) not just a long patch of very stormy weather, when their fantasy projects and hyper-power plans would succumb to certain formerly-denied realities — he saw that their

---

34 Alan Greenspan, 'An Update on Economic Conditions in the United States', available at the *Board of Governors of the Federal Reserve System* (www.federalreserve.gov/boarddocs/testimony/1998/19980610.htm).

self-generating catastrophes, and the interregnum they would create, were about to give the 'resistance' another opportunity to throw off liberalism's death-embrace — and, once the chaos passed, inaugurate a Fourth Age of European civilisation.[35]

MICHAEL O'MEARA
San Francisco, January 2011

Michael O'Meara, Ph.D., studied social theory at the École des hautes études en Sciences Sociales in Paris and modern European history at the University of California at Berkeley. He is the author of *New Culture, New Right: Anti-Liberalism in Postmodern Europe* (Arktos, 2013).

---

35 See Ted Sallis, 'The Overman High Culture: Future of the West' (21 October 2010), available at *Counter-Currents* (www.counter-currents.com/author/tsallis/); Charles Lindholm and José Pedro Zúquete, *The Struggle for the World: Liberation Movements for the 21st Century* (Stanford: Stanford University Press, 2010); and Michael O'Meara, 'Against the Armies of the Night: The Aurora Movements' (21 June 2010), available at *Counter-Currents* (www.counter-currents.com/2010/c7/against-the-armies-of-the-night/).

FOREWORD TO THE GERMAN EDITION

IT'S ABOUT THE PRIMORDIAL FIRE

In times of indoctrinated lies and well-bred civil cowardice, the courage to tell the truth mutates into a cardinal sin, as the few who take on the challenge must share the heretics' hopeless fate of banishment. Here Guillaume Faye steps forward from a newborn species of heretics, to show with the shrewdest of understanding and the boldest of determination that the phony peace of our Western civilisation represents the most malicious and dangerous 'state of war'. Should Europe not succeed in awakening its life-giving instinct for resistance, her peoples and cultures could be hopelessly lost forever.

But which destruction, which dangers, which death really threatens Europe? Just as the legendary hydra, these threats are like a multi-headed monster. Her decline is evident in the loss of her defining values: the fading away of an attachment to her people; a consciousness of her identity, history, and ethnicity; principles of selection, merit, and excellence; organic democracy; a will to power, an ethics of honor, and a striving to go beyond the human. The dangers, on the other hand, can be seen everywhere: toadying before the watchdog America; consumerism and mercantilism behind the grotesque face of *Homo oeconomicus*; emasculation and the cult of homosexuality with its various shades of degraded morality, universalism, globalism and mondialism[1] of all shades and with all prayer wheels; individualism and, as the lethal culmination of it all, ethnomasochism and xenophilia[2] of all origins and colours. This mental, spiritual and political degeneration into death knows many languages, names and forms, and then, at the very end, it rips its mask off: the demographic decline of the White peoples, the secret implantation of Islam — which will carry out its merciless assault once its time has come — and finally the planting of a genetic bomb, whose delayed detonation will inevitably lead to racial chaos and destruction.

Contrary to the suicidal opinions held by the sorcerers' apprentices of the multi-racial heresies, the analysis made by all experts on immigration, demographics and economics are symptomatic of an ever-widening gulf opening up between the clear vision of the scientists and the dementia of the dysfunctional political class. Herwig Birg, for example, the manager of the Institut für Bevölkerungsforschung und Sozialpolitik of the University of Bielefeld, gets straight to the point: 'Little by little we are moving this country towards the Second or Third World. I say this with conviction… Germany has much to lose — a culture admired around the world and a great prosperity which depends on this culture, and which will dissipate as the mass immigration from the Third World continues.'[3]

In view of the developments we can expect in the next four years, he has recently issued an even more urgent warning: 'In the larger cities of Germany, immigrants under the age of 40 will already make up

---

1 Globalism is the techno-financial machinery of planetary standardisation — an economic Leviathan erasing borders in the name of efficiency. Mondialism, its ideological twin, is the cult of universalism that dreams of dissolving all peoples into a single, deracinated mass governed by abstract humanitarianism. — Ed.

2 Xenophilia is the pathological adoration of the Other — a suicidal impulse of decadent civilisations that glorify the foreign while despising their own blood and soil. — Ed.

3 Herwig Birg, in *Aus Politik und Zeitgeschichte*, no. 20 (2003).

the majority of the population in 2010.'⁴ Fate's irony surpasses the most horrific scenarios we could have imagined as the guests of yesterday mutate into the new lords of the land, who then take charge of society. Then, Birg bluntly states, 'The issue for Germans will be [to ensure] that at least [the majority of the once-welcomed aliens] are not hostile to the Germans'!⁵ In plain language: the Germans should learn in which way to win the approval of the new rulers as soon as possible if they want to be tolerated in their own country in the future.

It is a fact: decadence is far more expensive than prosperity. The peak of absurdity, however, is the fact that the riches acquired through the labour of our people serve as, so to speak, credit cards for the multi-racialist political mafias. To put it another way: the victims finance the culprits, and voluntarily pay their executioners the highest salary for their march to the scaffold. Europe squanders her goods to cover the costs of her own extinction. Thus economic collapse precedes genetic ruin.

In a visionary book, the most creative and radical mastermind of *'Neue Kultur'*⁶ puts the imminent danger and the increasingly urgent necessity for an identitarian awakening into words: 'Giorgio Locchi had said to me that the latest World War was only the dress rehearsal and that Great Europe would have to suffer a final assault. He was of the opinion that no defeat is final, and that victory was possible even though we appear to be standing on the edge of the abyss. Giorgio Locchi, who was marked by the Roman tradition and the German spirit, asked me to continue his work in my own fashion — that is, in the French fashion. He was referring to the *furia francese*,⁷ which still

---

4   Dr. Krebs wrote this Foreword in 2006.
5   Herwig Birg, in the *Frankfurter Allgemeine Sonntagszeitung*, 1 April 2006.
6   *Neue Kultur*, or 'New Culture', is a term used to describe the various New Right movements throughout Europe. — Ed.
7   Italian: 'fury of the French'. This term was first applied to the French by the Italians during the Franco-Austrian War of 1859, which was fought in northern Italy, to describe the power of French infantry attacks. — Ed.

lives in some Gallic souls, and is marked by the will to resist by attacking; merciless, without fear and without empty talk. The war has only just begun. One has to ride the tiger.[8] The great confrontation announces itself: it contains both our death and our rebirth, even though, in fact, it is probably our last chance.'[9]

Why We Fight is truly a book in the tradition of the great preachers and prophets, a book that will hurt many readers with its relentless depiction of an all but hopeless reality, but which will also offer healing to many as they come to perceive the courses of action and methods that remain possible to restore Europe, and that could snatch her from the jaws of death, provided that the Europeans recognise that they want it, and that they make it possible. A book free from any doubts, containing brilliant ideas that are capable of inflaming the spirit of the Europeans' resistance and whose proposals for action aim at definitively uniting the European tribes from the coast of Iceland to the extreme border of Siberia. But not only that! It is also about the new definitions of key concepts on which this rebirth depends. It is an immense project which made the publication of a dictionary of 177 fundamental terms necessary, and which only Guillaume Faye's multifaceted nature could dare undertake, let alone successfully complete.

The ethnomasochists of the System — and this is important to know in this context — imitate Derrida,[10] the philosopher who tried

---

8   An expression coined by Julius Evola in a book of the same name to describe the problems faced by an individual who attempts to resist the norms and values of the modern world while simultaneously being forced to live in it. — Ed.

9   Guillaume Faye, *Avant-Guerre: Chronique d'un cataclysme annoncé* (Paris: Editions de l'Aencre, 2002), p. 9.

10 Jacques Derrida (1930–2004) was a French philosopher who is widely regarded as the most important of the postmodernist philosophers. His work has had an enormous impact on philosophy and literary theory since the 1970s. His work led to the technique of 'deconstruction', by which it is held that no text or idea can be reduced to a single meaning, but rather that every text can be interpreted in many different, and contradictory, ways, thus denying that an authoritative meaning can be claimed by any text. — Ed.

to deconstruct the world. First, one deconstructs language in order to destroy the means for expressing the traditions, institutions and laws of a people. This is a preliminary step in the radical deconstruction of our basic identitarian principles. It is intended to bring about the quick and complete extermination of all peoples and cultures before any resistance can be mounted.

The pen which wrote this book is an arrow and a scalpel in one. It strikes unerringly in the darkness of European decadence and, beginning with the decay of language, dissects all tumours, one by one. And then, one after another, he goes after the infections causing the dangerous disease that has sickened Europe: deceptive ideas are unmasked; all confusion, all semantic errors, and all false statements are located and cleansed — and so are the resulting un-values which paralyse our will and shut down our identitarian instincts. In other words, this is no book of rhetorical chatter, no book of intellectual gesture, nor a book of complacency, either for the author or the reader. Rather, it is a book woven exclusively from real ideas, ideas which are the maturation of new, bold spirits who are capable of will and, ultimately, action — since only a reawakened will is capable of saving our peoples, who are on the verge of an agonising destiny, from the decay of this epoch.

Only now do we understand better why the reconquest of ideas depends on the reconquest of the terms used to describe them and the reappropriation of their meaning: because one cannot awaken instincts without first dissolving the aberrations which have made the spirit lose its orientation. It would be just as impossible to remake the world without first defining the concepts to be used in its construction, or to reorient one's spirit without first correcting the distorted meanings of the words one uses. The willingness to redefine our terms thus implies a mental readiness to begin a counterattack against the political correct tyranny's aggressions and intimidations, these being nothing but a ruse by an enemy who knows full well that the more you pervert the language of a people, the more its spirit will be distorted and its resistance weakened.

The religious scholar and Germanist Bernhard Kummer[11] aptly said, 'He who knows the laws of our kind better than we ourselves can lead us wherever he wants.'[12] Language holds, without a doubt, one of these keys; as soon as it withers, the mind inevitably shrinks and the soul inexorably falls into dire distress. Hence it is high time to place our terms on solid ground and define them precisely, so that the ideas they describe may find their proper direction in order to counter the global deculturation of our people — the preliminary step towards its systematic genetic and identitarian destruction. Such resistance desperately requires a mental and semantic cleansing of the language — and that is precisely what Guillaume Faye has accomplished with this handbook.

This book, however, is more than just a book. It is many things at once: a handbook, a tool of critical observation, a strategic weapon, a compass of the spirit, and a leader of the struggle — and, because of this, predestined to become the reference work for all European identitarian forces of the Twenty-first century. Like the previous book in this series,[13] this is also written out of duty and inner necessity in the service of a strategy of awakening as well as to create a *corpus* for a common European worldview. These are war books that serve, one as well as the other, to constantly remind us that we are engaged with an enemy who threatens the very essence of our being: the inviolable right to be and become what we are, with an identity embedded in the legacy of our ancestors, whose biographies tell the most important part of world history. They tell of everything from the conquest of the Earth to the conquest of the stars with the millennia-old, unalterable

---

11 Bernhard Kummer (1897–1962) was a scholar of Old Norse language, culture and religion. He was active within the National Socialist Party both before and during the Third Reich and was a supporter of the German Faith Movement. — Ed.

12 Bernhard Kummer, *Anfang und Ende des faustischen Jahrtausends* (Leipzig: Klein, 1934).

13 The German edition of *Why We Fight* (*Wofür wir kämpfen*) was published by Dr. Krebs' Thule-Seminar as the second volume of their *Polemos* series. The first volume was Pierre Krebs, *Im Kampf um das Wesen* (Horn: Weecke, 1997). — Ed.

respect for the laws of life — against all criminal ideologies of racial and cultural extermination, whose handiwork is named miscegenation. By now it should be understood why such books are viewed as being of the worst sort by all who despise and destroy the races. It is because they teach about the right of peoples and the laws of life that govern them, which is everything that these destroyers are attempting to exterminate.

Granted, the System still holds all the political cards. But what is the most cunning game without the trump cards? We have nothing but our ideas, our convictions and our will — certainly not much, compared to the usurpers of power who daily confuse minds, poison souls and take all imaginable measures to initiate the destruction of all identities. We possess, however, the highest trump — the trump of trumps, which those who are attempting to erase all traces of their own blood do not possess and never can possess. We know where we are going because we know where we came from. We possess the memory of the history that is also the memory of the *mythos*[14] of our *ethnos*,[15] the consciousness of an unbroken line of ancestors from whom we have inherited the most valuable of all privileges: namely, the privilege to be like them.

Let us therefore immediately cease the endless debate over details — these are pursuits for the time after the rebirth of our civilisation. What we need are clear guidelines, unbending principles, uncompromising values, and an unshakeable belief in our culture and our people. Those are the indispensible conditions of victory! For we know one thing: we will remain forever, so long as we maintain the law of ethnic homogeneity without fail, against all propaganda to the contrary. We must also remain true to that indestructible heritage of the blood that transforms human beings without altering their essence. Our law stems from a divine will — from the only god whose name we know: heritage.

---

14   Classical Greek: 'story'. — Ed.
15   Classical Greek: 'nation', in the sense of an ethnic community. — Ed.

By following the teachings of this book, we allow this will to show us the way, to create a foundation and develop a vision for why we fight. We will together unleash the *furia francese* of which Guillaume Faye speaks, along with the *furia espanola, teutonica, italiana, russia, croatia* or *islandia* — and out of these *furia europeana*, new forces will coalesce that will put this world back on the foundations of Life. The time is short! The challenge is huge, yet it is from our enemies' folly that wisdom is born, from this will that life is passed on, and from this despair that hope rises: for only at the very epicentre of danger does that which saves continue to grow — provided one knows, believes and wants it. Summoning Nietzsche, who wanted to write on all the walls, wherever walls existed, we too are ready to write down for our brainless peoples, in marble letters that even the blind can read, the inviolable laws of the blood that maintain the Being of every people and house the Being of each culture. More than ever before, what is at stake is the primordial fire of our *genos*[16] and the Being of our *ethnos*. Yes: it is about the spinning wheel of our *germen*[17] — that which engenders the Being of our Soul and Spirit, both of which are indissolubly tied to the Being of the Race shaping them.

Long live the New Will perpetuating the Race, and may the Spirit triumph.

PIERRE KREBS
Kassel, Germany, 2006

Dr. Pierre Krebs, born in 1948, is the founder and Chairman of the Thule-Seminar, which he established in 1980. The Thule-Seminar, which describes itself as a group dedicated to research into and cultivation of Indo-European culture, remains the most prominent New Right organisation in Germany. Like Faye, it has worked closely with the Terre et Peuple group in France. Krebs graduated from the École Supérieure de Journalisme and the École des Hautes Études Sociales with degrees in philosophy, history and law.

---

16 Classical Greek: 'clan'. — Ed.

17 Faye defines this term in the dictionary. — Ed.

A NOTE FROM THE EDITOR

There were no footnotes to the French edition of this book. Therefore, all footnotes to Faye's text are my own, apart from those marked with 'Tr.', which were added by the translator. The footnotes to Dr. O'Meara's Foreword are his own, and the footnotes to Dr. Pierre Krebs' Foreword were also added by the author, with the exception of those marked with 'Ed.', which were added by myself. I would like to thank Robert Steuckers for contributing the information which I have added as footnote #46 in the 'Preliminary Elements' section. Wherever possible, references have been given to the English translations of texts; if a reference is to a work in another language, I was unable to locate an English version of it. All references to websites in the footnotes were verified as accurate and available during the period of February and March 2011.

This translation was made directly from the original French edition published in 2001, with the exception of the Foreword by Dr. Krebs, and the dictionary entries for ethnocracy and genopolitics, which were also added by Dr. Krebs for the German edition of this book that was published in 2006. A few changes that were made for the French version of Dr. Krebs' Foreword have also been incorporated into our version. I would like to thank Daniel Friberg for his input. The layout of the book was also modeled after the German edition, which we felt was superior to that of the French edition.

I would also like to thank Michael O'Meara for putting so much time and energy into this project. The time he spent on his Foreword, on checking and rechecking the manuscript, and on critiquing the footnotes went far beyond what is typically expected of a translator. Likewise I would like to express my sincere appreciation to Matthew Peters, who was originally only asked to proofread the manuscript, a task which he performed with great skill and alacrity. However, his contributions ended up going far beyond that, as he provided many valuable suggestions pertaining to the editing and footnotes of the present book. Sergio Knipe was also kind enough to volunteer some of his time to assist in reviewing the manuscript and he also contributed to the translation of the Foreword by Dr. Krebs. I thank all of you for helping to ensure that this is the best book possible.

JOHN B. MORGAN IV
Mumbai, India, April 2011

PREFACE AND PRECAUTION

Unite on the Basis of Clear Ideas Against the Common Enemy

The worst wars are the undeclared ones. They break out quietly, like an uneasy breeze, and are the harshest, most deadly.

Europe today faces the greatest danger in her history, a danger threatening the very existence of her civilisation. For **she is at war** and doesn't even know it. She may sense the danger, but refuses to see it, burying her head in the sand, like the ostrich, hoping to conjure it away.

We Europeans are rapidly and massively being occupied and colonised by peoples from the South and by Islam. We are subject to America's economic, strategic, and cultural New World Order. The two march hand in hand. We are emasculated by ideologies of decline and by those of a facile optimism, we are menaced by a regression of culture and education toward primitivism and by the faint simulation of prosperity.

Europe is the sick man of the world. It's obvious in her demographic decline, in her physiological devirilisation, and in the reigning ideology of ethnomasochism, imposed by politically correct censors and the controlled media. We are gnawed at from within and attacked from without. We are set upon by assailants, occupiers, and **collaborators**, who make up the majority of the political, media, and intellectual classes, whether of the Right or the Left. The people have yet to see it because their shopping carts are still full. And though everyone may secretly suspect that the war has begun, the majority denies it, because for the moment no one has the courage to fight it. For the moment...

The deepening crisis and the march toward the enveloping chaos are requisite to an awakening and a revolt. And we haven't seen anything yet. The tragedy is still early in its first act.

Like every war, the defenders' freedom of expression is compromised. There is no use complaining: such are the rules of the game. Throughout Europe, we possess immense resources. Nothing yet is lost and pessimism is no option.

In history it's always struggling minorities who make the difference, not the amorphous masses. And it's no longer a matter of Left or Right either, but whether **you're part of the resistance**.

Given the tragedy bearing down on Europeans and the futile disputes dividing identitarians, there's an evident need for a worldview powerful enough to rally the Continent — to rally our great fatherland, that family of kindred spirits, however politically fragmented, which is united on the essentials, favouring thus the defence of our civilisation and our imperilled identity, but especially favouring the principles of our regeneration.

Everywhere, one awaits a mobilisation based on a clear, federating discourse of resistance and reconquest — free of outdated ideas, sectarianism, and the paralysis of nostalgia. Never before has the urgency for such a discourse been so great. What matters most at this point is a **unifying ideological platform** that goes beyond sectarianism in the sincerity and lucidity of its reflections. When the house is on fire, domestic disputes are put on hold.

* * *

An **ideological regrounding** is necessary — a regrounding that is both a synthesising affirmation of a general doctrine and, at the same time, a rigorous definition of concepts, arguments, and propaganda. This is why the following manifesto takes the form, in large part, of a 'dictionary'.

Doctrinal confusion, phony debates, artificial oppositions, intellectual approximations and misunderstandings, sectarian skirmishes, the blunting of ideas for respectability's sake — they have gone on for far too long. What's needed is a **clear line.** A strongly formulated minimum around which the largest number of sensibilities and wills can coalesce.

We have entered a period when things no longer need to be said in half-measures, as we amuse ourselves with 'two-faced discourses'. What we need now is **radical thought** — not in the guise of extremist gestures, but in getting to the root of things. The truth is always a winner and it's the most effective ruse.

The time has come for identitarianism, in the broadest sense, to reaffirm itself as the most lucid and ambitious form of thought. The identitarian view of the world is simply more realistic and better adapted to the future than the dominant egalitarian and cosmopolitan ideology, which affects everyone from soft Rightists to the craziest neo-Trotskyites. All the facts, whether historical, geopolitical, demographic, ethnic, economic, or social, substantiate the identitarian and inegalitarian view of the world. Its vision — the **sole authentically rebellious and dissident form of thought** — is bound to prevail everywhere in Europe, for once the Twenty-first century succumbs to the approaching crises, the slate will be wiped clean — as ideological revisions, unexpected designations, and surprising radicalisations arrive with the force of circumstances.

* * *

Fifteen years ago, I published a small work titled *Pourquoi nous combattons* (*Why We Fight*), as well as *Petit Lexique du Partisan européen* (*A Small Lexicon for the European Partisan*), written in collaboration with Robert Steuckers and Pierre Freson. These two works have appeared in several pirated editions. But though they've retained much of their pertinence, they no longer quite fit the present state of emergency.

Since then, no comparable manifesto or ideological synthesis has been published — with the exception of Pierre Vial's last book, *Une Terre, un Peuple* (*One Land, One People*), a work whose conceptual and 'archeofuturist' orientations, in defending both ancestral traditions and an imperial future, are closely akin to our own idea of resistance and reconquest.

Beware of False Friends

Throughout Europe, young resisters and dissidents need to be wary not only of **cooptation by the system, but also by those posing as defenders of European identity**, the so-called 'artisans of renewal'. I'm thinking here of those de Gaulle described as 'kids jumping about crying: Europe! Europe! Europe!;'[1] talking of 'renaissance', but all the while defending decadent, permissive, censorious values that envisage Europe as a sort of 'tolerant' Disneyland, open to all the world, an ethnopluralist pandemonium — without a defining identity, an internal order, or a will to power. The ideological lure of such discourses is great, especially if conveyed in intellectually pretentious language. It's of utmost importance, though, that we resist such pseudo-identitarians, whose conformity and craving for respectability surreptitiously camouflage multiracial and multicultural dogmas in the form of a 'European idea' that actually dissociates Europe from her 'imperial idea'.

---

[1] From a presidential campaign interview given on 14 December 1965.

Anything can be found in today's supermarket of pseudo-rebellion: the anti-racist viaticum; a post-'68[2] 'anti-utilitarian' Leftism; a multicultural, multi-confessional, multi-anything ethnopluralism that discovered, thirty years later, the theses of American communitarians (somehow taken to be anti-American); an anti-liberalism derived from Bourdieu[3] and his friends; or else, at the other extreme, an ultra-free-marketism and a naïve, disarming idolatry of Americanism.

Even among regionalists one finds the cosmopolitan ideology of the far Left, which, in its pretence of fighting French Jacobinism, resolutely ignores the European character of the regionalist identity it defends.

We need, thus, to **watch out for false defenders of European identity,** those who have only formally broken with the Greens, Cohn-Bendit,[4] or José Bové.[5] For their fraudulent discourse is a simulacrum, which functions in the following manner: in the name of a repetitive, dogmatic, and badly argued anti-Americanism that invokes a convenient, neo-Marxist and economically superficial anti-liberalism, they pose as dissidents; they even label themselves European federalists,

---

2 In May 1968, a series of strikes by radical Left-wing student groups in Paris were joined by a strike of the majority of the French work-force, shutting down France and nearly bringing down the government of Charles de Gaulle. Although the strikes ended in failure and had evaporated by July, they are still seen as the decisive moment when traditional French society was forced to give way to the more liberal attitude that has come to define France in subsequent years.

3 Pierre Bourdieu (1930-2002) was a prominent French anthropologist, philosopher and sociologist who studied social dynamics. He opposed neo-liberalism and globalisation. He was also the foremost Marxist academic in France in his day.

4 Daniel Cohn-Bendit (b. 1945) is a leader of the French Green Party and has been a member of the European Parliament since 1994. He first came to prominence during the May 1968 student demonstrations in Paris.

5 José Bové (b. 1953) is a politician who has been an activist in agricultural causes, such as organic farming, and has also opposed globalisation and Israel's occupation of Palestine. He was elected to the European Parliament in 2009.

though they resist all thought of a powerful, imperial Europe; they pretend to be anti-globalists, proponents of the enrooted — identitarians — but at the same time they are 'open to all cultures', partisans of the 'cause of all peoples', and effectively pro-immigrant; they profess to be 'anti-progressive', but in the spirit of a vaguely realist 'sense of history', they judge every idea of Europe's ethnic reconquest as unrealistic; they say they are pagan, Christian, pagan-Catholic, or agnostic, depending on the restaurant, but applaud Islam's advance in the name of ecumenism — doing so, though, more out of conformity and ignorance than deception, etc. The most dangerous of these types are the pseudo-pagans, who systematically confuse things with their sophism and tolerant-mad polytheism — that is, with their anarchy. Sad to say, not a few Right-wing intellectuals have been snared in this way.

* * *

The mechanism is simple: they mount a **phony opposition to the system, attacking superficial aspects of it, but never challenge its foundation.** The threats presently facing Europe — notably, Europe's colonisation by the Third World and Islam, devirilisation, the decay of values, the Africanisation of culture, demographic decline, bureaucratic fiscalism and the metastasis of the regnant social democracy, triumphant homophilia — are prudently ignored by these fake resisters, who lack any geopolitical, strategic, economic, ethnic, or cultural vision of resistance — who lack a will to power. The principal enemy, everywhere known, isn't even mentioned.

These phony oppositionists excuse themselves by claiming to be thinking, but 'to think is not enough', as Jules Renard says, 'you must think of something'.[6]

There's another danger, the inverse of these: a nostalgic, pessimistic discourse steeped in sectarianism and impotence, marginality, and

---

6 Jules Renard (1864–1910) was a French writer whose journals were well known. This passage comes from *The Journal of Jules Renard* (New York: George Braziller, 1964), p. 117.

inept resistance. This is the logic of history's eternal losers, vanquished in advance, embittered and discouraged, seeing themselves as the *last line* of defence, rather than the *first*. **Every resistance not arising on a foundation of reconquest is destined to fail.**

* * *

We should also be wary of certain **spiritual, metaphysical, and so-called 'philosophical' tendencies.** Wary especially of those impostors who call themselves 'theologians' in the confines of their office... though a spiritual renewal is absolutely necessary — for the sake of Europe's rebirth — and against materialistic narcissism, which is the primal cause of her present tragedy.

Spirituality is not spiritualism. It isn't something to be decreed or instrumentalised, like a computer program. I'm a devoted reader of Evola,[7] particularly of his extraordinary political and social-philosophical texts, but **take heed of 'Evolianism'** (and the even more dangerous 'Guénonism')[8] that turns away from practical, tangible issues. Reflection must serve action and is not to be confused with metaphysical tautologies. I particularly address this warning to my Italian friends.

Distrust is no less warranted in respect to that artificial and instrumentalised 'paganism' that threatens to succumb to either a New Age disconnected from any worldly struggle, or worse, in the name of a badly understood polytheism, to *xenophilia* and a catastrophic 'Love

---

7   Julius Evola (1898–1974) was the most important Italian member of the Traditionalist school, which is to say that he opposed modernity in favour of an approach to life consistent with the teachings of the ancient sacred texts. His most important book, available in English, is *Revolt Against the Modern World*.

8   René Guénon (1886–1951) was a French writer who founded what has come to be known as the Traditionalist school of religious thought. Traditionalism calls for a rejection of the modern world and its philosophies in favour of a return to the spirituality and ways of living of the past (Guénon himself ended up living as a Sufi Muslim in Cairo). He outlines his attitude toward modernity in *The Crisis of the Modern World*, which is available in English.

of the Other'. I should add that I have long considered myself a pagan, fully pagan, allied to traditional Catholicism, and a friend of Hinduism, but a fierce adversary of the desert's totalitarian monotheisms.

A similar prudence is needed in respect to Catholic charismatic spirituality, with its enervating mysticism, and particularly its destructively pacifist dismissal of ethnicity and the will to power.

We need, in a word, to be alert to demobilising mysticisms, to a pretentious but hollow intellectualism, to easy refuge in a 'spirituality' or 'philosophy' whose attitudes, postures, and loopholes are ultimately tangential to the resistance.

I'm not at all disparaging spiritual or religious pursuits, which are one of the glories of European civilisation. Real spirituality, though, is possible only in combat. Few are those who find it in pure meditation. For the dangers of *disembodiment* are great and, in such cases, the most *profound* aspirations metamorphose into a form of prattle and a refuge from life's conflicts, part of history's flotsam. To give meaning to one's life one must struggle and take risks for one's ideals and especially for one's people. From such engagements there arises a true spirituality — an inner flame, not another bourgeois decorum. I think Evola, Heidegger, and Abellio[9] understood this, since **their spirituality stemmed from their engagements.**Spirituality is the enemy and opposite of spiritualism, just as intelligence is the enemy and opposite of intellectualism, and philosophy is the enemy and opposite of philosophism. Spirituality grows out of biological and ontological struggle, it neither precedes nor continues, but is linked to it and is coupled to it, like a nest of vipers.

---

9   Raymond Abellio (1907–1986) was the pen name of Georges Soulès, a French writer on mysticism. He worked for the Vichy government of occupied France and was the secretary general of the Mouvement Social Révolutionnaire, a French fascist party. After the war, he attempted to unite the forces of the far Left and Right in order to create a Eurasian Empire that would stretch from the Atlantic to Japan.

The word 'divine' refers, perhaps, to the end. But the divine is born only from the physical, concrete, practical ardour of men. It appears only if a humble, harrowing, but proud struggle has begun.

The physical and mental aptitude for struggle, the possession of a clear doctrine, the qualities of courage and resistance — are, for the moment, the stuff of fire and tragedy, far more important than any spiritualist soothsaying. *Mens sana in corpore sano*: a healthy mind in a healthy body. Let us not forget that Socrates was a hoplite and Xenophon a military magistrate.

* * *

Sterile disputes and sectarian divisions divide and neutralise those who ought to be in solidarity with one another. This contrasts with the enemy, who, however protean, knows how to close ranks. Our disputes and divisions are superficial — and cause us to spar with those sharing similar beliefs — those having the **same intuitive identitarian vision of the world,** designating the same enemy, and implicitly defending the same people and aspiring to the same goals — but who are still attached to unclear ideas, emotional conflicts, badly posed debates ('France' or 'Europe', 'sovereignism' or 'federalism',[10] 'Catholicism' or 'paganism', etc.). Without well-defined ideas, clear and unifying concepts, serene reflections, and a sense of urgency, it will be difficult to be understood and thus difficult to establish an effective ideological line. According to an old adage, whose origin I will not reveal, we need now to lay the basis, throughout Europe, for 'a form of positive, wilful thought creative of order'.

---

10 In the context of modern European politics, the conflict between notions of sovereignty and federalism is about the degree to which the various European nations should rule themselves independently, versus how much they should be subject to the authority of the European Union.

2

PRELIMINARY ELEMENTS

The history of the world is a history of the struggle between peoples and civilisations for survival and domination. It's a battleground of wills to power. It's an uninterrupted succession of prolific tragedies resolved solely through the creative powers of the determinant forces. Class struggle is no less a reality, but of a secondary order.

A people's long-term vigour lies in its *germen*,[1] i.e., in the maintenance of its biological identity and its demographic renewal, as well as in the health of its mores and in its cultural creativity and personality. On these two foundations a civilisation rests.

Contrary to the prevailing belief, it's not economic or military power, nor its social constitution or political independence, that in the last instance determines the longevity of a people or civilisation. These elements are extremely important, but they are part of the superstructure. **The base of everything is biocultural identity and demographic renewal.**

This is why the present situation in Europe is so tragic: for the first time in two thousand years, she is quite literally in danger of

---

1   Latin: 'seed' or 'germ'

disappearing. And this, at the very moment she is awkwardly trying to unite, as if she had the prescience to regroup against that which is threatening her.

Corrupted by the Western system she herself created, Europe is gnawed at from within and gnawed at from without. Domestically: by bourgeois individualism, the cult of short-term consumerism, infertility, devirilisation, xenophilia, ethnomasochism, and deculturation. Internationally: by a population-replacing colonisation, by the Islamic invasion, and by her strategic and cultural subjugation to Islam's accomplice, the American adversary.

Today, as night descends on them, European peoples need to consciously see themselves as **a people**, for they have less than a century to save their *germen* and their civilisation. The Twenty-first century will be **the decisive century**, specifically its early decades. More than ever, the old military adage — 'vanquish or die!' — assumes its pertinence. If the generation of native Europeans which turns 20 between 2000 and 2010 doesn't act, everything will be lost — forever — as the spirit of those who built the great cathedrals is finally extinguished. East Europeans won't even be able to aid their brothers in the West, for they too are sick.

The coming century will be a century of iron. It will bring about an archeofuturist return of ancient questions, of eternal disputes, after the short parenthesis of 'modernity', which lasted barely three centuries – a moment in history's course. **The coming age announces the titanic and the tragic** — as an overcrowded humanity, crammed on a sick planet, engages its decisive struggle for survival. End of a regime and interregnum.

The key issues facing the future won't be about financing *start-ups*, finding a place in the political system for women, or looking out for the well-being of the 'gay community', but rather about determining the outcome of the coming clash between Europe and the Islamic world colonising her: will Europeans remain the majority of the European population; will they be able to check the dramatic degradation of the

Earth's environment, etc.? This manifesto, and its dictionary, addresses these questions.

In the course of the coming century, all humanity, first in Europe, then worldwide, will confront **a convergence of catastrophes**. Nothing is likely to be resolved without a major crisis in which we are forced to act, once our backs are against the wall. The present system — this modern Western system — cannot be saved, contrary to the illusions of the Right or the optimism of the Left. **We need to prepare for the approaching chaos and start thinking in post-chaos terms.** Rationalising 'realists' have criticised me for a revolutionary, tragic vision. But my view is positive. History proves that intellectual 'realists', usually myopic experts, look at the world through the wrong end of the lens. They have even accused me of being an 'apocalyptic romantic'. But no, I'm a realist: I believe in the concrete. More paradoxical even, these reproaches are made by self-proclaimed 'philosophers' who pose as anti-progressives, yet have themselves succumbed to the worst liberal-Marxist illusions — in refusing to imagine the possibility of a catastrophe. They are like ostriches who bury their overdeveloped brains in the sand — or like the eyeless sea creatures in Marianne's[2] sewers … History is not a long, tranquil river, but is rather a series of falls, rapids, and, would you believe it, mouths.

Why do we fight? We don't fight for 'the cause of peoples',[3] because the identity of every people is its own concern, not ours, and because history is a cemetery of peoples and civilisations. **We fight only for the cause of our own people's destiny.** Our political activities — the most quotidian cultural or metapolitical, the most down-to-earth,

---

2   Marianne, symbolising Liberty and Reason, appears on the emblem of France, therefore Faye is referring to the sewers of France.

3   'The cause of peoples' is a slogan coined by Alain de Benoist's GRECE, by which it is meant that the cause of the New Right should be to preserve the unique ethnocultural identity of all groups, not only that of the Europeans. Faye has written an essay on the subject entitled 'The Cause of the Peoples?' for *Terre et Peuple*, which has been translated by the *Guillaume Faye Archive*, available at guillaumefayearchive.wordpress.com/2007/07/07/the-cause-of-the-peoples/.

the most humble activities, even in the formulation of our practical programs — are guided by the imperative of all Grand Politics: that is, by the struggle **for the heritage of our ancestors and the future of our children.**

The Logic of Decline

European civilisation is gangrened with the cosmopolitanism that comes with the Western system, which it helped create, as Nietzsche saw in an earlier phase of its decay. Europe's destiny in this sense is tragic.

The main cause of her decline is the maturation of those Eighteenth century ideas of equality and individualism that came at the expense of our communal, national, and ethnic consciousness. Another cause is the secularisation of Judaeo-Christian universalistic — and egalitarian — values. A third is the materialistic frenzy constitutive of the bourgeois spirit.

Europeans as such are themselves responsible for the ills afflicting them: the ills of the declining birth rate, Third World and Islamic colonisation, deculturation, American domination, strategic feeble-mindedness, etc. They have, in effect, allowed their enemies to pollute their spirit and corrupt their body.

Narcissism, consumerism, devirilisation, homophilia, social egoism, xenophilia (improperly called 'anti-racism'), demographic decline, cultural neo-primitivism, a rejection of aesthetics and the will to live, hatred of aristocratic and warrior values, the cult of the economy (secular monotheism), the disfiguration of classical humanism and true spirituality, the triumph of a vulgar, hypocritical humanism — these forces contributing to the diminution of the European's character have been at work for more than a century. Largely invisible until now, the virus of this decay has at last completed its incubation and begun to burst forth.

Ethnic Colonisation

More than 'immigration', we need to speak of mass colonisation by African, Maghrebian, and Asian populations, acknowledging that Islam is seeking to conquer France and Europe; that 'the delinquency of youth'[4] is the first step toward ethnic civil war; that the invasion is as much about maternity wards as it is about porous borders; that, for demographic reasons, **Islamic power is threatening to install itself in France,** first at the municipal, then, perhaps, at the national level.

The public schools are floundering, prey to the violence of 'Beurs' and 'Blacks',[5] the new conquerors. 'No-go zones' have passed the thousand mark. For several years now, the number of immigrants, either legal ones with visas or illegal ones, has exploded. These new arrivals are not employable workers, but immediate candidates for the dole. We're standing at the edge of an abyss: if nothing changes, in two generations France will no longer have a majority European population, and this for the first time in her history. Germany, Italy, Spain, Belgium, and Holland are on the same catastrophic path, just a few years behind us. Not since the fall of the Roman Empire has Europe known such a cataclysmic situation. And it's occurring with the complicity of our clueless, ethnomasochistic political class and with the criminal collaboration of the immigrationist lobbies.

The growing ethnic chaos in Europe risks abolishing our civilisation; this threat is graver than any of the previous plagues and wars that Europe has known. And we shouldn't forget that **this colonisation and Islamisation serves the interests of the United States** and that the integration/assimilation of the invaders, like multi-ethnic communitarianism, is, in actuality, utterly unfeasible. There is, moreover, an alternative: *reconquest*.

*

---

4 I.e., immigrant youth. — Tr.
5 North African Arabs and sub-Saharan Negroes. — Tr.

Never has the ethnic and cultural identity of Europe, the basis of her civilisation, been so gravely menaced, exacerbated by the collaborationist and suicidal complicity of the media and the politicians. Laurent Joffrin[6] could thus write this stupefying phrase in *Le Nouvel Observateur*: 'The extreme Right thinks it can ameliorate the disorders of the liberal future with a remedy that is as false as it is murderous, opposing its own aggressive ethnic identity to the inevitable mélange of cultures.'

The fatalistic belief here in the inevitability of race-mixing is simply unsupported by the facts. It's no 'mixing of cultures' that we're experiencing in France, but rather the destruction, the eradication, **the ethnocide of European civilisation for the sake of Americanisation, on one side, and Islamisation and Afro-Maghrebisation, on the other.**

Under cover of their integrationist ideology, which has never been realised anywhere in the world, our enemies, loyal to the Trotskyism of their origin, endeavour to abolish our ancestral culture, which they consider intrinsically perverse.

'Ethnic identity' and its defence are thus designated as an Evil — having become symbols of aggression, in Laurent Joffrin's term. The defence and affirmation of one's culture in this view is nothing but a form of racism.

Far from becoming a 'planetary civilisation', a global village, the planet is today being organised into competing ethnic/identitarian blocs. **The mixing of cultures and the abolition of identities are not part of the Twenty-first-century's project.** India, China, Black Africa, the Arab-Muslim or Turkish-Muslim world, etc., are affirming their identities, tolerating neither a colonising immigration nor a cultural mélange on their soil. Only our pseudo-European elites defend the dogma of a 'mixed planet', which is pure illusion.

Europe is losing its ancestral heritage, while the official defence of the national 'patrimony' is nothing but a museological enterprise. For

---

6 Laurent Joffrin (b. 1952) was the editor of the Left-wing daily *Libération*. He left this position in March 2011.

cultural identity, like biological identity, is fundamentally archeofuturist: that is, it stems from an ongoing renaissance of forms and generations, beginning with the original *germen*. Permanent biological and cultural renewal and the ongoing assertion of the will to power: such is the law of all long-living peoples. **Identity is inconceivable without the complementary notion of continuity.**

The struggle against identity has become the watchword of the dominant egalitarian ideology. This entails abolishing both our memory and our blood. School programs testify to it, for in class they'd rather discuss an African folk tale than sing the old French songs. Céline's prediction of a 'tom-tom' invasion is coming true.[7]

*

This colonisation by alien populations is deeply rooted in our mentality. **The French themselves are the artisans of France's destruction.** If she is the country most assaulted by the alien invaders, it's because her cultural and ethnic identity is the most impaired.

The problem goes far back. Since the Revolution of 1789, Jacobin France has thought of herself as 'the republic of the human race', 'the country of all men', in imitation of the United States, which had just gained its independence. But only in the United States, this country founded on immigration and the destruction of its aboriginal peoples, is the formula true, whereas in France, a land of enrooted peoples and ethnicities, this universalistic formula is dangerously false. **From the start, the French Republic was based on the dogma of a non-ethnic state.**

---

7   Louis-Ferdinand Céline (1894–1961) is considered by many to have been one of the greatest French authors of the Twentieth century. He was also an unapologetic racist and anti-Semite. He outlines the idea that 'tom-tom' culture will infiltrate the West in his book *Trifles for a Massacre* (1937). 'Tom-tom' is slang for African-style drumming.

After the defeat of 1870,[8] the Republic's ideologues, with Renan[9] at their head, opposed Germany, a nation 'constituted by an original people, speaking an original language', in contrast to the allegedly more civilised France, founded not on a specific race, an enrooted history, or an inherited identity, but on a social contract and 'a political desire to live together'. Since then there has prevailed this disastrous French ideology, which denies its own ethnic reality and makes **the republican half-caste (métis) the model citizen.**

In 1914, again in 1940, Germany was perceived as a hereditary enemy, representing a people of a distinct stock — a primitive, identitarian people — who were to be defeated by French republicans, detached from all blood relations and linked to their fellow citizens solely on the basis of a social contract.

By way of a historical boomerang, today's anti-ethnic and anti-identitarian republican ideology, after having tried to destroy the historical personalities of France's various provinces, is failing to assimilate and integrate her millions of immigrants — or rather her new colonisers. These latter have conserved their identity, whereas the native French have lost theirs! **In effect, French ideology is destroying France.**

Founded on a hopeless cosmopolitanism, this French ideology is deeply rooted in the mentality of bourgeois governance: hence the

---

8   This is the Franco-Prussian War, which was fought in 1870–71 between France and several of the German states under the leadership of Prussia. The German victory in the war led to the collapse of the Second French Empire and the unification of the German states into one nation for the first time.

9   Ernest Renan (1823–1892) was a prominent French philosopher. Initially sympathetic to the ideals of German philosophy, his views changed drastically following the French defeat in 1871. His opposition to the German concept of nationalism was outlined in his 1882 essay 'What is a Nation?', in which he contrasted the idea of the nation as a 'daily referendum' to the nation as the product of a shared cultural, historical and linguistic heritage. The essay is available through the University of California Paris: ucparis.fr/files/9313/6549/9943/What_is_a_Nation.pdf.

nearly unanimously passed 'anti-racist' laws of Pleven (1972),[10] and Gayssot (1990),[11] which have, by governments of the Right and Left, established a thought police, innumerable pro-immigrationist measures, and a renunciation of border controls. Generally speaking, **France's bourgeois elites, whether political or mediacratic, lack either an ethnic or identitarian consciousness.**

They are indeed complicit with the present colonisation and invasion, both through their support for anti-racist activities and through their quasi-religious ideological belief that 'identity' is an evil, like every other political doctrine linked to ethnicity. And the most dangerous of these collaborators, in my view, are those on the 'Right', because they disarm and demobilise the instinctive resistance of healthy young people.

*

Such culpatory anti-identitarian activities ought to be seen as a form of *xenophilia* — that is, as a fascination for the Other, for the stranger — rather than as an 'anti-racism', which even touches the heart of those political and cultural movements claiming a French and European identity, though they demonise all forms of ethnocentrism. The evil is profound, the virus is lodged deep within the organism.

The house is on fire, but no one is saying anything. In respect to certain so-called 'identitarian' philosophers — who defend 'communitarianism', minimise or deny the effect of immigration/colonisation, and howl with the wolves against 'racism' — it's neither intellectual credulity, ignorance, nor cosmopolitanism that motivates them, but simple *cowardice*, born from a desire to appear socially respectable, to submit to the thought police, to 'correctly protest' without ever crossing

---

10 The Pleven Law was passed by the French Parliament in July 1972, making it illegal to incite racial hatred either through speech or writing, or to use language that is perceived as racially defamatory.

11 The Gayssot Act, which was enacted by the French Parliament in July 1990, makes it illegal to deny or question the severity of the Holocaust.

the cordon. Such treasons are so crude that even the cosmopolitan Left despises them. Yes, the enemy despises its own collaborators.

The enemy respects only those resisters who actively rebel.

The Blocked Society[12]

More than ever, society is 'blocked' and becoming sclerotic: as evident in the enormous benefits received by public functionaries who are resistant, of course, to all reform — evident also in the government's impotence whenever it's challenged by unions, pressure groups, the street. All this indicates the appearance of a **new form of class struggle.** And it's the Leftist electorate that stands here on the side of the exploiters. We find ourselves today in a situation where there are:

1. 'Guaranteed salaries' for public functionaries, who benefit from lifetime employment, full social coverage, and innumerable privileges; immigrant colonisers, who receive guaranteed welfare benefits, unlike natives, and practice their parasitism with impunity; and the great bourgeois fortunes (allied with the intellectual-media sphere), which have been turned into a new class of speculators.

2. A less and less protected middle class in full decline (short-term contracts, redundancy plans, cost cutting, etc.), increasingly precarious yet responsible for financing the state's growing deficit.

3. An expanding native proletariat, unemployed or partially employed, faced with intractable poverty and insecurity. The famous *exclusion*[13] touches mainly these native Europeans, not the immi-

---

12 This term was first coined by French sociologist Michel Crozier in a 1970 book, translated as *The Stalled Society* (New York: Viking Press, 1973). He used it to describe France's tendency to have too much bureaucracy which stifles social change, leading to problems that can only be resolved in times of crisis.

13 *Exclusion*, in the contemporary French context, means those who are entirely divorced from the labour market and mainstream society, particularly, but not limited to, those of the unemployed whose social benefits have expired.

grant colonisers, who are the beneficiaries of public and communal assistance.

The protected classes in this way live at the expense of the active but non-protected classes they exploit. Those who write the legislation and administer it evidently belong to the protected classes.

We're seeing as a consequence **the flight of our most talented people — prelude to our Third-Worldisation**. Fleeing from a blocked, indebted and overtaxed society, in which the state pressures rather than aids the vital forces, thousands of young minds are expatriating themselves every year. Who will replace them? Not unskilled, unproductive, and extremely costly immigrants, since the majority of them are welfare recipients.

Corrupted by the oligarchic careerism of professional politicians, democracy is being disfigured by a republic of judges and by increased censorship of the 'politically incorrect' and of whoever diverges from the opinions of the ruling party — and by an oligarchy whose indifference to the people's welfare is now eating away at the legal foundations of the state. Electoral abstention has reached unprecedented proportions. Governments are increasingly based on minority coalitions. Once it's realised that Greens or Communists, who represent but a splinter of the electorate, have managed to impose their laws, things become immediately more understandable.

It's as if Western 'democracy' had adopted a soft model of Stalinism (itself inspired by the despotic masters of the French Revolution). The anti-populist and anti-demagogic intellectual-media managerial class opposes all direct forms of democracy and has developed, especially on the Left, a distrust, a contempt, and a phobia of the people. **The West's pseudo-democracy is actually a neo-totalitarian oligarchy.**

A **soft totalitarianism** has, in effect, been installed under the guise of 'democracy'. The political arc of the reigning political parties of Europe (based on fabricated majorities and a fabricated opposition) form **a single party** — for they all, with certain nuances, subscribe to the same ideology. Direct democracy, like that of the Swiss, is considered illegitimate and the people's opinion is treated as if it were something immature and dangerous. One party, Austria's Freedom Party (FPÖ),[14] is officially treated as if it were illegitimate, though it's regularly re-elected at the polls.

Paradoxically, the greater the institutional laxity regarding mores, delinquency, and immigration, the greater the political repression, the computer monitoring, and the fiscal burdens on native citizens. *Big Brother* is making himself into *Ubu Roi*[15] and vice versa. There's a corresponding deterioration of society's vital forces, of its muscles and skeleton, as ossification sets in.

In economics, **we have combined the disadvantages of both capitalism and socialism,** without receiving the advantages of either. From capitalism, we've retained free trade and open borders without the benefits of free enterprise; from socialism, we've retained only statism, trade union corporatism, high taxation, and bureaucracy, without social justice, solidarity, and full employment.

It's false to say, as do the theoreticians of the Right and Left, who lack economic expertise or entrepreneurial experience of any kind, that 'liberalism is the main enemy' or that we live in a brutal, ultraliberal society. This is an old canard of Left analysis.

First of all, **it's unbridled global free trade that needs to be combated and not the play of interior market forces** within a protected European continental space. To demonise the 'market' plays the game of a sclerotic and communising corporatism. Though criticising

---

14 The Freedom Party of Austria (Freiheitliche Partei Österreichs, FPÖ) is a Right-wing populist party founded in 1956, known for its nationalist and anti-immigration stances. As of 2025, the FPÖ remains active and influential, having won the largest share of votes in the 2024 legislative elections.

15 *Ubu Roi* is a well-known play by Alfred Jarry written in 1896. It is regarded as one of the primary precursors of the Theatre of the Absurd. Ubu, the main character, is depicted as the culmination of all of the flaws of modern man, being selfish, cruel, vulgar and dishonest, and manages to become king by murdering his predecessor.

'market society' and the 'reign of money', we must not forget that performance, economic energy, and innovation are the principal motors of *competition* and that the maximisation of gain (not virtue) was — and will always be, whether it is deplored or not — the basis of dynamism.

Criticising 'market society' ought not, then, to be a critique of the market and its liberal principle, but rather an opposition to its possible dictatorship and to the speculative forces. It's necessary thus to demand the presence of a sovereign function to operate above the market — a political decisionism,[16] as well as the correcting mechanisms of social solidarity, to aid those of our people who cannot subsist solely on the basis of their labour.

The real problem in our society is not an excess of liberalism, but an excess of socialism! And it's the worst sort of socialism: not the socialism of Proudhon[17] or Blanqui,[18] but Communist-inspired trade union corporatism, protected privileges, colossal pay cheque deductions. Such excesses are remote to any idea of social justice — an idea frequently proclaimed though rarely practiced.

The great institutions of the public sphere — the basis of every civilisation (schools, hospitals, the army, the police) — along with the constitutive principles of every living society (security, public health, the transmission of knowledge, etc.) — are slowly beginning to decline.

---

16 Decisionism, or *Dezisionismus* in the original German, was a term first coined by the German legal scholar Carl Schmitt. According to Schmitt, the validity of a particular moral or legal precept has nothing to do with its specific nature, but only depends on the authority from which it was issued.

17 Pierre-Joseph Proudhon (1809–1865) was a French politician and philosopher who opposed capitalism and did not believe in state ownership of property, instead believing that property should belong to workers' groups.

18 Louis Auguste Blanqui (1805–1881) was a revolutionary activist. His version of socialism, however, differed greatly from Marx's, especially in that he believed that a socialist revolution would not be brought about through a mass movement of the workers, but rather by a small elite who would enact the revolution by imposing a temporary dictatorship.

Society, however, still stands, like a straw man in a field ravaged by crows. This is the 'new society', of the 'new modernity', which thinks itself strong and healthy (there's the Internet, isn't there?), but whose interior is gangrened, like a dead tree, whose bark is still intact but whose fall will come with the first storm.

With the drying up of the inner sap — that is, with the loss of the values and biological forces counteracting the forces of desiccation — administration hardens and blisters, the heart stops, the blood wears thin, enthusiasm and liberty die off. **A fake civilisation emerges from the collapse of real culture.**

*

One must always hope. Our people still possess immense resources. Despite the ongoing subversion, the tragic creativity of European civilisation has yet to be extinguished.

France or Europe?

Several impertinent questions merit posing:

Does being French still mean anything once one assumes a European identity? A related question: should we remain French, in the actual legal sense of the term, or should we become European? Can we still construct Europe while preserving the French state? Does the disappearance of the French state signal the end of France? Is such an end inescapable and desirable — in a context where we seek to create a powerful, sovereign, identitarian Europe? Is the ideology of the French state, with its Jacobin centralism and cosmopolitan universalism, even compatible with a European identity?

Will the failings and profligacies of the European bastard born at Amsterdam in 1997[19] return us to the past or will it provoke a flight forward, toward a sovereign Federation?

---

19 The Treaty of Amsterdam was a revision of the 1992 Treaty of the European Union.

Should the European Union now under construction be seen in a Machiavellian sense, as a necessary stopgap, part of an inevitable but provisional process? An imperfect construct built by 'useful idiots', which is nevertheless indispensable, though it will have to be renovated from top to bottom? Is European Federation — a veritable historical revolution, undoubtedly the most important event of the last 1,500 years — the sole way to ward off the fatal dangers facing Europe? Should the European revolution be accelerated, to liberate us from the American yoke, to remedy the terrible problem of immigration and Islamisation, to check our demographic decline, to ward off the advent of an already visible economic crisis of massive proportions, to rediscover the brilliance and power of our civilisation? Or is it necessary to renounce the utopia of European Federation, considered by some inherently impotent, and save Europe by returning to the sovereignty of the European nation-states, whose relations will be governed by simple treaties, in the old way? Such are the key questions urgently in need of addressing.

We are entering a period of great storms, as we've long anticipated, a historical cyclone which, in an earlier work, *Archeofuturism*,[20] I called the 'convergence of catastrophes'.

La Grande Europe will in no case be 'the first step toward a World State' — but rather toward **a New Nation, federal and imperial, based on Europe's historical regions, not her presently inadequate nation-states, and rooted in her ethnic unity.** We need, thus, to struggle against both the old nation-states (which no longer defend us because they've become so weak and inadequate) and against the false ideal of a cosmopolitan Europe.

*

---

20 Published in English as *Archeofuturism: European Visions of the Post-Catastrophic Age* (London: Arktos, 2010).

I've always been a 'nationalist' — never a 'French nationalist', but rather a **'European nationalist'**. Despite dreams of grandeur (which have eluded her), France is too small. To exist, to defend ourselves, to assert ourselves in an increasingly hard world, it's necessary to regroup at a larger level, as a continental bloc. Certain French virtues (the imperatives of independence and influence, strategic power, state sovereignty...) need to be extended to the European level, while at the same time avoiding certain failings of the French state and its ideology: an inveterate cosmopolitanism, a suicidal religion of human rights, bureaucratism, fiscalism, egalitarianism, extreme centralisation, the dogma of *jus soli,* the conservatism of 'acquired advantages', social blockage, etc.

European nationalism is far more acceptable to an Italian, a Belgian, an Austrian, or a Spaniard than to a Frenchman. Yet it was the French who initiated the process of European construction, which even de Gaulle[21] didn't try to arrest ... Paradox of history: certain Frenchmen, unconsciously perceiving France's insufficiency and dreading the thought of a servile destiny, such as England's *vis-à-vis* her American overlord, didn't hesitate to lead her former hereditary enemy, Germany, into constructing what, in effect, is a neo-Carolingian[22] community.

Having long opposed the rest of Europe and the Ghibelline[23] idea of empire and having adhered to the cult of the Jacobin state, France

---

21 As President, Charles de Gaulle presided over France's participation in the formation of the European Community (forerunner of today's European Union). While he did not attempt to stop the development of the EC, it is true that he went to great lengths to manipulate it to ensure France's independence from it and the other members, including withdrawing French participation in the EC altogether.

22 The Carolingian Empire was ruled by Charlemagne and his successors during the Ninth century. At its height, the Empire comprised most of Western Europe, and is seen by historians as begetting the modern states of France and Germany.

23 The Ghibellines were one of the two main factions of the Holy Roman Empire. They favoured the imperial power of the Hohenstaufen dynasty, in opposition to the Guelphs, who supported the idea of papal authority.

became the paradoxical creator of a future European federated community: a dialectical reversal explainable, perhaps, in terms of her peoples' unconsciousness. It's as if this nation, the ethnic résumé of Europe, sensing her powers declining after 1945 and again after decolonisation, had wanted to project herself onto a Europe conceived as a 'France on a larger scale', pursuing, in effect, a variant of the Napoleonic dream. The history of this effort has already worked out quite differently than the French intended: Europe is not going to be a *Grande France* — it's going to be herself, something unprecedented in history. And it's up to us to see that Europe becomes authentically imperial and does not fall into some sort of political chaos opened to all the world, to all peoples, to all denominations, and to all dangers. Nothing is inevitable.

To take a larger view, we might consider European unity today as a counterpoint, 1,700 years later, to the breakup of the Roman Empire and the slow birth of nations — and thus **the reconstitution, in a different form, of a lost unity,** of which Medieval Christendom was also an effort.

*

Today, fifty years after the Treaty of Rome, who doesn't see that the EU's nation-states are in the process of withering away, devoid of substance? Should we try, then, to re-animate these states or, through a historical metamorphosis, try to create a real Great Nation?

These questions are especially painful for French patriots. But there are moments when it's necessary to make heartbreaking revisions, in order to remain who we are — in order to defend the essential.

Eminently respectable, the 'idea of France' is nevertheless not as important to me as the idea of 'Europe'. **Besides, as presently practiced, the 'idea of France' seems profoundly harmful to the people of France.** In this period of mass immigration and deculturation, even 'French nationalists' — supreme irony of history — appeal to the folklore of Alsace, Provence, Brittany, etc., that was once brutally assaulted by the Jacobin state, in order now to recover a 'French identity' that official France no longer recognises.

An Antwerpian of Belgian nationality, a Catalan of Spanish nationality, a Lombard of Italian nationality ... are my compatriots. They are fellow Europeans. But a West Indian, an African, an Arab, or a Chinese who possesses a French National Identity Card are not my compatriots, though in strictly judicial terms they may be considered French. They themselves see things in this way, contrary to the wishes of assimilationists and other pathetic defenders of the 'republican model of integration'.

To see things as such is to react in the way any person or people on Earth would react. Ethnicity is the sole stable basis of human community, as Claude Lévi-Strauss argues in *Race et histoire* (*Race and History*).[24]

The Algerians refused to designate certain former colonials who considered themselves Algerian as 'Algerian', because they quite rightly considered them European. Today, the majority of immigrants with French citizenship refuse to see themselves as 'European' and still identify as Africans or Asians. This shows that they understand 'European' in ethnic terms. In the United States, where pragmatism rules, the term 'European' is officially used to designate those descended from white European immigrants.

From an archeofuturist perspective envisaging the future as a return to archaic principles, once the universalism of modernity fails, the following question about European unification inevitably arises: will Europe be constructed on a model of ethnic chaos, according to the utopian model of communitarian cohabitation that has failed everywhere, or will she be constituted as **an organic regrouping of kindred cultures possessing a common will — a central brain**, if you will?

---

24 Claude Lévi-Strauss, *Race and History* (Paris: UNESCO, 1952).

Related to this question is the necessity of distinguishing between Europe's principal enemy and her principal adversary. **Her principal enemy is the South, assembled under the banner of Islam, which, through a colonisation from below, is endeavouring to permanently establish itself there. Her principal adversary is the United States**, which, in its double-game, has allied with Islam, as evident in NATO's aggression against the Serbs.

Islam strives for revenge and conquest. The United States — logically from its geostrategic perspective — endeavours to neutralise Europe, whose unification threatens American hegemony and economic interests on the Continent. To divide Europeans in order to better rule them, the U.S. endeavours to foster war and discord, it favours Islamic immigration, it seeks to prevent a European alliance with Russia and the Slavs, it keeps us under its military tutelage, and it forces us to open our markets without reciprocating, all the while proclaiming that it's our protector: this is the logic of America's perverse hegemony in Europe, which the Europe of nation-states, no less than the Europe of Maastricht and Amsterdam,[25] is unable to defend herself against, because she lacks the will to do so.

A third way might be considered, which would be a nightmare for both the principal enemy and the principal adversary: **a democratic, sovereign, powerful, but decentralised European Federation — economically based on 'the autarky of great spaces'**, refusing Islamisation and Third Worldisation, equipped with an independent military force, and aspiring to integrate Russia into the greatest imperial ensemble that humanity will have ever known — **Eurosiberia** — seeking, in the process, to arrest its demographic decline, ally with China and India, and thus break with the Islamic and American worlds.

*

---

25 The European Union.

The tragedy of our age is positive to the degree it offers Europeans, and especially European youth, a way of escaping the torpor of consumer society. As Sartre (who rarely understood the measure of his words) once naïvely observed, it's in adversity, in the urgency of battle and war, that joy is born.

The European revolution: this is the fuse that needs to be lit, this is the single glimmer in a world darkened by stormy skies, this is the sole hope.

Economic Principles

For Nuclear, Not Petroleum Energy

The disaster of the oil tanker *Erika* in 1999[26] reminds us that petroleum energy is the most polluting in the world. The pseudo-ecologists, however, reserve their thunder for nuclear energy, the least polluting form of energy! The reason: **oil is a pillar of American hegemony and the financial basis of the Muslim states.** Nuclear power, moreover, would make Europe energy independent, which is seen with a jaundiced eye. **There exists, as such, an objective alliance between Trotskyist Greens, American interests, and the Muslim states.**

*

Nuclear energy has been demonised in Europe because it evokes the 'atomic bomb' and Hiroshima. Another symptom of magical thought. This energy source, however, is the least dirty of all, the least dangerous, contrary to the twittering of propagandists and ... despite Chernobyl.

*

---

26 The MV *Erika* was a Maltese tanker that broke in two and sank during a storm in the Bay of Biscay on 12 December 1999. It killed a lot of marine life and polluted the shores of Brittany. It remains the largest environmental disaster in French history.

Nuclear energy, if it is properly mastered, is perfectly respectful of the environment. Classic thermal plants or hydroelectric dams massively pollute the atmosphere and destroy forests and other vegetation.

Barring accident, a nuclear plant is not ecologically harmful. Since 1950, the very rare cases of nuclear accident (Three Mile Island, Chernobyl, Fukuyawa, etc.) have caused a thousand times less damage than petroleum accidents. Another example: German Greens massively mobilised against the transport of nuclear materials from France to Germany or to Japan, though there has never been an accident. At the same time, they are virtually silent about accidents and disasters caused by the ground transport of oil products or by oil pipelines! The precautions involved in nuclear production are qualitatively more rigorous than those of the oil companies. But the petroleum industry stands at the centre of America's military-industrial complex, generating vast profits from which many benefit, including Greenpeace and the Greens.

Following the stupid German decision, made under the pressure of philo-American and philo-Islamic Trotskyist ecologists, the government of Gerhard Schröder was compelled to abandon nuclear power. Claude Allègre, the former French Minister of National Education, reacted by declaring, 'Once the question of waste disposal is resolved in the coming decade, nuclear energy will become the most reliable and least polluting of energy sources. The Germans haven't told us how they are going to generate their energy. All sources emitting carbon dioxide in the atmosphere will dangerously modify the climate. My concern is maintaining France's energy independence.'[27]

Fossil fuels (petroleum, coal, and gas) emit millions of tons of carbon and nitrogen oxides into the atmosphere, which cause cancer (more than the mythical radiation) and diminish the ozone layer, responsible for the greenhouse effect, which raises temperatures and causes climatic disturbances. In France alone nuclear energy avoids

---

27 From *Le Figaro*, 20 July 2000.

emitting 78,000 tons of dust, 1.1 million tons of nitrogen dioxide, 2 million tons of sulphur dioxide, and 337 million tons of carbon dioxide, the gases that are the most polluting and the most destructive to health. Thanks to her nuclear capacity, France has reduced 70 percent of the polluting gases that come from electrical production, while the other 30 percent are emitted by gas-based motors and cars, which is more than all the waste produced by her industry! Thanks to nuclear energy, France (whose electrical production is the most advanced in the world) pollutes the atmosphere less than any of her EU partners: 6.9 tons of carbon dioxide per inhabitant, against the European average of 8.15 tons and the German average of 11 tons.

*

The Greens and the ecological lobby always play the petroleum card, which is the most polluting! They have, for example, succeeded in stopping all nuclear construction in Germany, Sweden, and Italy.[28] These nuclear power sources have been replaced by gas or fuel-powered electrical generators, which are extremely polluting. The 'energy savings', demagogically promised by the Greens, was limited to emissions. A second example: the Greens — in this case, the catastrophic Madame Voynet[29] — succeeded in shutting down the Rhine-Rhône canal, allegedly because of its negative effect on the scenery. The result: freight costs between the Rhine and Rhône basins have increased 4 percent annually, as has the pollution caused by the trucking

---

28 As of April 2025, Germany has completed its nuclear phase-out, shutting down its last reactors in 2023, and remains committed to renewable energy despite some calls to revisit nuclear power. Italy, after decades without nuclear energy, approved a plan in 2025 to reintroduce it using advanced technologies like Small Modular Reactors, aiming for operation by the early 2030s. Sweden, which once planned to phase out nuclear power, now supports building up to ten new reactors by 2045 to meet energy demands and climate goals.

29 Dominique Voynet (b. 1958) is a French Green Party politician who served as environment minister and senator before returning to national politics in 2024 as a member of the National Assembly.

replacing it. Similarly, the Greens have never raised a finger against the development of unnecessary highways (such as the Paris-Troyes A3 or the Rouen-Tours A28, which are always empty). In contrast, they protested against the high-speed train lines (TGV)[30] between Marseilles and Valence ... Never have the Greens shown even the least support for 'rail-piggybacks' (trucks on trains). Petroleum-based electricity and transport are what these impostors support in practice.

*

It's quite possible that the Greens and the ecological lobby have 'rolled over' for the oil companies and the American interests to which they are closely linked. For the United States, ally of the Muslim oil producers, has a vested interest in Europe's abandonment of nuclear power.

The world petroleum lobby is threatened by nuclear power, as well as electricity-powered transport. 80 percent of the petroleum industry is controlled by Anglo-American companies. And let's not forget the British oilfields in the North Sea ... Another thing: American support for the Muslim Chechens, like that of Europe's pro-American Left, has been partly motivated by its desire to control the pipelines linked to the Caspian Sea oilfields. Similarly, the principal producers of natural gas (Algeria, Indonesia, and Central Asia) are Muslim countries. **Oil-gas production is largely in the hands of American-Muslim interests. Nuclear-generated electricity in Europe would be an economic catastrophe for them.** So much for the environment. And this with the blessing of the pseudo-ecologists, who have probably been bought off.

Their anti-nuclear aggressiveness may also have something to do with their globalist vision of the economy, which again serves American interests at Europe's expense. Petroleum implies dependence on foreign sources, while nuclear energy relies on small quantities of easily available uranium (of which Russia has vast supplies).

---

30 *Train à grande vitesse* is French for high-speed train.

The idea of European energy independence is incompatible with such interests. Besides, to deprive Europe of competence in nuclear civil engineering would deprive her (especially France) … of the ability to produce weapons-grade uranium, and thus deprive her of an independent deterrent. This is part of both American and Muslim geopolitics. In many other areas as well, **ecologists, Trotskyists, the Pentagon, and Islam wage the same struggle against Europe.**

*

What disturbs our neo-Leftist ecologists is the objective power (military and economic) and independence that nuclear power offers Europe, as well as its technological implications. There's a distinct logic to the Left's struggle: weaken the *European devil*, censure her traditions and ancestral memories, defuse her technological and military power, smother her independence, corrupt her mores, and destroy her ethnic *germen* through immigration. Its anti-nuclear and pro-petroleum stances are but part of a concerted, multifaceted **strategy to destroy the identity and continuity of European civilisation.** The Left's environmental concerns and defence of public health are simply crude, oily pretexts.

What serious counter-propositions can be made against these anti-nuclear impostors? Energy production has two principal applications today: electricity and transport.

What energy types are presently available to produce electricity?

1. Classic coal, oil, and gas-based power plants, which are largely dependent on foreign suppliers and cause massive pollution (atmospheric emissions, oil spills, etc.).
2. 'White oil', that is, dams, of which there aren't many and which flood large natural areas — like the present scandalous dam at Guiana,[31] against which the ecologists uttered not a word.

---

31 Faye is referring to the Barrage de Petit-Saut dam in northern French Guiana.

3. Tidal power plants, like the one in Rance (Brittany), the sole such plant in the world,[32] are not just a rarity, but create great, problematic accumulations of silt.

4. Geothermal energy, which is very costly to produce.

5. Energy from solar panels, whose output is slight.

6. Solar ovens (or cookers), which are dependent on the weather.

7. Wind farms, which require large areas and produce a mere fraction of the energy that comes from a nuclear plant.

8. Aquatic (or hydroelectric) energy, produced by turbines in rivers with strong currents, have generally low outputs and are limited by a lack of appropriate sites.

For transportation, there are the following energy sources:

1. Polluting internal combustion engines.

2. Electric motors which pollute very little or not at all.

We can't get away from internal combustion engines (in planes, ships, diesel locomotives, etc), but they can be limited, though this has never been seriously tried. Everything has happened as if, lacking research or serious investment, alternative petroleum-based transportation, especially in relation to automobiles, has been systematically discouraged, despite the evident problems this has created.

*

---

32 The Rance Tidal Power Station in France, operational since 1966, was the world's first and remained the largest until South Korea's Sihwa Lake facility surpassed it in 2011. As of 2025, countries operating tidal power stations include France, South Korea, China, Russia, and the UK — where Scotland's MeyGen project is expanding. While Canada and the U.S. have tidal projects in earlier stages or pilot form, countries like India and the Philippines are planning future installations.

It's not a matter of succumbing to the dogma of 'all nuclear', in the way we succumbed to the dogma of 'all oil'. Every form of energy production has its disadvantages, but nuclear for the moment offers the fewest. These are:

1. In case of war or terrorism, electricity production concentrated in a small number of ultra-powerful plants is vulnerable.
2. There is the problem of storing radioactive waste for very long periods, though if careful precautions are taken (such as storing at great depths), the risks of radiation are minimised.
3. There's also the risk of accident or the escape of radioactive gases into the atmosphere. In the fifty years that nuclear plants have operated, there has, however, been only one such failure, Chernobyl, whose negative effects on public health were qualitatively less than the colossal emissions of carcinogenic gases produced by petroleum energy or by oil spills on the high seas. Nuclear energy can be mastered and improved, but not oil energy.

Here are several proposals for an energy strategy and a transport policy aimed at **the dual goal of causing the least pollution and ensuring Europe's energy independence and autarky.**

For electrical production, the basis should be nuclear, a policy which doesn't presently exist in France. A new type of Franco-German plant, still in the planning, will reduce electric costs by a quarter. The Greens are doing their best to torpedo the project. At the same time, **supplemental sources need to be developed to provide for local, decentralised use** in order to diminish the fragility of 'star networks'.[33] These might include wind farms and river and sea turbines. The general rule should probably be to avoid gas, coal, or oil-based plants.

In respect to transport:

---

33 Centralised networks. — Tr.

1. Systematise the use of electric-diesel engines, or better, GPL/electric engines (which pollute very little) and more thermal fuels made from vegetable oils.
2. Impose a policy of 'piggybacking', as in Switzerland and Austria, where trucks are mounted on trains.
3. Extend the network of high-speed trains (TGV) throughout Europe, with numerous connecting links, to alleviate the massive inconveniences of continental air traffic.
4. Develop a systematic policy for rail and canal freight.
5. Use wind energy (wind turbines or semi-rigid sails) in commercial shipping, which would permit a 40 percent reduction in fuel consumption.
6. Invest in the new German blimp technologies as a means to transport freight.

With an eye to larger strategic policy concerns, it would also be useful to invest in 'second-generation nuclear power' — that is, in nuclear fusion rather than fission (where atoms are joined, not split), for the theoretical basis of fusion is already known and with it there's no risk of radiation (since its combustibles can be any metal, instead of uranium). Oil lobbies, however, have everywhere, especially at Brussels, tried to limit research and investment in new energy and transport technologies. It's in their interest to maintain Nineteenth-century fossil fuel energies.

A little common sense: acid rain that kills forests, miners who die from black lung, oil slicks that ravage coasts, cathedrals and historic monuments that are blackened and eroded by auto exhaust, respiratory illnesses and cancers caused by carbon or sulphur emissions, European dependence on American-Muslim oil suppliers and interests — all these things, it might be argued, pose a far greater threat than the alleged dangers of nuclear power.

The Imposture of the 'New Economy'

Everyone talks about the 'new economy'—that is, the economy based on multimedia telecommunications and information services provided by the Internet, which have supposedly ushered in a second Golden Age. **This magical talk, with its euphoric sensibility, simply reiterates the old progressive, scientistic illusions.** In fact, it's just another neo-liberal imposture, whose modernist hegemony is presently coming to an end. For the 'new economy' may well culminate in disaster...

*

The Internet and the 'new technologies' are no 'revolution', but a simple evolution and, undoubtedly, one of great fragility. Founded on the globalisation of trade, techno-science, and the instantaneity of information, the 'new economy' is actually more than a century old.

Online sales, for instance, are only an improvement of the older forms of mail order sales introduced around 1850, and correspond to no *structural change*. Similarly, not the Internet, nor multimedia cell phones, TV networks, smart cards, the general 'informationisation' of society, or genetic engineering represent a fundamental structural change, but are, rather, the 'elaboration' of already existing things. For none of these so-called new technologies are comparable to the real upheavals, the real techno-economic metamorphoses, that occurred between 1860 and 1960—and completely revolutionised life and society—with internal combustion engines, electricity, the telephone, the telegraph, the radio (far more revolutionary than television), the railroad, the airplane, penicillin, antibiotics, etc. The new technologies are behind us! There has been **no fundamental innovation** since 1960: computers have only been reconceived, and made faster and cheaper than what already existed. In contrast, the automobile, antibiotics, telecommunication, and air travel were authentic revolutions making possible things that had previously been impossible.

Another reason not to succumb to the siren songs of the 'new economy', which has supposedly brought an end to crises, is that just the opposite risks happening.

The economist Frédérique Leroux, who has criticised the presently fashionable mirages of the 'new economy', writes, 'The dominant thought of market economists lacks all the breath of inspiration. Yoked to the prevailing conformities, they have abandoned every critical perspective ... Their linear projections are now the stuff of all reference ... We are rapidly approaching the zero degree of economic thought'.

Criticising those who think the Internet and *start-ups* have inaugurated a new era without recession and cycles, she notes, 'The new economy — about which we know little to the degree it designates new technologies or new modes of economic functioning (perpetual growth without inflation or boom-bust cycles) — accounts for everything because it allows everyone to speak with an expert's enthusiasm about something which no one has bothered to understand'. The new economy is simply a term that refers to no actual reality, it's a pseudo-concept, one of neo-liberalism's ideological ruses. 'The new economy is simply an expression used to justify our renunciation of all effort to economically conceptualise it, preferring non-reflection. It is the marketing standard of those who have opted for compliance out of ignorance, convenience, laziness, or hazard.'[34]

Like Francis Fukuyama,[35] with his idea of the 'end of history' (following Communism's fall and the belief that a world unified on the

---

34 From *Le Figaro*, 24 July 2000.
35 Francis Fukuyama (b. 1952) is an American political philosopher who is best-known for his 1992 book, *The End of History and the Last Man*, which postulated that with the triumph of liberal democracy at the end of the Cold War, humanity had attained the perfect form of government and that the remnants of other ideologies would soon pass away. It was viewed by many as the credo of America's political and economic dominance of the world during the 1990s.

basis of a universalistic liberalism will be a world freed of political conflict), the apostles of the new economy want us to believe that we've entered a marvellous new era of **perpetual growth**, without crisis or recession.

Thanks to the Internet, *start-ups*, data processing, globalisation, etc., it's imagined that the economy has freed itself of crises. But this is a religious — a redemptive — vision of the economy. The 'economic cycle' is alive and well, for the economy is human, purely psychological, and not something simply 'technological'. After the euphoria comes the inevitable panic and despair.

*

A number of factors suggest that **we're actually living through the end of a cycle of false growth and entering a period of economic catastrophe that may well be worse than that of 1929, because the world economy is now more fragile, more globalised, and more speculative than ever before.** It's the logic of a house of cards. We haven't entered a completely new era, as neo-liberalism's sorcerer's apprentices claim. Previously, in the 1920s, it was also believed that the new technologies (automobiles, radio, airplanes, telephones, electricity, etc.) had ushered in an age immune to crisis and recession. And we know how that ended ... Today, with computers and the new economy, we've succumbed to a similar *belief in miracles*.

Toward a Planetary Economic Crisis?

The present 'growth' is actually quite superficial and will prove to be ephemeral for the following reasons, all of which suggests the possibility of a general collapse:

Initially associated with American neoconservatism, Fukuyama later distanced himself from the movement, particularly criticising its militaristic foreign policies in his 2006 book *America at the Crossroads*.

1. **The fragility of a stock market economy.** The present world economy is founded, even more than the economy of the 1920s, on the speculative frenzy of transnational stock markets, a totally unreal world: the Dow Jones, Nikkei, or CAC 40[36] direct the economy toward ultra-short-term considerations and day-to-day speculative spirals (generating immediate profits, panics, and sudden euphoria), while any notion of political economy is abandoned and long-term realities neglected.

    With the slightest bad news, speculative investment, the motor of the new economy, risks collapsing. We've already had a warning shot with the 'Asian crisis' of the 1990s.[37] Frédérique Leroux writes, 'With the intrusion of the smallest grain of sand into the gears, the virtual mechanism comes to an immediate halt.' It's like the 'butterfly effect' in weather: the most minor event can provoke an investors' panic. A speculative world economy is nothing but a giant with feet of clay. 'Given the ephemeral nature of its economic nirvana, the tiniest changes turn an 'irrational exuberance' into an anorexic depression ... We've reached that critical point in the long economic cycle today where the stock market, this jittery entity to which we have abandoned ourselves, has taken over the economy.'

    Growth, fundamental to the economy, has completely escaped government or public control. It's now at the mercy of those euphoric or depressive moods particular to speculation. It's significant that Europe (unlike the United States) no longer has a monetary policy, a first in her history. Based entirely on speculation,

---

36 The CAC 40 is the French stock market index.

37 The Asian Financial Crisis began in July 1997 in Thailand when the government, faced with bankruptcy due to its massive foreign debt, switched the national currency from a fixed to a floating exchange rate, causing its collapse. The crisis then spread throughout Asia, resulting in massive inflation, which continued to affect many nations until the end of 1998. Indonesia was particularly impacted, culminating in widespread rioting and the resignation of President Suharto.

the so-called 'new economy' is simply an aggravation of financial economics, speeded up by digital technologies.

2. **The exponential growth of world debt, public and private.** All the countries of the world, rich and poor alike, are in deficit and there's talk of annulling Third World debt. Who is going to pay the bill? The world economy resembles an enterprise on the verge of bankruptcy, but one always supported by some virtualist banker. The bulletin of the brokerage firm Prigest, hardly anti-capitalist, noted in July 2000, 'Private debt is rising at a frenzied rate. It has become a circular transmission belt, linking rising stocks and economic activity. And it's making the system increasingly fragile, however much it gives the impression of increased growth.' The bulletin also speaks of the new economy's irrational exuberance as it glides along the chasm. An economy based on debt (a monetarist dogma) — and not on labour or non-market considerations (demographic, ecological, energy, etc.) — is bound to be short-lived.

3. **The demographic ageing of Europe and other advanced industrial countries, compounded by economic and immigration burdens.** For the moment, we can bear these blows, but it won't last. The paucity of active workers, pension obligations, and health costs will, beginning in 2005–2010, gravely aggravate Europe's economic burdens. Productivity gains and advanced technologies (a favourite remedy) will then cease covering the costs of the changing demographic situation. Far from compensating for the decline of an active native workforce, Europe's colonising immigration will present her with the problems that come with unskilled workers and massive welfare payments. Immigrants, moreover, are going to become increasingly more expensive (in terms of insecurity, criminality, and urban policy).[38] The economic collapse of Europe,

---

38 Faye's prediction seems to be well on its way to being fulfilled. In France alone, the large-scale riots of 2005 and 2007 by Muslim immigrant youth, the mass protest in 2006 against the government's attempt to deregulate labour, the 2010

the world's foremost economic power, will bring down the United States and the other advanced economies.

4. **Contempt for ecological limits.** The extensive pollution caused by the planetary development of mass industrial economies (nowhere resisted by the ecological impostors bought off by the oil barons) is already starting to take its toll, which keeps rising in the form of catastrophic climate changes, exhausted fishing reserves, desertification, diminished fresh water supplies, destroyed forests, and the depletion of sea phytoplankton responsible for renewing the Earth's oxygen, etc.

*

Despite the infantile euphoria of the 'new economy', the Internet, and the purely conjunctural upswing, **the world economy is in the red and will likely lead to a gigantic world economic crisis early in the Twenty-first century.** Our civilisation — based entirely on the exaltation of market society, monetary values, and economic primacy (whether socialist or capitalist) — risks perishing from the economic functions upon which it rests.

---

revolt against pension reform, and the EU's sovereign debt crisis sparked by the Greek collapse all signaled deepening cracks in the European socio-economic order. More recently, the 2023 nationwide protests in France against raising the retirement age from 62 to 64 — despite elite insistence on its economic necessity — drew millions into the streets, paralyzing infrastructure and revealing a vast generational divide. The same year saw the eruption of days-long riots following the police killing of 17-year-old Nahel Merzouk, the French-born son of Algerian and Moroccan immigrants. Over 12,000 vehicles were torched and thousands of buildings damaged, highlighting the very 'insecurity, criminality, and urban policy' burdens Faye warned would follow from mass, unassimilated immigration. Far from compensating for the decline of an active native workforce, this colonising immigration has produced social fragmentation, cultural alienation, and escalating state expenditures — fulfilling Faye's vision with eerie precision. — Ed.

The situation is analogous to that of a militaristic society that perishes because of the ongoing wars it wages and eventually loses. Those who actually know something about the economy (such as Maurice Allais[39] or François Perroux)[40] have warned us about idolising it — like those soldiers who warn civilians about the dangers of militarism.

Structural factors (notably demographic and ecological ones) are never taken into consideration by those fixated on immediate, short-term results.

The apostles of the new economy are like children masquerading as adults. The new world economic order these false prophets extol is nothing but the swansong of the old order.

---

39 Maurice Allais (1911–2010) won the Nobel Prize in Economic Sciences in 1988. In his later years, he often criticised the economic and legal foundations of the European Union.

40 François Perroux (1903–1987) was a French economist who was best-known for his criticisms of economic policies involving the Third World, which he felt were too centred on Western interests and concepts.

3
STRATEGIC PRINCIPLES

With the end of the 'Soviet menace' and the subsequent pressures Islam and the South bring to bear on Europe (with American approval), the geostrategic situation has been thrown into upheaval. New concepts — **a Eurosiberian alliance, a 'domestic front', and rearmament, including nuclear weapons** — are accordingly rising to the fore.

The geostrategic situation of the Twentieth century has been transformed by two factors: first, the end of the Cold War, which makes possible a Russo-European pact against the American superpower; and second, 'from below', an American-supported colonising offensive by Arab-Muslim peoples, allied with the Global South against Europe.

America and Islam Against Europe

The Pentagon's nightmare is an ethnocentric Eurosiberia. That is, a long-term union of West and Central European peoples with the Russian Federation — a union free of Islamisation, American hegemony, and non-European colonisation.

America's thalassocracy[1] would like to control this vast region and prevent any rival power from rising there. Since 1945, the United

---

1   A thalassocracy is a state which depends primarily on the sea for its power, either economically or strategically.

States, through NATO, has sought to be 'the foremost European military power'. As an organisation designed as a defensive alliance against possible Soviet aggression, NATO no longer has a role to play, except to keep Europe strategically and militarily subordinated to the United States. This is evident in the alliances NATO has formed with the former Soviet satellites. Incapable of adopting a common defence policy and of saying 'no' to their American nephew, Europeans are alone responsible for their subjugation. France abandoned de Gaulle's strategic independence when it participated in the Gulf War[2] and again when it joined American-led NATO forces against Serbia. No one forced her to do this.

*

American geopolitical objectives in Europe are:

1. To militarily and strategically weaken Russians and Serbs, the sole peoples to have resisted their Muslim enemies (Kosovo, Chechnya, Central Asia, etc.).

2. To create dissensions among Orthodox Slavs and other Europeans in order to divide and rule them. European participation in the bombardment of Serbia, militarily futile but politically symbolic, was directly aimed at compromising us.

3. In the spirit of 'the Islamo-American pact', **the U.S. seeks to weaken Europe by favouring her Islamisation and her transformation into a multi-racial, Africanised society.** To this end, it promotes an Islamic bridgehead in the Balkans (Bosnia, Albania, Kosovo) and pressures the EU to admit Turkey, and after that, Morocco. When we were told that the bombardment of Serbia was a failure because it failed to establish a multi-ethnic society there, this was a distortion, for it was actually a success. In accord with other Muslim states, the U.S. goal was to establish a mono-ethnic

---

2   Faye is referring to the Gulf War of 1991.

Kosovar state in the heart of Europe. In exchange, Middle Eastern states were persuaded not to attack Israel, to accept Iraq's embargo, and, thirdly, to leave their oil assets in Anglo-American hands. It might be added that the Pentagon has consistently supported the arming of anti-Russian Muslim terrorists — everywhere from Afghanistan to Chechnya.

In the spirit of their ancestral Qur'anic tradition — 'the slightest resistance today for the sake of a greater domination tomorrow' — **Islamo-Arab governments accept their provisional subordination to American interests for the sake of American aid in conquering Europe.**

4. The United States welcomes Europe's Islamic colonisation. The enormous cost of this colonisation has had the effect of diminishing European competitiveness. Millions of Third World welfare recipients have poured into Europe, while Europe's young, creative economic elites are leaving for the U.S. The United States has a vested interest in this Third Worldisation of Europe's economy, just as it has in the loss of Europe's cultural, ethnic identity *vis-à-vis* Islam and the African masses.

Americans have congratulated the French on becoming a multi-racial society, just as the spider flatters the frog in order to better deceive him. As Thomas Sancton writes in a *Time* article[3] with the hallucinatory title of 'A French Renaissance', 'The French don't like to admit it, but decades of immigration have produced a multi-racial society that is reviving the nation'.

If the hypocritical Casanova in the White House is to be believed, the American government apparently now wants a rapprochement between the EU and Russia. In June 2000, Bill Clinton declared that it was 'very positive that Russia had adopted a long-range approach to the EU, with the aim of entering it and NATO'.

---

3   *Time* magazine, 5 June 2000.

In this way the Americans endeavour to recuperate the idea of a continental union for the sake of neutralising it. 'Unify, but under NATO's leadership — that is, under our authority'. Their objective is a destabilised Continent — Americanised, Islamised, and strategically directed by the U.S.

This is a completely logical strategy. There's no need to morally reproach the U.S. for it, as our passive, deranged anti-Americans do. Europeans themselves need to take matters into their own hands.

The Dangers of European 'Disarmament'

The present whim of European governments is 'disarmament' — the drastic reduction of conventional and especially nuclear arms. This stems from the dogma that, since the fall of the USSR, 'Europe no longer has any enemies' — a dogma exploited by the European political classes and by a cynical Pentagon.

The call for 'disarmament' rests on two prejudices. The first is that security is possible without maintaining a large armed force. The only thing that counts is 'the power of economic interests', with war now seen as an 'archaism'. But force and the threat to use it are one of the constants in human societies. The warrior function has never been replaced by the economic function. This is especially the case since **our enemies, given the nature of their ancestral culture, respect nothing but force and its threat.**

The second prejudice is the superstitious fear of 'nuclear', which is refuted by history. Nuclear arms are essentially dissuasive. And nothing can prevent their proliferation.

What is America's military doctrine regarding Europe? It's diabolically clever: first, to feign approval for the creation of a common (but small) European military force, a simulacrum of a common European army ('Eurocorps'), but one which in reality would be totally subordinated to NATO, even if formally separated; second, to limit European forces to 'peace-keeping' operations under UN or NATO auspices, sending European troops to replace the 'boys' on the ground, 'protected', of course, by U.S. airpower; third, European forces would thus have **no role to play in any real defence of the Continent,** which would remain under NATO and U.S. authority. This is all very well thought out geopolitically. We will be left with only peace-keeping and policing forces fit for a banana republic.

France is the turkey in this farce: she has unilaterally renounced nuclear testing (while the U.S. Senate has refused to ratify the suspension of American tests, which could start up again at any time); she has thus unilaterally reduced her nuclear arsenal. The U.S. has not ended its nuclear program. In accord with the SALT accords, it has reduced its 'overkill' capacity, but without impinging on its global capacity. Even better: in violating its treaties and despite vain Russian and French protests, Americans continue to work on developing an 'anti-missile shield', which would undermine the deterrent purpose of nuclear weapons.

In sum, the Pentagon hasn't at all prevented the proliferation of nuclear weapons (notably among its Israeli and Islamic friends), but has, instead, sought to disarm France and Russia in order to make itself invulnerable to nuclear attack.

Notions of the 'Menace from the South' and the 'Domestic Front'

The principal potential military threat to Europe comes from the Arab-Islamic world. Soon Iraq,[4] Iran, eventually Algeria, and already Pakistan possess or will soon possess rudimentary but devastating nuclear arms capable of reaching Europe. From this perspective, France's nuclear force no longer functions as a deterrent of 'the weak against the strong' (as was the case with the former Soviet Union), but as 'a deterrent of the strong against the crazy'.

---

4   This was written prior to the American invasion of Iraq in 2003.

On the hinge of the Twentieth and Twenty-first centuries, we are going to experience a **geopolitical and geostrategic change of dramatic proportions.** The danger will no longer come from the East, but from the South. The great fractures won't be inter-European but inter-civilisational. It will be a return of a long-past situation, a return to archaism: to the Eighth century of Charles Martel.[5]

The maintenance and development of an independent nuclear military capacity for Europe, based on France's nuclear arsenal, and eventually linked to Russia's, will be indispensable to the Continent's defence. In awaiting the creation of a viable European executive, the French government needs to preserve and maintain its strategic and tactical nuclear arsenal. It's never too late to revoke a bad decision.

Just as nothing is ever excluded from history. **The possible conjuncture, in the course of the Twenty-first century, of an ethnic civil war in France and Europe, along with a military threat from Arab-Islamic countries, is no longer automatically excluded from consideration by our more lucid military planners.** Supported by tactical forces, a nuclear deterrent will be indispensable against our enemies in the coming century.

Similarly, notions of an 'interior enemy' and an 'interior front' are increasingly viable and irrefutable. Against a possible 'Kosovarisation' of Europe, encouraged by the Muslim states, our geopolitical and strategic orientations have got to change.

---

5 Charles Martel (ca. 688–741), which in English means Charles the Hammer, was a great Frankish military commander who fought under the Merovingian kings, defeated a Muslim invasion and thus prevented Europe's Islamisation, and helped to lay the groundwork for modern Europe.

Toward a Eurosiberian Strategic Doctrine: The 'Giant Hedgehog'[6]

Our future strategic doctrine is clear. Here are its principal axes:

1. Europeans need to form a **land army, made up of native Europeans and adequate to fighting a possible religious-ethnic civil war.** But is this possible with the professionalisation of the military and the abandonment of conscription? Everything depends on the criteria used to select recruits. The stakes are high. The massive presence of non-indigenous elements within the present armed forces makes them a possible fifth column.

2. Europeans need to develop an **autonomous nuclear capacity, complete with full tactical and strategic assets.** Given that nuclear arms are credible only when there's a unity of decision-making behind their possible use, there will have to be a common sovereignty, and if this is not possible, then France and Russia will have to assume a 'defensive and deterrent pact' for Europe, like the present American nuclear umbrella. Since Great Britain is not an independent nuclear power, but a U.S. appendage, it will have to be excluded from such a pact.

3. Because a Russian alliance is preferable to an American alliance, Europeans need to stop seeing themselves as 'the pillar of NATO'

---

6 'The "Giant Hedgehog" refers to a celebrated poster made at the time of the huge demonstrations against American missiles in the early 1980s. The poster, drawn by the Flemish cartoonist "Korbo", represented a joyful laughing hedgehog walking along and saying "Pacifist but ready to defend myself". It was a plea for a well-organised defence according to the Swiss or Yugoslavian model. Once the hedgehog raises his quills, he cannot be captured by a predator. So Europe had to leave NATO and adopt a Swiss citizens' army able to "network" (*maillage* in the French terminology of General Brossolet) the territory in a locally-based defence system. General Jochen Löser, with whom I worked for a short time, wrote his thoughts down in several papers about this kind of alternative defence system.' Courtesy of Robert Steuckers.

and start **dismantling NATO** for the sake of an integrated military alliance (including the defence industry) that links the EU, Eastern Europe, and the Russian Federation. As the strategic prelude to Eurosiberia, this geopolitical vision of 'armed neutrality', perfectly anti-imperialist and defensive, corresponds to the 'giant hedgehog' doctrine that Robert Steuckers has formulated in his many geopolitical writings. Quite simply, we need to form **a new Warsaw Pact, from the Atlantic to the Pacific!**

4. Threatened by Islam and the South and by the U.S., Eurosiberia has a long-range interest in forming military and economic alliances with China and India, for they too have the same enemy as us: Islam.

5. Again, in the long-term, a future Great-European diplomacy will need to **persuade the Americans that they are on the wrong path in allying with Islam and the South, and in playing their anti-European card.** Even in their own strategic terms, they will not always be a thalassocratic superpower. From a visionary historical perspective, it would seem that their vocation is to return to the bosom of their motherland, Great Europe. This would be like the return of the prodigal son, as European-Americans finally realise the error of their secession. But that's something for the day after tomorrow.

6. **Good relations with the Arab-Islamic world cannot but take the form of an armed peace that never lowers its guard.** The *sine qua non*[7] of such a condition will entail the end of its colonisation of Europe. As the *Qur'an* says, Islam needs 'to put down its hand to avoid having it cut off'. It won't do this if there's a sword in its hand. The idea of a 'European-Arab Mediterranean alliance' based on allegedly common interests is a fool's errand, without any historical or economic basis. Europe has no need of Africa or the Middle East, which are a drag on her, a financial, economic, and human

---

7   Latin: 'an essential element' or 'prerequisite'.

burden, and increasingly a menace. Russia is overflowing with oil, gas, and nearly inexhaustible uranium mines. It's toward the East, toward the rising sun, that we must turn.

Our future strategic doctrine is clear. **Eurosiberia will have need of no one. It would threaten no one, and no one would be able to threaten it.** 'At the European level', as Pierre Vial puts it in *Une Terre, un people* (*One Land, One People*), page 134, 'Europe's objective is to form a Eurosiberian union, an imperial confederation, based on military, diplomatic, monetary, and commercial competencies, constituting a vast market in the form of a self-centred space. Capable of showing its teeth whenever necessary, such a giant power would be able to convince the other continental blocs to give up their colonising schemes — doing so without excluding the possibility of establishing bilateral relations that would serve each of their interests.' This says it all, for only in this way can humanity's great civilisations, each in conserving their distinct identity, cooperate to preserve the common human heritage of this planet we call 'Earth'.

Eurosiberia is obviously a long-term perspective. A heartland to hold, an objective comparable to a ship sailing toward its destination, to the inspiration of pioneers conquering an unknown land. Such a *Grand Political* perspective will undoubtedly make myopic 'specialists' and bourgeois politicians (always fooled by history) turn away in fright. As yet we still don't know how we're going to realise this great Eurosiberian project, which will entail a true metamorphic — and archeofuturist — renaissance of the ancient European idea of Empire. The road will be difficult — and stodgy intellectuals, as well as 'realistic' politicians, will never cease objecting to it — like sailors refusing to take to the sea because of an unfavourable wind.

Evoking a future historic alliance between Europe and Russia, Gorbachev, the visionary, spoke of 'constructing our Common House'.[8]

---

8   Gorbachev had used the phrase earlier but is most famous for using it in an address in Prague in April 1987, in which he was calling for an end to the partitioning of Europe between East and West.

4

METAPOLITICAL DICTIONARY

Here, in the form of a dictionary, is a synthesis of our conception-of-the-world and our historical perspective, for it's on the basis of keywords and concepts that we inevitably organise ourselves. There's no need to read it in linear fashion. The index at the end of this book will help you select the ones you wish to consult.

A

Aesthetics

According to its Greek etymology, 'that which evokes a strong sensation'. Aesthetics is linked to notions of beauty, harmony, achievement of form.

Contemporary egalitarian ideology abhors and implicitly demonises aesthetics. It associates (rightly) the will to power with discipline, which it considers morally unacceptable, 'fascist' in effect. **This ideology opposes aesthetics to 'ethics' and situates itself in ethics' iconoclastic tradition.**

With the plastic arts, architecture, cinema, literature, theatre, even fashion, the ugly, the unachieved, the unformed, the most far-fetched nonsense, the shady and the watered down are now preferred to the aesthetic, which is made synonymous with a menacing 'order'.

Since the mid-Twentieth century, contemporary arts, encouraged by the dominant ideology, have rejected any notion of aesthetics. Instead of harmony, the power of forms, the exaltation and elevation of sensation and beauty — notions of abstract 'conceptual art' are preferred, which becomes a pretext for degeneracy, wilful ugliness, and subsidised incompetence. Abstraction accordingly reigns, just as a jargonising meaninglessness and obscurity enthrals the intellectuals. The genuine aesthete, the authentic artist, is ostracised or marginalised — as if he were politically incorrect. Hence, the paradox of a society that strives to be 'moral' and humanistic, but ends up privileging barbarism, the inversion of values, and new forms of primitivism.

We're witnessing **the simultaneous cohabitation of (1) abstruse 'contemporary' art subsidised by the system, (2) a cult which turns the 'past' into museum pieces, and (3) a commercial and consumerist subculture.** Contemporary art has become the very opposite of avant-garde art. Its sad impostures haven't budged for a century. It combines a dull *academism*, imposture, an absence of talent, and financial speculation. Instead of aesthetics, the system prefers pessimistic or suicidal values of representation, those that come from chaos and deformity, nonsense, pathological abstraction, regression, infantilism, scatology, a psychotic pornography: the exaltation of primitive forms (what the visionary Céline called 'the tom-tom cult' or what Chirac calls 'primitive art'[1]). Accompanying this wretchedness, this impotence of old men, there's the vulgar, artificial boom of costume-culture, which is to culture what costume jewellery is to jewellery.

---

1   French President Jacques Chirac was one of the primary proponents of the Quai Branly Museum, an art museum dedicated to presenting the works of indigenous cultures from around the world, located near the Eiffel Tower in Paris. The museum opened in 2006.

The rejection of aesthetics is crucial to the dominant ideology. For aesthetics, at root, is aristocratic, opposed to massification and fake elites.

*

In its historical essence, the political is a declension of aesthetics. 'Grand Politics' aims, in effect, at forming a people in history, making civilisation a creator of great works, turning civilisation itself into a work — a work of art. This conception opposes the modern doctrine that reduces the political to the administrative, that hollows out the notion of a people's destiny, and rejects the creative projects of the statesman for the sake of the career politician.
(see **neo-primitivism; politics**)

Alien

Within a given population, those who are culturally and biologically of non-indigenous origin.

Today it would be better to talk of 'aliens' (*allogènes*) than of immigrants born in Europe of non-European parents, insofar as the majority of them are not ethnically European, but are considered 'nationals' solely on the basis of *jus soli*.[2] Since Antiquity, as Aristotle, Thucydides, and Xenophon noted, it's been known that every nation that takes in large number of aliens is destined to perish, for these aliens progressively replace natives, who are culturally and/or physically destroyed by them. Such a process is underway now in several parts of France.

At the beginning of the Twenty-first century, the notion of the alien has lost all currency in Europe, either legally, linguistically, or nationally. **The law, though, should designate every resident not of**

---

2 *Jus soli*, or birthright citizenship, is the official policy of France and the U.S., automatically granting citizenship to anyone born within their respective territories. In contrast, most European countries have a policy of blood citizenship in which one's eligibility depends at least partially on one's ethnicity.

European origin as an alien. A Belgian, Italian, or Russian of European origins residing in France is not an alien. The key point is that a people submerged by aliens eventually becomes a minority, strangers in their own land. Such is the logic of the colonisation we're now experiencing. **In the end, the alien becomes the native.**
(see **colonisation**)

Americanism, anti-Americanism, philo-Americanism, the American-sphere, Americomorphosis

Americanism is the ideological affirmation of the general domination exercised by the United States and its social-cultural model — which are seen as the apotheosis of modernity and Western civilisation.

Americanism is a mental attitude, a consequence of Americanisation, which causes Europeans to lose their identity and sovereignty, **but it also comes from the European's voluntary submission to it, rather than from 'American imperialism'.**

Americanisation is linguistic, dietary, cultural, vestimentary, musical, audio/visual, etc. It substitutes American myths and imaginations for European ones. It's also evident in Europe's refusal to assume her own defence (NATO) or practice protectionism to counter American protectionism.

But how appropriate is anti-Americanism, on the Right or Left?

Very little. The danger of anti-Americanism is in the virulence of its jeremiads, which are irresponsible and turn its proponents into hapless victims. Europeans are the leading actors in their Americanisation, in their submission to the United States — for **the latter is strong only to the degree we are weak.** From its own perspective, the cultural, economic, and strategic domination the U.S. exerts in the world is a normal part of its role as the liar's poker of history. It's not in the name of some moral imperative, then, that America is to be opposed, but rather as part of the normal process of competition. Rather than being anti-American, we need to be **non-American and Eurocentric.**

Philo-Americanism (an idolatry of things American) is often based on an overestimation of American forces and a fascination with it supposed status as the 'lone superpower' — an overestimation that ignores its many weaknesses.

In politics and culture, the philo-Americans are the agents of their own deculturation and domination. They are the ones who have Americanised their own culture. For this reason, one can't actually speak of American imperialism in the same way one spoke of Soviet imperialism. **It's the absence of European resistance, of self-affirmation, of will and creativity that best explains America's cultural and strategic hegemony.**

On the other hand, an overly obsessive anti-Americanism, often ignorant of America, has the paradoxical effect of reinforcing Americanism! For such a mania weakens its cause by infantilising its grievances. In demonising America, it thus actually valorises and magnifies it. Similarly, its negative discourse closes off any affirmation of its own culture and interests, and refuses to take responsibility for itself.

Anti-Americanism is demobilising. Protests against 'the monopolistic power of American subculture' are made, for example, without ever considering that it might be France's self-proclaimed elites who are responsible for the declining influence of her culture. How, after all, can American hegemony be explained, especially its cultural and economic hegemony, if its civilisation is such a nullity?

As mentioned earlier, America is our **principal adversary**, not our *principal enemy*. The latter is the mass of alien colonisers, the collaborators (foreign states and fifth columnists), and Islam.

The **American-sphere** designates that ensemble of countries, principally in Europe, which overestimates American power and its 'model', and *willingly submits* to American hegemony (NATO, commercial *diktats*, etc.) — unlike the countries of the former Soviet bloc, which were *forced to submit*. There's also **Americomorphosis,** that is, the systematic mimicry of American cultural forms — that reflect of every colonised mentality. Along with this deculturating tendency comes a not unrelated 'Afromorphosis', since the Americanisation of mores encourages Europe's abandonment of her own ethnic identity.

What's needed are Eurocentric practices — not an ineffectual anti-Americanism.

(see **competition; designation of the 'enemy' and the 'friend'; ethnocentrism**)

Anti-Racism

In the guise of combating racism and xenophobia, this doctrine encourages discrimination in favour of aliens, the dissolution of European identity, the multi-racialisation of European society, and, at root, paradoxically, racism itself.

Like the Greens, whose ideological demands do nothing to protect the environment, but surreptitiously promote a concealed Trotskyist agenda, **anti-racists use their fake struggle against racism to destroy the European's identity, as they advance cosmopolitan and alien interests.**

Anti-racism, moreover, translates into a racial obsession and contradicts itself, since its partisans deny the existence of races. In promoting open borders and dogmatically encouraging multi-racial society, anti-racists end up objectively provoking racism.

The dominant ideology imposes a quasi-religious anti-racist faith that promotes integration into its politically correct society. **Anti-racism is quintessentially a form of intellectual terrorism.** Whoever disapproves of immigration or affirms the superiority of European civilisation — and identity — whoever denounces the evils of multi-racial society, whoever observes the ethnic character of the growing criminal element — is demonised and branded by media, society, and the law as a 'racist'.

Touchstone of the self-righteous, anti-racism is the most advanced expression of postmodern totalitarian ideology. It demonises all forms of rebellion and anti-system opposition. Similarly, it neutralises and keeps potential dissidents within the system's ideological bounds. A certain intellectual Right, hoping not to alienate the ruling powers, has in this way been recuperated, marginalised, and subjected, losing in the process any hope of being publicly recognised. In effect, it endeavours to collaborate with the enemy and obey its dictates, somewhat like the Orthodox Church under Stalin. This egghead Right (it's necessary to mention it, for it's a textbook case) is not content with publicly declaring itself to be 'anti-racist', but goes so far as to denounce whoever publicly defends his European identity as a 'racist'. Incredible, but true.

This all goes to show the paralysing and integrative power of anti-racist dogma, which demands that its collaborators become informers — which probably isn't a very sound calculation.
(see **xenophilia**)

Archeofuturism

The attitude that approaches the future in terms of ancestral values, believing that notions of modernism and traditionalism need to be dialectically transcended.

Archeofuturism opposes both modernity and conservatism, seeing them as versos of one another and believing that **modernity is backward-looking,** having failed to realise either its ideals or great projects. Techno-science, for example, is incompatible with modernity's humanitarian and egalitarian values. The Twenty-first century will see the resurgence of struggles that bourgeois and Western cosmopolitan ideology thought it had long ago buried: identitarian, traditionalist, and religious conflicts; geopolitical fissures; ethnic questions posed at the planetary level; battles over scarce resources ... no

need to develop the concept here, since I've devoted an entire book to it — *Archeofuturism* — to which one can refer.
(see **progress, progressivism**)

Aristocracy, new aristocracy

Literally and etymologically, 'the government of the best'. Second meaning: 'The class of the best'. The problem is defining the 'best' and determining if it actually governs society.

For the Greeks, aristocracy was first of all a mode of government based on the rule of the nobles and the most competent. For Aristotle, aristocracy and democracy did not oppose, but complete and integrate one another according to the complementary logic of apparent opposites.

The idea of hereditary aristocracies is a constant in human societies…even in certain Communist regimes (North Korea), where hereditary power is practiced by a caste of pseudo-aristocratic parvenus, the *apparatchiks*. The notion of hereditary aristocracy should be treated carefully, for it can lead to sclerosis. A true aristocracy is founded not on the power of money, nepotism, or family filiations, but rather on character and ethics. **Those who defend their people before their own interests, those who respond to real anthropological and cultural criteria:** this is the criteria for defining aristocrats. An aristocracy has a sense of history and blood lineage, seeing itself as the representative of the people it serves, rather than as a member of a caste or club. Today every traditional European aristocratic family, without exception, has been wiped out or turned into an object of mediacratic manipulation.

To recreate a **new aristocracy**: this is the work of every true revolutionary project.

What are the qualities of a true aristocrat? Attachment to one's people, who are served with courage, impartiality, modesty, creativity, taste, simplicity, and stature.

The figure of the bourgeois is very unlike that of the true aristocrat. The decline of European aristocracies, then their disappearance, came once they merged with the bourgeois dynasties. An aristocracy is not juridicially hereditary, for a hereditary aristocracy always decays, and eventually becomes extinct. Every generation of aristocrats, through their acts, must prove that they are worthy of their status. In an archaic and futurist inegalitarian vision of the world, aristocrats would have more rights than others, but also more duties. The principle of heredity is acceptable if it facilitates the selection of elites: that is, if it weeds out the incompetent and helps incorporate capable newcomers. Today, the mere idea of aristocracy is incompatible with the dominant ideology. But every people needs an aristocracy. It's an integral part of human nature and can't be dispensed with. **The question then is not 'For or against aristocracy?' but 'What kind of aristocracy?'**

The 'nobility' of today's media is a caricature, a total renunciation of the aristocratic spirit, a bourgeois instrumentalisation of the tattered remnants of the 'great families'.

A true aristocracy embodies a people's essence. It's not formed by money, but in service to and in leadership of its people. Its rule is one of disinterest, courage, efficacy.

Every aristocracy, such as those we have in Europe, is bound to become confused with an 'economic elite' once it degenerates. What's most needed today is **the creation of a new European aristocracy**. The only possible workshop in which such an aristocracy can be created is war. Aristocrats are born of war, which is the most merciless of selection processes.

(see **circulation of elites**)

Assimilation, assimilationism

The belief that the immigrant masses can become French or European if they renounce their cultural origins.

Assimilationism is, at root, a disguised form of racism. It's also a utopia. The doctrine of assimilation was born from the quasi-religious and universalist ideals of the American and French Revolutions, as well as the Russian Revolution. It supposes that there are no peoples, that ethnic realities are a fantasy, and that the only thing that counts is the individual as consumer.

Only small minorities can be assimilated. Never in the history of mass immigration has a people been assimilated by those among whom they've settled. Faced with the present failure of assimilation, the public powers have adopted a strategy of 'integration' and 'communitarianism'. But here too they have failed.

Worse: Muslim and alien 'minorities' have ceased, in many areas where they live, to be minorities and have turned the tables on Europeans, who are compelled to assimilate the culture and mores of the colonisers! **All assimilation is equivalent to cultural genocide, for the assimilator or the assimilated.**
(see **communitarianism**)

Autarky of Great Spaces

The organisation of the world economy into autonomous, self-centred great spaces, in opposition to globalism's capitalist and free trade dogmas.

Autarky, as defended by the German school of *Grossraumautarkie*[3] and today by the French Nobel Prize recipient, Maurice Allais, is a **response to globalist economics.** The autarky of great spaces is no obsidional

---

3 'The autarky of great spaces'. This is a reference to the Historical school of economics, an approach to economics and its administration that arose during the late Nineteenth century in Germany and persisted until the Third Reich. Its adherents maintained that economics could only be understood within the cultural context of a specific historical era, and not using standardised formulas or theories. Its members were also often concerned with the plight of the common workers. Joseph Schumpeter, Werner Sombart, and Max Weber were all members of the school.

closure, but an exercise in contingency: only those things that can't be produced domestically are imported. International exchanges are thus limited, but not suppressed. The objective is political and energy independence, as well as the protection of native industries. At the same time, autarky resists the extremely fragile 'new economy', which comes with globalisation, limiting the participation of transnational firms and extra-European financial powers within the European economy. It also concerns itself with the workforce, preventing the employment of non-Europeans, except in special, highly select cases, which can't be filled by Europeans. Autarky would avoid dependence on imports, creating a vast interior market (Great Europe), capable of absorbing its own products, thus immune to foreign economic reprisals. Autarky's principle is not the exclusion of imports, but of dependence.

Autarky cannot be practiced solely by France, but must assume a European continental dimension. It's the inverse of free trade — for it rejects the EU's open borders, which contributes to unemployment and renders economic revivals ephemeral and haphazard, impinging upon European economic independence. Autarky also has the advantage of discouraging outsourcing, avoiding its multiplier effects within protected economic spaces.

Free trade critics of autarky contend that it would ruin the European export market. This is false: autarky would promote the multiplication of inter-European commercial flows based on commercial preferences for community-made products. A French enterprise would accordingly be obliged to furnish products for European rather than for international markets (if these products are available).

To be viable, the planetary economy needs to be organised into relatively impermeable continental spaces that regulate the exchange of merchandise and capital, as well as labour, organising itself into regional modes of production and consumption. Such a model would also combat the cultural homogenisation that comes from concentrated modes of production and consumption, permitting each 'great space' (especially in the Third World) to maintain its own economic identity and autonomy.

In respect to energy (and thus ecology), the autarky of great spaces would maximise one's own resources, freeing it from the present 'all oil' logic. Autarky would also affect the cultural realm, policies that in Europe, for instance, would lead to an extension of the idea of 'cultural exception',[4] particularly in the field of audio/visual media. After all — it goes without saying — this is already the standard practice in ... the United States.

Like the formation of Eurosiberia, this vision of autarkic great spaces would undoubtedly be a nightmare for the U.S., for such a self-contained continental space would be perfectly autonomous, especially in respect to energy (oil, gas, etc.) — and no longer dependent on the rest of the world.

Free trade and a single planetary economy have weakened economies everywhere, profoundly hurting European interests and creating economic situations that can't possibly last. The autarky of great spaces, along with a 'two-tier' economy, are a revolutionary response to the impending catastrophe of global free trade.

(see **economy, organic; economy, two-tier; liberalism, managerial; Eurosiberia**)

---

4   'Cultural exception' was a concept introduced by France in the 1993 GATT (General Agreement on Tariffs and Trade) agreement in the United Nations in 1993. It called for cultural products to be treated differently from other types of goods, allowing France to maintain tariffs and quotas designed to protect its television and film markets from domination by the United States.

B

Belief in Miracles

The general prejudice inherent to egalitarian and humanitarian utopias, as well as the philosophy of progress — which holds that 'one can have everything at the same time' and that reality is no obstacle.

We can have both guns and butter. One imagines, as liberals do, that an 'invisible hand' is at work spontaneously re-establishing a harmonious equilibrium. Here are some examples:

- Belief in the dogma that unlimited economic development is possible in every country without causing massive pollution and without ecologically disastrous consequences. **This is the illusion of infinite development.**

- Belief that a permissive society doesn't lead to a social jungle, and that one can have both libertarian emancipation and self-disciplined harmony. Hence, the dramatic shipwreck of public education, whose violence, insecurity, ignorance, and illiteracy stem **from pedagogical illusions** that banish all sense of limits.

- Belief that one can maintain social security and medical assistance to the elderly in a period of demographic decline by remaining committed to a system that fairly distributes aid. This is **the illusion that comes from the Communist conception of solidarity.**

- Belief that the mass immigration of aliens is compatible with 'the values of the French Republic' and the preservation of European peoples and nations; the belief that Islam can be secularised and assimilate republican values. Belief that the active population can be regenerated by importing immigrants, even though most of them are unskilled welfare recipients. Belief that it's possible to normalise the status of clandestine immigrants, that they can be integrated, and that in this way one can avoid the arrival of new immigrant waves, even though the reverse is everywhere obvious. **This is the illusion of immigration as a benefit.**

- Belief that aliens can be assimilated and integrated, as they defend and maintain the specificities of their original culture, memories, and mores. This is **the communitarian illusion,** one of the most noxious of all, particularly dear to our 'ethnopluralist' intellectuals.

- Belief that cancelling the Third World debt will enable it to economically 'take-off' and avoid future debt. **This is the Third World illusion.**

- Belief that nuclear power can be abandoned and replaced with oil and coal plants, while reducing carbon emissions. **This is the ecological illusion.**

- Belief that a world economy based on short-term speculation, a generalised indexation of computerised stock markets, and the replacement of monetary policy with the hazards of financial markets promises new and lasting growth. **This is the illusion of the new economy.**

- Belief that the reinforcement of democracy and 'republican values' will eradicate 'populism', that is, the direct expression of the people's will.

*

The list could be extended. In each of these cases, the belief in miracles is explainable by **the hapless optimism that comes from the secular religion of egalitarian progressivism;** but it also comes from the fact that the dominant ideology, being at an impasse, doesn't dare to deny its dogmas and make drastic revisions, clinging as it does to the idea that there 'will be no storm' and that everything is explainable by the sophisms of its fake experts, whose inevitable conclusion is that all will turn out for the best, that things will continue to improve, and that the situation is well in hand. It's a bit like the driver, running a red light at a hundred kilometres per hour, who explains that the faster he goes, the less time he will be in the intersection and thus the less risk he has of collision.

(see **convergence of catastrophes; progress, progressivism**)

Biopolitics

A political project oriented to a people's biological and demographic imperatives.

Biopolitics is today demonised everywhere in Europe, for it implicitly supports the idea of **a people's biological longevity in history**, without limiting itself simply to its 'public health'. Nothing could be more politically incorrect. Biopolitics is a policy devoted to **the long-range preservation and improvement of a people's biological germen.** Biopolitics is premised on the principle that a people's biological health is essential to its survival and social harmony.

Biopolitics includes family and population policy (totally abandoned today), restricts the influx of aliens (who threaten a people's biological-anthropological core), and addresses issues of public health and eugenics — that is, the improvement of the people's genetic quality. Today, both China and India actively practice biopolitics.

Biopolitics possesses considerable techno-scientific means (genetic engineering) to compensate for Europe's weak demographics. There's little question that these will pose grave problems — but lacking a 'natural' solution, how else are they to be solved? In any case, we need to approach the issue from a political rather than an 'ethical' perspective. Techno-science proposes, politics disposes. In awaiting a future biopolitics — a matter of some urgency for Europeans — it will be necessary to address two major issues: **reinvigorating the European birth-rate and reversing the Third World invasion.**

(see **eugenics**)

Born Leader

A creative personality imbued with a historical vision of the world.

To be historically fertile, a political movement or regime needs a leader, that is, a head. Even if elected or chosen, the leader is nevertheless predestined to the divine spark, if he's not already genetically imbued with it. **History is the fertilisation of a people's passive soul by the active soul of its born leaders.**

Man or woman, the born leader is a recurring and necessary figure in history — a notion rejected by Marxist egalitarians (attached to their dogmas about the 'masses'), though they too depend on such leaders.

The born leader brings the danger of despotism, but of destiny as well. History refuses to conform to the vision of our humanitarian egalitarians. The born leader is a man of storms, but also a man of extraordinary creativity. He appears where he is not expected, whatever the ideology he animates. He seizes hold of reality and transforms it. He seduces the people, like a snake paralyses the bird. He is **history's surprise,** whether he's divine or dramatic and bloody.

The born leader is an indispensable, as well as a tragic figure. He can lift up and liberate (Charles Martel, Joan of Arc, Mustafa Kemal,[5] etc.), doing so like a tyrant (Lenin, Stalin, Mao…) or a conqueror (Alexander, Napoleon, Abd-el-Rahman[6]…). **He's an inescapable given in the lives of a people faced with constant dangers or in pursuit of a great ambition.**

---

5   Mustafa Kemal Atatürk (1881–1938) was a Turkish military officer in the First World War who led the Turkish national movement following the collapse of the Ottoman Empire, later becoming the first president of modern Turkey. His reforms laid the foundation for the secular, democratic Turkish government which has existed up to the present day.

6   Abd-el-Rahman al-Ghafiqi was the Arab military leader who led the Muslims into battle against the Frankish forces of Charles Martel in 732. His army was defeated and he himself was killed by the Franks during the battle while attempting to stop his men from retreating.

*

In our decadent, nearly exhausted civilisation, born leaders no longer appear because the natural elites have been turned away from politics and no longer serve the people (confused with the 'state') — the people has been abandoned to careerist functionaries. In the present situation, only a tragic crisis will permit a born leader to emerge. He alone can **cut the Gordian knot** of what historically appears as an inextricable situation. Robert Steuckers thus writes, in reference to Carl Schmitt, that the latter 'wanted to restore the personal dimension of power because this personal dimension is alone capable of responding to a state of emergency. Why? Because the born leader can act more rapidly than slower procedural mechanisms'.[7]

*

The born leader accordingly has a dictatorial character, but in the positive sense. **A dictator is not an oppressive tyrant, but one who 'dictates', who cuts through and saves things in a state of emergency.** The born leader appears thus as a people's supreme protector, disinterested, the ultimate symbol of true democracy, 'populist' democracy, in the Hellenic political-philosophical sense.

The born leader is he who both **sets a people in motion and protects its ancestral character, its identity.** He is the one who breaks the system for the sake of a futuristic dynamic that paradoxically preserves the archaic, that soul of a civilisation. He is both Agitator and Dictator.

The born leader is a figure of individualism, in the positive sense, as in 'altruistic individualism'. In a given period, at a tragic or fertile point in history, he crystallises and formulates the unconscious will of the people. Muhammad was probably the greatest born leader of all time, having, in a few decades, set the world ablaze with his religious and warrior doctrine, which, today, constitutes for Europeans, as it

---

7   From *Vouloir*, January-February 1995.

does for many other peoples, the greatest of dangers — the principal enemy — that which is to be contained and hurled back.

Europe has need for born leaders today, for she will be saved neither by intellectuals nor politicians nor entrepreneurs, but only by those embodying the People's Soul.

Remember, though: there are no generals without an army — no chief without a tribe.

(see **aristocracy; democracy; elite; personality, creative**)

Bourgeoisism

The mental characteristics of the petty bourgeoisie, extended to the whole of modern society irrespective of social class.

Bourgeoisism designates the negative traits of the bourgeois spirit, minus the entrepreneurial mentality of the great bourgeoisie, which today is in decline. Opposing the popular spirit, like it opposes the aristocratic spirit, bourgeoisism dominates our market society, with its morality of self-interest, its individualist pursuit of security and immediate well-being, its susceptibility to ephemeral fashions, its refusal of risks, its passive and conspicuous consumption, its conformity to the reigning doctrines, its concern with maintaining politically correct appearances, its total lack of patriotism and ethnic consciousness, its cultural snobbery, its spirit of calculation, its compromising conception of human relations, its narcissism, the preponderance of money in its scale of values, its indifference to communal solidarity, its superficial humanitarianism, its insensibility to the sacred and poetic sentiments, and its aesthetic inaptitude, etc. Bourgeoisism has even abandoned its earlier familial spirit, with its sense of generational continuity.

The modern petty bourgeoisie or middle class dominating present-day society tries to be 'trendy', but betrays an extraordinary **conformity**. It's both the target and the principal actor in the ideological/intellectual establishment of the reigning soft totalitarianism.

(see **economism**)

C

Chaos, Ethnic

A historical situation in which a people or civilisation loses its ethnic basis due to the mass immigration of aliens.

Ethnic chaos was a factor in the decomposition of the Roman Republic and Empire, Pharaonic-Egyptian civilisation, and many ancient Greek cities. Europe is presently in the grip of a colonising settlement by overseas peoples. A civilisation disappears once it loses its original ethnic basis. It becomes a patchwork quilt in which any idea of city, community, and destiny is impossible.

Ethnic chaos signals the pure and simple disappearance of a people and a civilisation — and of true democracy — as all the classical Greek philosophers warned.

An ethnically heterogeneous population — a kaleidoscope of communities — becomes an anonymous society, without soul, without solidarity, prone to incessant conflicts for domination, to an endemic racism ('every multi-racial society is a multi-racist society') — ungovernable because there's no shared vision of the world. Ethnic chaos is an open door to tyranny.

In the name of multi-racialism, capitalism and democracy have made ethnic chaos part of their program. Men are stripped of their attachments and remade as consumers, each interchangeable with the other, each without an identity. But this is stupid. Man never actually loses his memory or ancestral identity. A society of ethnic chaos leads in the long run not to prosperity, harmonious individualism, or republican rule, but to political and social disorder. We're now catching the first glimpses of this chaos. From it, there will perhaps come the post-chaos — that is, regeneration — a return to homogeneity.

(see **culture, civilisation; communitarianism; colonisation; germen; philia**)

Chaos, post-Chaos

Chaos is that state of disorganisation and anarchy affecting a collectivity of any sort, once it's beset by catastrophe. The post-chaos is that phase when a new order is reconstructed on the basis of a revolutionary, metamorphic logic.

It's the eternal cycle of life, death, and rebirth, as expressed in Nietzsche's theory of the eternal return of the identical,[8] as well as in René Thom's mathematical theory of catastrophes.[9] The society we know can't be fixed, the system can't be saved. This is the illusion of every conservative tendency. The sole solution to the present situation will come from chaos — from civil war, economic depression, etc. — that overthrows established mentalities and makes acceptable and indispensable that which was previously unimaginable. Only in situations of chaos are the given variables changed and does it become possible to establish another order — the post-chaos. **Only in crisis, then, will a solution be found.** To construct a new home, it's first necessary that the old one collapses. It's not a pessimist but a realist who sees this.

(see **convergence of catastrophes; interregnum**)

---

8 'What if some day or night a demon were to steal into your loneliest loneliness and say to you: "This life as you now live it and have lived it you will have to live once again and innumerable times again; and there will be nothing new in it, but every pain and every joy and every thought and sigh and everything unspeakably small or great in your life must return to you, all in the same succession and sequence..."' From Friedrich Nietzsche, *The Gay Science* (Cambridge: Cambridge University Press, 2001), p. 194. This is one of Nietzsche's central ideas.

9 René Thom (1923-2002) was a French mathematician who is best-known for his development of catastrophe theory. The theory is complex, but in essence it states that small alterations in the parameters of any system can cause large-scale and sudden changes to the system as a whole.

Circulation of Elites[10]

An expression of the sociologist Vilfredo Pareto[11] to designate the process by which elites are renewed, new blood brought in, and incompetence shed.

A people that does not renew its elites sinks into a 'blocked society'. A sclerosis of the elites is a very French malady, for in France the privilege of acquired advantage has always kept good company with a paralysing egalitarianism. Both before and after the Revolution... The circulation of elites requires a principle of rigorously selecting the best and most deserving, in a word, it's an 'intelligent inegalitarianism' founded on justice. The selection of elites, like the notion of aristocracy, is based on principles of freedom and competition: 'The best wins'.

Social egalitarianism **rejects the principle of selection** (the great legacy of May 1968) and instead favours 'positive discrimination' and quotas for ethnic groups, which leads not to social justice, but to the promotion of mediocrity.

For thirty years, our system of national education has abandoned principles of selection and discipline, blocking the democratic process by which elites circulate and by which the best from the unfavoured classes are recruited into the ruling classes. In effect, the public school

---

10 Pareto coins this term in *The Mind and Society* (New York: Harcourt, Brace & Co., 1935), vols. 3 and 4, to describe the transference of people that he saw taking place between two groups in society: those with fixed economic means, and those whose income is variable and depends upon their own ingenuity to be maintained. Pareto believed that some people remained influential in society only because of their situation as part of the former group, while others became influential through their drive to attain more wealth and power. Individuals from the latter group would sometimes cross from one group to the other as a result of their efforts. The degree to which this process takes place, Pareto asserted, determines the qualities of a civilisation. See *The Mind and Society*, Sections 2026-2029 and 2233-2235.

11 Vilfredo Pareto (1848-1923) was an Italian sociologist whose lack of faith in democracy was highly influential upon the Italian Fascists, and later, the European New Right.

system has been massively devalued and is no longer able to fulfil its role in facilitating social advancement. Only money now enables access to a quality education. This anti-selective egalitarianism leads to corporatism, nepotism, and the blocked circulation of elites.

(see **aristocracy; competition; democracy; meritocracy; selection**)

Civil War, Ethnic
The grave and foreseeable confrontation between native Europeans and the alien colonisers, mainly of Afro-Maghrebian origin — a confrontation that threatens to break out in France and Belgium early in the Twenty-first century.

In Europe, especially in the two above-mentioned states, we have, in respect to Islam and its alien populations, passed from the stage of friction and minor delinquency to the stage, beginning in the 1990s, of **pre-civil war**, linked to the aliens' territorial and demographic conquests.

Alas, it's only the outbreak of a real civil war that will resolve the present problems of colonisation, Africanisation, and Islamisation — the greatest tragedy in European history and one which completely escapes the perspicacity of her 'elites', who are either blind or enemy collaborators.

Ethnic civil war is the sole means of treating a problem 'hotly' that can never be resolved 'coldly', within the state's system of law or through its democratic procedures. Make no mistake: I'm not calling for war, but I consider it inevitable, something almost automatic. Solutions based on 'rational and peaceful coexistence', as advocated by our communitarians, belong to the realm of infantile belief, distinct to dreamy, rationalising intellectuals, who know nothing of sociology or history.

It's only when their backs are against the wall, faced with an unavoidable emergency, that people find solutions that in other times are unthinkable. It was through armed reconquest that Spain threw off her Arab-Muslim occupation. But this took time — though, with history's present acceleration, it will probably take less now. The important thing is to be prepared for the inescapable.

Conditions for civil war are still not quite ripe, given the apathy of Europe's anaesthetised population (anaesthetised by market society and various guilt-inducing ideologies). These conditions will soon ripen:

1. **Once the state starts falling into the hands of Afro-Maghrebian and Muslim 'communities'.** This is already beginning to happen, as municipalities, followed by regional legislatures, allow the 'immigrant vote', and local, eventually national, powers fall to the colonisers.

2. Once **the degradation of the people's economic situation** (provoked in part by the ageing population) is compounded by a conspicuous increase in Afro-Maghrebian criminality, as it reaches insupportable levels and is linked to more and more pronounced alien conquests of the national territory. One never revolts when the shopping carts are full.

It's all a matter of reaching that stage where the population clearly sees the danger. **There will be no European rebellion until Afro-Maghrebians hold power and are seen thus as oppressors and occupiers** — not until the **economic catastrophe** resulting from immigration and demographic decline breaks out. This is slowly beginning. One resists an authority, in effect, only if it is seen as alien and illegitimate — one doesn't resist social facts, a particular kind of society, or national forms of power.

(see **colonisation; convergence of catastrophes; resistance and reconquest; state of emergency**)

* * *

Colonisation

The occupation and permanent installation of a people (or several peoples) on another people's homeland. This term is preferable to that of 'immigration'.

This is what Europe is presently suffering: a **massive colonisation by alien peoples**, which makes it the greatest tragedy in her history, because it threatens to destroy her ethnic stock. This colonisation is far more serious than a military occupation, because it's potentially irreversible. At the same time, this colonisation threatening an Islamic conquest of Europe is carried out with the complicity of the United States.

From a tactical perspective, it's necessary to **speak of colonists rather than of immigrants,** and to stop affirming that the latter are victims of 'exploitation'. Just the opposite, these colonists have come to Europe to live at our expense. Their invasion comes from both the maternity wards and porous borders (30 percent of French births are now of alien parentage and, if nothing changes, by 2010 Islam will become the largest practiced religion in France).[12] **We are suffering 'a colonisation from below', very different from the former European colonisation of the Third World.** The gravity of the phenomenon has been compounded by Europe's demographic collapse.

European colonisation was civilising: it brought many things to the countries involved and, contrary to the dogmas of the xenophilic Left (dogmas echoed by Right-wing Parisian intellectuals), it had little effect on native culture. Rather, it (stupidly) reinforced Islam, laying the basis for its current historic assault on Europe.

---

12 As of 2023, Islam is recognised as the second-largest religion in France, with approximately 10% of the population identifying as Muslim. Catholicism remains the largest religion, with about 29% of the population identifying as Catholic. However, when considering religious practice, Muslims are more observant than Catholics. Approximately 5.8% of the French population are practicing Muslims, compared to 4.35% who are practicing Catholics.

In every realm, resistance to this colonisation and reconquest constitutes the single overriding objective of every European political project of the Twenty-first century.
(see **ethnomasochism; resistance and reconquest**)

Communitarianism

The doctrine that diverts and disfigures the notion of 'community'. Of American origin, communitarianism is a doctrine advocating the cohabitation of different ethnic communities within the same society, each with its own laws, imagining that harmony between these different communities is possible.

It's the very negation of the idea of a people — it's a variant of apartheid. Hardly possible in the United States, communitarianism is completely unrealisable in Europe. Touted as an alternative to forced assimilation, communitarianism is unfortunately defended by certain stargazing intellectuals of the *Nouvelle Droite*.[13] It's a delirious and abstract understanding of social polytheism and derivative of the notion that Empire is a '*pluriversum* of peoples'.[14] As practiced by the French state today in regards to Muslim and Afro-Asian aliens, communitarianism has the effect of fragmenting society into an array of ethnic ghettos. It's derived from the Rousseauian idea ('social contract') that cohabitation between different ethnic groups is possible within a single political entity, through the magic of 'education' and 'political reason'.

Defended by recent Parisian Right-wing converts to Rousseauianism and anti-racism, this thesis simply doesn't hold up. No people can be an amalgam of different ethnic communities, the product of some miracle carried out under the state's beneficence. Our intellectuals are not only dreamers, but historical ignoramuses, like everybody else

---

13 French: 'New Right'.

14 As opposed to a *universum*, which denotes something that is present everywhere, a *pluriversum* was defined by New Right author Julien Freund as a 'plurality of particular and independent collectivities or of divergent interpretations of the same universal idea' ('Schmitt's Political Thought', *Telos* 102, Winter 1995, p. 11).

today. They want to fabricate homogeneity from heterogeneity, mixing sulphur and saltpetre, hydrogen and oxygen without setting off an explosion. In respect to immigration, communitarianism is the stupidest possible response, based on the most infantile utopia ever conceived by Western intellectuals and bureaucrats. Their theoretically 'harmonious' solutions have been a disaster in practice.

The communitarian doctrine and those who defend it are, objectively, complicit with ethnic colonisation and the Islamic invasion. The worst aspect, in the case of the Right-wing communitarians, is the vanity of their explication (that of Bouvard and Pécuchet,[15] the two kindred 'philosophers', unable to distinguish thought from reality), while the Left's explanation is simply a cynical calculation. Neither matters: the facts suggest that communitarianism ends in civil war.
(see **assimilation; resistance and reconquest**)

Community, community-of-a-people

A group whose organic bonds are animated by the sentiment of belonging, homogeneity, heritage, and wanting to live together and share the same destiny.

The notion of community opposes that of 'society', whose essence is mechanical, heterogeneous, and based on a social contract. Community is the most natural way to group humans, since it's based on ethnic and spiritual kinship — which establishes a harmonious equilibrium between its members and serves as the most propitious expression of their culture. Community pre-exists its specific forms of organisation and institution, for its essence is historical, innate, and non-contractual, unlike society.

---

15 Bouvard and Pécuchet are the main characters in a novel by Gustave Flaubert, published in 1881: *Bouvard et Pécuchet*. The two title characters are office clerks who become friends and, out of their shared enthusiasm for learning, attempt to master all of the various branches of knowledge. All of their efforts are unsuccessful.

Community, though, never exists in a pure state; it always includes certain social relations. One speaks thus of a 'communitarian model', whether of the **nation as a community-of-people**, of family, clan, association, army (community of combat), etc.

The communal model radically opposes the social model of egalitarianism and individualism. In the communal model, human relations are hierarchical, interdependent, and multi-functional. The community is not limited to the present; it has a history and a destiny. Its being transcends individual existences, imbuing it with meaning. The social model, in contrast, is purely contractual, mechanistic, and abstract, with the individual isolated, easily excluded, and the whole ensemble prone to rapidly descending into a jungle. The nihilism of contemporary market society is unthinkable in the communal model.

From this perspective, **the community-of-a-people is organically subdivided into encompassing sub-communities**: nations, regions, towns, clans, families, etc. **True democracy, in the classic Greek sense, is only possible within such a communal context.** This follows the implications and co-responsibilities of communally-related individuals; of their common ethnic bonds; and the common projects and memories linking them. The social model, on the other hand, is prone to ethnic chaos and its individual members are indifferent to one another, solidarities are purely artificial, self-discipline is impossible, democracy a simulacrum, and order a constraint. **A community-of-the-people — given that solidarity, social justice, freedom, security, defence, and the transmission of values are possible within it — operates with at least a minimum of ethnic unity and a sense of innate belonging.**

In defining the *Ummah*[16] as a community of believers opposed to the Western individualist model of anonymous society, Islam finds in its communitarian nature a very powerful and effective idea. Despite

---

16 As understood in Arabic, the *Ummah* designates the whole of the community of adherents of Islam wherever they are in the world, regardless of ethnicity or national boundaries. The term originates in the *Qur'an* (3:110).

the good sense of its social and philosophical precepts, Islam nevertheless remains the enemy, for its totalitarian and obscurantist ideology is totally incompatible with the European mentality of the *liber civis*: the free man. This is not a matter of disputing Islam's critique of the West, but of denying it the right to offer us its solutions. Each must find it in himself, in his own way.

It's possible that the idea of community among ethnic Europeans will be reborn only in misfortune.
(see **people**)

Competition, struggle for life
The clash of living-forms for supremacy and survival.

Competition, or the struggle for life, constitutes the principal motor force of evolution in everything from bacteria to humans, as well as history. Even the most fanatical pacifists acknowledge it.

Competition affects every domain of existence; it's observable between individuals and between groups. **Communal solidarity is the sole element mitigating its harshness.** In blunting the individual's egoism, its goal is to ensure the superiority of the community over other communities.

Even religions that 'submit to God' (Islam, for example), which might appear to renounce competition, appeal to it. For an individual or for a people, decay sets in once one starts believing that competition and the struggle for life are 'unjust', that enmity toward the Other is 'abnormal', that the state of peace is natural and war unnatural, and that the Garden of Eden is possible on Earth. Competition, the struggle for life, is the normal, permanent state of all living things — pacifism renounces life; it's a morality of slaves.

There's no use complaining about enemies: we should instead take satisfaction in fighting and eliminating them, knowing that **they will always be with us.** Those who declare that they have no enemies, that they aren't in competition, that peace is perpetual, have succumbed to the entropy of extinction and death, which will pitilessly eliminate them. Even the most sincere cooperation is never definitive. An individual or a group or a people not in competition with one another are threatened in the long run by dying off. **Vital forms of harmony are paradoxically born as much from struggle as from concord. And the choice of one's friends is inextricably linked to the designation of one's enemy.**

The enemy is never wrong, if he wins. A 'superior people', a 'superior individual', a 'superior group' (whether military, economic, religious, etc.) operates not with abstract, ontological principles, but on the basis of the concrete results that come from competition. This is the case for all living things. One is never 'intrinsically superior' to others. One is superior only in successfully achieving supremacy.

It's the law of the strongest, the most capable, the most flexible that always dominates. Vae Victis, death to the vanquished: such is the law of life; there has never been born a philosopher who could prove otherwise. If an individual possesses talent and will, he can defeat multitudes. Competition is economic, political, ethnic, etc. It's based on an alliance of will and talent. One ought never to complain about being dominated. It simply comes from not being strong enough — not effective, not clever, not wilful enough.

The key to victory in any competition, as Robert Ardrey[17] saw, is the **combatants' solidarity**. For humans, competition and the struggle for life are not primarily individual, but collective. In this way, the

---

17 Robert Ardrey (1908–1980) was a widely read and discussed author during the 1960s, particularly his books *African Genesis* (1961) and *The Territorial Imperative* (1966). Ardrey's most controversial hypothesis, known as the 'killer ape theory', posits that what distinguished humans' evolutionary ancestors from other primates was their aggressiveness, which caused them to develop weapons to conquer their environment and also leading to changes in their brains which led to modern humans. In his view, aggressiveness was an inherent part of the human character rather than an aberration. However, Ardrey's theories are no longer upheld by the mainstream scientific establishment.

friend-enemy polarity is formed, a polarity which is the source of life itself.

(see **selection**)

Conception-of-the-World

The ensemble of values and interpretations of reality — implicitly or explicitly distinct to a specific human group — whether a people, a civilisation, a family of thought, political or not, a religion, etc.

One speaks, almost indifferently, of a 'worldview'.

The conception-of-the-world transcends — goes beyond — political doctrines, as well as ideologies, and can even comprise several antagonistic ideologies, often based on the same principles. For example, the liberal Right and the socialist Left, progressive Christians and atheistic cosmopolitans, share the same general conception of the world. A conception-of-the-world comprises the intellectual and spiritual, rational and intuitive facets. It's different from culture, in which several conceptions of the world can coexist within it. A conception-of-the-world implies a political and historical project, along with a specific view of man's nature.

In the European, Western universe, there are two opposed conceptions-of-the-world. The dominant one, issuing from Judaeo-Christianity, is egalitarian, individualistic, and cosmopolitan. The other, more or less censored today, and derived from ancient European paganism, can be called inegalitarian, communalist, and ethnic. With Nietzsche, the latter achieved conscious philosophical formulation. Certain people, like Christian traditionalists, share aspects of both conceptions of the world, living an inner contradiction. It's the war over conceptions-of-the-world, to which myths are evidently associated, that ultimately affects history's course.

(see **Judaeo-Christianity, paganism**)

Consciousness, Ethnic

The individual or collective consciousness of the necessity to defend the biological and cultural identity of one's people, the indispensable condition for the longevity and autonomy of its civilisation.

This is what today's European, deformed by bourgeois individualism and universalism, lacks the most.

Ethnic consciousness clashes with the prejudices of modern anti-racism and ethnomasochism, both of which afflict Europeans. The dominant ideology demonises ethnic consciousness and equates it with a racist perversion and a will to persecute. **Europeans are thereby denied the right to an ethnic consciousness, a right which every other people has been granted.**

Bourgeois individualism is the principal ideological obstacle to the rebirth of ethnic consciousness. This individualism goes hand-in-hand with forgetting one's roots and identity. The absence of ethnic consciousness is a collective mental affliction, associated with the pathological refusal to accept that one is a product of a certain ancestral heritage — a refusal born of that narcissistic individualism of which the West is so fond. The notion of ethnic consciousness will dominate the coming century. Jews, Chinese, Arabs, and Indians understand this well. Europeans alone have failed to see its appeal.

Democracy is real only among an ethnically homogeneous people, conscious of its ethnic identity. **Ethnic consciousness is the democratic foundation for justice and social solidarity between members of the same people,** as the Greek tradition understood it.
(see **democracy; ethnosphere, ethnic blocs; philia**)

Consciousness, Historical

The consciousness of belonging to a civilisation and to a people long inscribed in a distinct history and destiny.

Historical consciousness ought to be the basis of the political. Its aim is to ensure the long-term survival of a human ensemble, integrating it with the destiny of future generations. Unlike Muslims, Chinese, and others, European leaders lack historical consciousness. History no longer exists for them, neither in the past nor the future. Their temporal horizon extends only as far as the next election. **This absence of historical consciousness will undoubtedly become the tomb of Western civilisation, incapable as it now is of envisaging the future or measuring up to the stature of its past — and thus unable to ensure its own survival.**
(see **people; long-living, short-living people**)

Consumerism

Choice of a society founded exclusively on the quantitative dimension of its members' material consumption — to the detriment of all other considerations.

Consumerism is the lowest degree of materialism and economism, since it's uninterested in long-term economic power, neglects the economy's ecological effects, and focuses exclusively on the mere volume of immediate consumption. Consumerism is a form of slavery, to which the mass men of our civilisation have succumbed, these mass men who are neither citizens, nor actors, nor responsible individuals, but rather passive, domesticated beings. Questions of an ecological, ethnic, or political nature hold no interest for the consumer. Even his personal security takes second place to his standard of living. **A goose in the barnyard of a foie gras**[18] **producer.**

---

18 *Foie gras*, or 'fat liver', is a dish prepared from a duck or goose liver that has been purposefully fattened.

Consumerism stems from a certain mental pathology — as Thorstein Veblen,[19] Guy Debord,[20] and Jean Baudrillard[21] have shown. It's a matter of accumulating objects, things, but it lacks a sense of ends, even in matters of pleasure or well-being.
(see **economism**)

Convergence of Catastrophes

The converging lines of civilisational rupture that in the course of the Twenty-first century will consume the 'modern world' in a great planetary chaos.

For the first time in history, humanity as a whole is threatened by a convergence of catastrophes.

A series of 'dramatic lines' are coming together and converging, like merging river streams, in a perfect concomitance of ruptures and chaotic upheavals (between 2010 and '20). **From this chaos — which will be extremely painful at the planetary level — there will emerge**

---

19 Veblen (1857–1929) was a prominent American economist and sociologist. He is best known for his 1899 book *The Theory of the Leisure Class*, in which he postulated that the emerging upper class of modern society was unique in that it consumed a great deal, but contributed little toward the maintenance or advancement of civilisation.

20 Guy Debord (1931–1994) was a French Marxist philosopher and the founder of the Situationist International. His ideas have become influential on both the radical Left and Right. The spectacle, as described in his principal work, *The Society of the Spectacle*, is one of the means by which the capitalist establishment maintains its authority in the modern world — namely, by reducing all genuine human experiences to representational images in the mass media, thus allowing the powers-that-be to determine how individuals experience reality.

21 Jean Baudrillard (1929–2007) was a French philosopher and cultural theorist who is regarded as one of the most important postmodernist thinkers. In his early works, he analysed consumerism and concluded that capitalist societies instill false needs in the minds of consumers by linking the consumer's identity to a fetishised object which will give him social prestige if he acquires it

the possibility of a new post-catastrophic world order — the painful birth of a new civilisation.

Briefly summarised, here are the principal lines-of-catastrophe:

The first of these is **the cancerisation of Europe's social fabric**. The colonisation of the Northern Hemisphere by peoples of the South — which is becoming more and more imposing despite the media's reassuring affirmations — is creating an extremely explosive situation; the failure of multi-racial society, which is already increasingly multi-racist and neo-tribal; the progressive ethno-anthropological metamorphosis of our Continent, a veritable historic cataclysm; the return of poverty to the West and the East; the slow, but steady progression of criminality and drug use; the continued fragmentation of the family; the decay of the educational system and especially the quality of instruction; breakdowns in the transmission of cultural knowledge and social disciplines (barbarism and failing competence); and the disappearance of popular culture for the sake of that mass cretinisation which comes with 'spectacular' culture. All this suggests that European nations are headed toward a New Middle Ages.

Factors of social rupture in Europe will be aggravated by an economic-demographic crisis that will culminate in mass poverty. Beginning in 2010, the number of active workers will no longer be sufficient to finance the baby-boomers' retirement. Europe will teeter from the weight of its senior citizens. Her ageing population will then experience an economic slowdown, handicapped by the need to finance the health needs and pension requirements of her unproductive citizens; such an ageing population, moreover, will dry up techno-economic dynamism. Add to this the Third-Worldisation of the economy that comes with the uncontrolled mass immigration of unskilled populations.

A third dramatic line of the modernist catastrophe: **chaos in the Global South.** In pursuing an industrialisation that comes at the cost of their traditional culture, the countries of the South, despite their deceptive and fragile growth, are creating social chaos that will only get worse.

The fourth dramatic line of catastrophe, recently explained by Jacques Attali,[22] is **the threat of a world financial crisis,** which promises to be qualitatively more serious than that of the 1930s, bringing another Depression. Stock market and currency collapses, like the East Asian recession of the late 1990s, are signs of what's coming.

The fifth line of convergence: **the rise of fanatical, fundamentalist religions, especially Islam.** The upsurge of radical Islam is a repercussion of modernity's excessive cosmopolitanism, which has imposed on the whole world its model of atheistic individualism, its cult of merchandise, its despiritualisation of values, and its dictatorship of the spectacle. Against this aggression, Islam has been radicalised, as it returns to its tradition of conquest and domination.

The sixth line of catastrophe: a **North-South confrontation, highlighting ethnic-theological differences.** With increased probability, this confrontation will replace the former East-West conflict. We don't know the exact form this confrontation will take, but it will be very serious, given that its stakes are much higher than the former, rather artificial conflict between U.S. capitalism and Soviet Communism.

The seventh line of catastrophe: **the uncontrollable pollution of the planet,** which threatens less the planet (which has another four billion years before it) than the physical survival of humanity.

---

22   Jacques Attali (1943-) is a French economist who was an advisor to Mitterrand during the first decade of his presidency. Many of his writings are available in translation. Faye may be referring to Attali's article 'The Crash of Western Civilisation: The Limits of the Market and Democracy', which appeared in the Summer 1997 issue of the American journal *Foreign Policy*. In it, Attali claimed that democracy and the free market are incompatible, writing: 'Unless the West, and particularly its self-appointed leader, the United States, begins to recognise the shortcomings of the market economy and democracy, Western civilisation will gradually disintegrate and eventually self-destruct.' In many ways his arguments resemble Faye's.

Environmental collapse is the fruit of the liberal-egalitarian (as well as the Soviet) myth of universal economic development.

To this should probably be added: the likely implosion of the European Union, which is becoming more and more ungovernable; nuclear proliferation in the Third World; and the probability of ethnic civil war in Europe.

The convergence of these factors on our extremely fragile global civilisation suggests that the Twenty-first century will not witness a progressive extension of today's world, but rather the insurgence of another. We need to prepare for these tragic changes, lucidly.
(see **chaos, interregnum, modernity**)

Cosmopolitanism

The belief that the systematic mélange of cultures is preferable to the identity of each culture — the belief that comes from the prejudice that some sort of world civilisation is necessary.

Etymologically, cosmopolitanism is the establishment of a 'world city', whose every inhabitant is a citizen, no matter his origin. Cosmopolitanism is a pillar of the dominant Western ideology. Islam exploits Western cosmopolitanism in order to establish itself in Europe, but it lacks cosmopolitan ideals, for it strives to be culturally hegemonic and monopolistic. Islam is 'universalistic', but not cosmopolitan.

Cosmopolitanism is nothing but a failed differentialism. Its ideal of mixing cultures for the sake of creating a single world culture is essentially totalitarian. With its simulacrum of heterogeneity, there lurks the will to uniformity.

*

Classical Greek democracy fiercely opposed cosmopolitanism, for since Pericles[23] it rested on the rights of blood and on ethno-cultural

---

23 Pericles (495?–429 BCE) governed Athens during its 'Golden Age' between the Persian and Peloponnesian Wars, when Athens made many of its greatest

homogeneity. Only in the Eighteenth century, with the Enlightenment, was democracy associated with cosmopolitanism, this same cosmopolitanism which the Greeks saw as a source of political chaos and thus tyranny.

Cosmopolitanism's principal argument is that 'the mixing and mélange of cultures is an enrichment'. As an example, Nineteenth-century Vienna and its flourishing culture are often cited. This, though, is sophistic, for what is here held out as cosmopolitan was not at all cosmopolitan, for Vienna was solely about the peoples and cultures of Europe, and was thus rooted in her native substrata.

The present European discourse on cosmopolitanism insists on a necessary Africanisation, as if it will be some sort of godsend.

In reality, Europe's cultural wealth owes little to extra-European contributions, despite the claims of the official vulgate. Today, cosmopolitanism seeks to dissolve European originality and specificity into a jumble of world cultures. It has no future. There's never been a 'world culture'. **Europe is the sole victim of cosmopolitan propaganda for a future 'mixed world'; everywhere else there's been a reinforcement of identity and ethnic blocs.**

(see **miscegenation; people; universalism**)

Cultural Struggle

The defence and creative assertion of threatened European cultures.

Political struggle is sterile without a cultural struggle to support, accompany, and justify it. A dynamic, identitarian culture, buttressed by its native biological stock, is essential to the survival of a people or a civilisation. All political movements neglecting cultural struggle, all states rejecting a policy of cultural identity, operate in a void.

Cultural struggle is not restricted to the defence of the patrimony, the maintenance of tradition, or dialogue with the historical memory — it's also **creative**. For it's not enough to denounce the destruction of European culture in order to save it — we need a counter-offensive.

*

To this end, cultural struggle needs to address: Americanisation, Islamisation, Africanisation, as well as society's present neo-primitivism. Cultural struggle is polymorphic, both defensive and offensive. It involves the school, no less than the plastic arts, music, audio/visual, language, literature, etc. It must **reject both cosmopolitanism and antiquarianism.** With the present censorship and subversion, cultural struggle has a vested interest in attack and imagination, as it continues to transmit the common heritage.

Cultural struggle also resists the **substitution of memory** (to which Europeans have been victim) and the effort to make alien cultures preferable to our native culture; it resists replacing pride with guilt and repentance, and resists all effort to make ethnopluralism (which demotes the significance of European culture) everywhere hegemonic.

At the same time, it's necessary to beware of pseudo-identitarians, the system's secret collaborators and hirelings, who endlessly profess their admiration for 'all the cultures of the world', even those hostile to us and seeking the destruction of our culture.

Cultural struggle doesn't entail defending all cultures, only European culture, which it assumes is superior to other cultures. (see **culture, civilisation; ethnocentrism; neo-primitivism**)

Culture, Civilisation

Culture is the compass of a people's mentalities, traditions, mores, and values. Civilisation is the tangible material expression of the culture, representing culture's practical realisations.

As an ethnic group, a people can superficially adopt the civilisation of another group, but it can never be integrated into the culture, since the latter ultimately rests on a hereditary or biological disposition.

A civilisation grows out of a culture's mental and spiritual stock, whose ethnic disposition is largely inherited. Language is an attribute of civilisation, but not culture, except insofar as an acculturated population can adopt the civilisation and language of another people by reconstructing it in an ethnicised and hence deviant way (French-speaking or American-speaking Blacks, for example). **Culture is the basis of civilisations, but culture also rests on a people's genetic capacity — that is, on its bio-anthropological substrata, its germen.** Civilisation is the material, exterior aspect, or projection, of a culture. Contrary to the illusions of Marxist and liberal philosophers, culture is not some sort of superstructure produced by a given techno-economic condition, but is, instead, the mental infrastructure determining social and economic forms.

*

As an integral part of man's physiological nature, culture is the 'grid' upon which man interprets the world in terms of his heredity and milieu. The West has tried to impose itself as a homogenising world civilisation', founded on economic materialism, plutocratic democracy, and the egalitarian humanitarianism of human rights. But it has failed. The revival of Islam and several other ethnospheres (India, Black Africa, China, Latin America…) demonstrates that **the plurality of civilisations, produced by distinct races and cultures, like the conflicts that divide them, are intrinsic to humanity.**

The Twenty-first century heralds a **clash of civilisations** — not the advent of a unified, humane civilisation, as modernists believe.

'Western civilisation' is not actually a civilisation at all, but rather a technical mode of life, lacking depth, based exclusively on a quasi-Pavlovian domestication of material habits; and, as such, it's ephemeral, for it rests on no memory, no tradition, no cultural substance, but rather on modes as fleeting as a cumulonimbus cloud,[24] on the most superficial forms of conditioning.

Islam denounces Western civilisation, like it formerly denounced Communism, and for good reason. But what it proposes in its stead is something even worse: another form of totalitarianism. Above all, its civilisational project is totally incompatible with European culture, for it's founded on the notion of absolute submission and lacks, as a consequence, an organic, harmonious accord between freedom and order.

Today, the two principal adversaries of European culture and civilisation are American-Western civilisation and Islamic civilisation.

*

Nothing is ever permanently acquired. Everything can be lost. A people can see its culture die, either through a modification of its ethnic substrata (colonisation), a loss of its inner substance, or through decadence. The latter is explainable only in terms of the psycho-biological decline of its life force. European peoples today are threatened by the exhaustion of their identity and cultural vigour (by cosmopolitanism, Africanisation, Islamification, and the transformation of their culture into a folkloric remnant), but the principal cause of their decline resides in themselves and not in the aggressions assaulting them. In dereliction, one is rarely an innocent and almost always a consenting victim.

(see **decadence; deculturation; germen; West**)

---

[24] A cumulonimbus cloud is the type of cloud which is conducive to thunderstorms. They tend to have very short life spans.

D

Decadence

The weakening of a people or civilisation resulting from internal causes that leads it to lose its identity and creativity.

The causes of decadence are usually the same throughout history: excessive individualism and hedonism, the softening of mores, social egoism, devirilisation, contempt for heroic values, the intellectualisation of elites, the decline of popular education, the abandonment of or turning away from spirituality and the sacred, etc.

Other causes: modification of the ethnic substrata, the decay of natural aristocracies, the loss of historical memory, and the forgetting of primordial values. Decadence ensues whenever concern for the community-of-people in history fades, whenever the communal lines of solidarity and lineage slacken. One could say, in effect, that decadence occurs whenever apparently contrary symptoms combine: the **excessive intellectualisation of elites,** more and more cut off from reality, and **the people's primitivisation.** *Panem et circenses...*[25]

Europe today knows such a situation. Most of the time, decadence is not seen as such and thus denied. Those who denounce it are stigmatised as prophets of doom. **Periods of decadence sometimes even initially assume the guise of a renaissance.** Such periods seek to conjure away the real, occultating its negative symptoms in order to reassure everybody.

No decadence is irreversible. We would do well to cultivate Nietzsche's *tragic optimism*.

---

25 Latin: 'bread and circuses', a term first coined by the Roman poet Juvenal to describe the entertainments which Romans used to distract themselves from dealing with the larger problems of the Empire. It has come to refer to any such entertainments which serve to divert people's attention away from social problems.

(see **devirilisation; individualism; neo-primitivism**)

Deculturation
The loss of memory and cultural references.

There are several forms of deculturation: first, there's the American-Western model that afflicts Europe (much more severely than African, Arab-Muslim, Chinese, Indian, etc., cultures); then there's the deculturation that comes from our Islamic colonisation. These two types of deculturation can be combined, as in the **Afro-Americanisation** of present-day youth (rap, raï, hip-hop, etc.).

We need to give up the myth that immigrant youth, the 'Beurs-Blacks', are victims of deculturation. Just the opposite: like the mentality of other colonisers, they've developed an identitarian counterculture (music, language, clothing, etc.), which is both Afro-Arab and American — and, as such, radically opposes French and European culture. **French youth**, in contrast, who adopt the Beur-Black counterculture through imitation or ethnomasochism, are **the real victims of deculturation.**

The dominant ideology wilfully contributes to the present deculturation, to the de-Europeanisation of youth, because it wants to detach youth from their roots and cause them to lose their identity, which is reputedly dangerous. Illiteracy, the abandonment of the study of history and classical humanism are well-known examples. The present deculturation of European youth is pursued not for the sake of a superior, more elaborate culture (which was the case when primitive populations encountered Europe's superior culture in the Nineteenth century), but for the sake of **an inferior, massified, and neo-primitive culture**: that of *zapping*, video games, tom-tom, degenerate pop art (the opposite of 'popular art'), etc.

The struggle against deculturation is not merely a matter of re-enrootment or teaching history, but also of identitarian creation and imagination.

(see **culture**)

Democracy, democratism, organic democracy

A political system in which the people is sovereign and governed by its elected representatives.

Etymologically, democracy, as it appeared in Athens, was the 'power of the *demes*', administrative units in which only members of the *demos* (free citizens) were eligible to vote and hold office, unlike the *metics* (*métoikoi,* 'strangers'). Democracy differed from tyranny or oligarchy. It was originally a constitutive part of the European tradition (Hellenic, Germanic, Scandinavian, Celtic), unlike Oriental political systems based on despotism.

Reappearing with the Eighteenth-century Enlightenment, democracy has since been largely corrupted — not only in the 'popular democracies' of Soviet Communism — but no less so in the present Western democracies. **Democratism is now a world dogma, but it's a sham democracy, for it neglects the people's interests. Western democracies are actually oligarchies that conceal their betrayal of the Hellenic-Germanic tradition of democracy.**

What's wrong with Western, and especially French, democracy?

First off, it has been transformed into a **plutocracy** ('power of wealth'), in which access to power and its exercise are conditioned by money. Second, it's dominated by a political class that has been institutionalised as a largely corrupt careerist caste. Third, real power is not exercised by the people's so-called representatives, but by unelected technocrats (at the national and European level) and by financial and economic decision-makers, pressure groups, and corporate and minority organisations. The people has lost control of its destiny and a disguised totalitarianism has come to control it: in the guise of a false plurality, **the parliamentary Left and Right function almost as a single party,** dealing with issues only if they are politically correct.

That is, only if they serve the interests of the oligarchy and the dominant ideology.

Democratism is becoming all the more virulent given that real democracy has been eliminated by the system. The system, in fact, refuses real democracy since with it the people might express dangerous or morally condemnable opinions. **Democratism openly violates real democracy and accuses true democrats of being 'populist'**, which has been given a pejorative connotation. The refusal to hold referendums on the death penalty or immigration; the incessant attacks on the Swiss model of direct cantonal democracy in which naturalisations are submitted to the people's vote; the demonisation and illegal exclusion of Austria from the European Union after Haider's FPÖ, a democratically-mandated party, though reputedly one of the 'far Right', was let into the government; the system's presumption that 'nationalist' parties, however legally and democratically represented, are illegitimate; state indifference to the mass influx of aliens (everywhere opposed among the population), and contempt for the 'law and order' demands of the popular classes — this all suggests that the dominant ideology may be **democratist but it's hardly democratic**. Though the principle of democracy is always acknowledged in discourse, it's not in practice. Democracy, as such, is acceptable only as simulation.

In Western Europe, the best illustration of democracy's absence is the fact that the established powers objectively favour our replacement by non-European, Islamic colonisers, without ever having consulted native Europeans. **The people's destruction, its ethnocide, is indeed programmed by the present pseudo-democracy.** This makes it completely anti-democratic, since it destroys what needs conserving. Besides, it's always on **questions of secondary significance** that the people or its representatives are consulted. Important issues are settled elsewhere. France's Constitutional Council is the very emblem of our anti-democratic institutions: being an assemblage of notables, appointed, not elected, who are empowered to judge the constitutionality of laws voted by the people, doing so in the name of so-called constitutional principles that are, in reality, purely ideological.

*

Should we be anti-democratic? No, we should instead revive the **organic democracy** deeply rooted in the European tradition Such a democracy, as the Ancient Athenian political philosophers held, is **possible only among ethnically homogeneous people.**

The notion of allowing aliens to vote negates the very idea of the nation and democracy. The participation of everyone in the exercise of power, in making political decisions affecting the whole, is possible only within a human ensemble possessing the same values, memories, and culture. **A multi-racial, multi-confessional society can in no case be democratic,** since it lacks commonly shared references. Such a society would be endemically oppressive and culminate in a caste system.

Organic democracy, in contrast, embraces the principle of aristocracy. That is, 'the selection of the best to rule'.

Organic democracy thus presupposes a meritocracy, not a plutocracy, as we have today. It's also necessary to understand that the form of government is not all-important. The opposition between a hereditary monarchy and a republic is mainly a matter of semantics. The existence of a hereditary king, a royal family, would contribute to ensuring continuity, tutelary protection, and the spiritual perspective of the people's will. But this is a question that history alone will decide, for a 'ruling family' isn't always necessary to assure a people's spiritual and historical continuity.

*

Organic democracy is not egalitarian. It has need of leaders, ones who serve the people, not themselves. In the Oriental tradition, which has contaminated us today, the governing elites serve their own interests, their own vanity, their own sinecures. In the European tradition, the leader, the king, the emperor, the elites served their people, being part of it, like the brain is part of the body. Hence its 'organic' character.

Organic democracy, finally, doesn't consider immediate interests alone, but the people's historic destiny, taking account of its memory and its future generations, abiding by the imperatives of sovereignty and independence, along with a faith in the longevity of its collective, biological, and cultural identity.

*

In a word, organic democracy is founded on the following, ostensibly contradictory, but in fact complementary notions: **ethnic homogeneity, the primacy of the popular will, aristocratic and meritocratic selection, and historical destiny.**
(see **aristocracy; born leader; meritocracy; populism**)

Designation of the 'Enemy' and the 'Friend', 'enemy' and 'adversary'

The enemy is one who physically poses a danger, who endeavours to eliminate you by making you disappear; the adversary dominates and weakens you.

It's totally erroneous to designate an abstract entity, a doctrine, or a system (like liberalism or socialism) as an enemy, even if one thinks it ought to be resisted. **The enemy is someone.** Carl Schmitt[26] has said of the enemy that he is 'the shape or configuration of our own question'.[27]

---

26 Carl Schmitt (1888–1985) was an important German jurist who wrote about political science, geopolitics and constitutional law. He was part of the Conservative Revolutionary movement of the Weimar era. He also briefly supported the National Socialists at the beginning of their regime, although they later turned against him. He remains highly influential in the fields of law and philosophy.

27 From *Theory of the Partisan* (New York: Telos Press, 2007), p. 85. A footnote to this phrase in the Telos Press edition of this work notes that its meaning is explained in Schmitt's postwar notebooks: '*Historia in nuce* [history in a

Also: 'Woe to him who has no enemy, for I myself shall be his enemy on Judgement Day'.[28] Whoever, in effect, has no enemies and sees no dangers will always be defenceless against a cynical enemy: as is the case today, in the Europeans' confrontation with their Third World colonisers.

Europe's principal enemy at present is the alien, the colonising immigrant masses, and Islam. Her principal adversary is America, which allies with Islam to weaken and dominate Europe.

In opposition to liberalism, which understands the essence of politics as mere state management, Carl Schmitt defines it in terms of 'designating the enemy': a definition that is true but insufficient. **The political also entails designating the friend,** that is, designating allies, but even more, designating one's co-religionists, comrades, and ethnic brothers, those who possess the same interests, the same origins, and the same values.

Decadent civilisations designate their friends as enemies and their enemies as friends. Thus it is that Europe's governing elites demonise and ostracise as 'fascists' whoever opposes the alien ethnic colonisers, even though these alleged 'fascists' defend their people's identity and survival. By the same turn, the elites designate as friends and protect the alien masses colonising her.

*

nutshell]. Friend and Enemy. The friend is he who affirms and confirms me. The enemy is he who challenges me (Nuremberg 1947). Who can challenge me? Basically, only myself. The enemy is he who defines me. That means *in concreto*: only my brother can challenge me and only my brother can be my enemy.' From *Glossarium: Aufzeichnungen der Jahre 1947–1951* (Berlin: Duncker & Humblot, 1991), p. 217.

28 From *Ex Captivitate Salus* (Cologne: Greven Verlag, 1950), quoted in Gopal Balakrishnan, *The Enemy: An Intellectual Portrait of Carl Schmitt* (London: Verso, 2000), p. 132.

A striking but clarifying example: **Arabs and Muslims could be our geopolitical and cultural allies if they remained in their own lands, but once installed in Europe they are our enemies.**

America, similarly, is an **adversary,** though it is not intrinsically and eternally so. The adversary endeavours to weaken and dominate, but not physically colonise and annihilate. This is why those intellectuals who designate America as the 'principal enemy' commit the grossest of logical errors.
(see **ethnomasochism; xenophilia**)

Destiny, becoming
The way of a people in history or of a creative personality, determined by Providence, will, and capacity.

Destiny is the spark that lies within a people (or an exceptional individual), that is, it's a projection of oneself into the future, as well as an invisible pact with a transcendent power and a struggle against the hazards of time.

Only long-living peoples and great creative personalities have a destiny. It's the *fatum* of the Romans and the *moïra* of the Greeks, this unknown but very real force that bends the backs of the gods themselves. Destiny is the sombre light that enabled Ulysses to find his way back to Ithaca and Penelope, Agamemnon to conquer Troy, Romulus to found Rome, Charles the Hammer to defeat Abd-el-Rahman. The rage of destiny has been embraced by Buddha, Confucius, Christ, Muhammad, and many others.

The mystery of destiny is both biological and spiritual, it reunites hazard and will to power in the same concentration of strength. But destiny is not haphazard or random; **a good part of it is willed.** It doesn't suffice just 'to be', it also needs 'to become'. As Robert Steuckers puts it, **identity is inconceivable without continuity** and the latter must be willed. Said differently: in the European tradition, destiny isn't passive but active. It's a response to an appeal, a **positive response to** a predestination, a call to the divine. For 'he who has a destiny is possessed', as Shakespeare put it; he who possesses a destiny, it might be added, responds to inner forces that possess him and call him to act. A people unconscious of its destiny is a people destined to disappear. (see **history; people, long-living**)

Devirilisation
The declining values of courage and virility for the sake of feminist, xenophile, homophile, and humanitarian values.

The dominant Western ideology fosters this devirilisation of Europeans, though it doesn't touch the alien colonisers. Homophilia, like the feminist fashion of false liberation, the ideological rejection of large families for the sake of the unstable nuclear couple, the declining birth rate, the preference of photographers for the African and the Arab, the constant justification of miscegenation, the denigration of warrior values, hatred for every powerful, forceful form of aesthetics, as well as the prevailing lack of courage — are some of the present characteristics of this devirilisation.

Confronted by Islam's conquering virility, **the European feels morally disarmed and confused.** The prevailing conception of the world — whether it comes from the legislature, public education, the Church, or the media — is deployed to stigmatise all notion of virility, which is associated with 'fascist brutality'. Devirilisation has become a sign of civilisation, of refined mores, the paradoxical discourse of a society, half of which is sinking into violence and primitivism.

Devirilisation is linked to narcissistic individualism and the loss of communal identity, which **paralyses all reaction to the assaults of immigrant colonisers and the party of collaboration.** This also explains the feeble repression of immigrant delinquency, the absence of European ethnic solidarity, and the pathological 'fears' haunting Europeans.

In no case ought the notion of 'virility' be confused with 'machismo' or with the stupid demand for some sort of 'masculine social privilege'. There are women whose quotidian behaviour is more 'virile' than many men. **The virility of a people is a condition for its maintenance in history.**

(see **ethnomasochism; homophilia; xenophilia**)

Discipline

The regulation and positive adaptation of behaviour through sanction, reward, and exercise.

Discipline is the basis of all education and every civilisation. Permissive 'pedagogical' theories cannot but lead to the **failure to transmit knowledge,** as is so evident today.

The belief that 'self-discipline is possible for all' is a tragic perversion of aristocratic individualism. Only superior beings are capable of self-discipline, not the common man. But, against common sense and overwhelming evidence, egalitarian ideology refuses to acknowledge that there are differences between those capable of self-discipline and those who aren't.

The refusal to accept legally-established disciplines leads to the most savage oppression, to a law of the jungle. Egalitarian ideology associates discipline and order with their excesses, that is, with arbitrary dictatorship. But just the contrary is the case, for **freedom and justice are founded on rigorous social discipline.** The anthropologist Arnold Gehlen, like the ethologist Konrad Lorenz, has shown that man, by his very biological nature, is 'a being of culture' (*Kulturwesen*), that is, 'a being of discipline' (*Zuchtwesen*). It's patently obvious that so-called defenders of freedom (actually license) challenge social disciplines in the name of freedom and the rule of law, but the social and political model they advocate has the effect of destroying all freedom, all law, all social justice: as seen in the spread of delinquency and insecurity, the collapse of public education and equal opportunity, the toleration of delinquents and gangsters, privileges for influential or violent pressure groups, etc. — all this comes at the expense of the citizen's security. **We shouldn't be afraid to say that every society refusing to uphold law and order, that is, collective discipline, is ripe for tyranny and the loss of public freedoms.**

*

The judicial imposture of the dominant ideology endeavours to make us believe that the absence of social discipline is a guarantee of public freedoms, insofar as it wards off the spectre of a 'police state'. But just the opposite is true. **The ideology of license is the foundation of contemporary despotism.** The greatest of liberalism's impostures has been to **confuse indiscipline with freedom and freedom with anarchy.**

The anti-disciplinary societies of today are hardly exempt from repression and other, more cloaked, forms of totalitarianism. Repression has merely changed its object and nature. The rigours of the law, fiscally and punitively, now fall on the 'transparent citizen', but the number of no-go zones keeps expanding, just as delinquency and other criminal activities are increasingly tolerated. Indeed, all kinds of violent delinquencies have grown. 'Hate speech' (i.e., identitarian speech) or 'homophobia' is strictly repressed, as the thought police demand, but drugs are decriminalised, the threshold for urban delinquency is raised, secularism is violated in favour of Islam, terrorists and urban rioters are appeased, etc.

These are the signs of a society whose fundamental values have become **suicidal** — a society which represses and censors everything that is vital and encourages everything that is culturally and biologically pathological.

(see **order; personality**)

Disinstallation

The typically European penchant to abstract oneself from one's own framework without denying one's traditions — doing so for the sake of curiosity, conquest, and adventure.

'Disinstallation' (*désinstallation*), this neologism coined by Robert Steuckers, is neither a form of deracination nor of nomadism. It motivated Europe's colonial era, but eventually turned against Europe: the spirit of disinstallation needs to be reoriented today. A good example of this is the conquest of space, whose inspiration is purely European.

The bourgeois spirit is simultaneously cosmopolitan and 'installed', while the aristocratic spirit is both enrooted and disinstalled. Disinstallation is a Faustian and Promethean mark of European culture. Conquests, scientific discoveries, and explorations are examples of disinstallation. Through atavism, the majority of other cultures live a static enrootment, while European enrootment has always been dynamic, disinstalled, and accustomed to the idea of **movement**.
(see **enrootment; Promethean**)

Domestication

Mental and behavioural submission to a social and ideological system, accompanied by a loss of will and proper judgement, and a physical dependence on material conditions.

This term was originally used in reference to domestic animals — incapable of autonomy and entirely conditioned by man. According to ethologists, man is 'self-domesticated' to the degree his behaviour is yoked to culture rather than to his impulses. For us, however, 'domestication' has a slightly different sense, **designating that situation in which Western man's passivity and dependence renders him incapable of reacting to the system, however noxious it becomes.**

*

Its symptoms are innumerable: susceptibility to ideological conditioning (audio/visual, scholastic, professional, etc.), dependence on consumerist ways of life, loss of independent judgement in respect to propaganda and culpability, the banishment of all spirituality (replaced by the media gnosis), etc. Domesticated man is a conformist, he doesn't revolt, he never resists, even when he engages in the simulacrum of emancipation and originality. For the sake of social rewards, he blindly follows his many inculcated prejudices. He sees the global catastrophe provoked by the immigrant colonisation, but doesn't dare rebel and instead takes refuge in flight. He's the perpetual *victim of fashion*. Above all he doesn't want to feel 'Other', independent, for that would mean *being excluded* (the great contemporary terror). The system provides his dog food, his minimal subsistence, a financial pittance — in return he abdicates whatever critical spirit might touch him. Domesticated man is profoundly attached to the social structures conditioning him, devoid as he is of all revolutionary spirit and historical vision. Whether at the top or the bottom of the social scale, he is **a human type incapable of autonomy, the model citizen of our neo-totalitarian age, the modern figure of the slave.**

The paradox of the domesticated man is that he has been made to feel that he is an 'individual'; and indeed narcissistic individualism has become his sole horizon. He's a little like the artificially bred pig who is force-fed in his cramped cage. **The individualism of this domesticated creature, though, actually conceals his submission to the herd's morality.**

How many intellectuals, artists, and brilliant philosophers, on the Right and the Left, have been domesticated (that is, sterilised by the dominant ideology and the fear of displeasing it), made to stand at attention, to dissipate their talent, and act as *muzzled watchdogs*? What a terrible price to pay for renouncing oneself and sabotaging one's talent.

This sort of human being has unfortunately become the dominant type. In case of shock, serious crisis, or system failure, the model he represents will simply collapse — and then he will have to count on those minorities who, in every society, are never domesticated.

One should also consider the **false resisters** — those who 'resist', in private, in words, but from whom nothing consequential ever follows. The system has already got to them, these domestics. They can accommodate anything, provided they are fed. But they aren't important. The best case against domestication is found in La Fontaine's fable of 'Le Chien et le loup' ('The Dog and the Wolf').[29]
(see **bourgeoisism; devirilisation**)E

Ecology, ecologism, ecological productivism

Ecology is the science of the natural environment and the concern to preserve it for the sake of human societies. Ecologism is a political doctrine that in the name of ecology pursues quite different aims.

The word comes from the Greek *oïkos,* meaning 'home', 'habitat'. The ecological imperative is foundational, but not so much for preserving Gaia,[30] the Blue Planet (which still has four billion years ahead of it), but for the sake of preventing the human race from destroying itself by polluting its biosphere, the habitat in which it lives. It's not nature 'in itself', this misty metaphysical concept (with nothing to fear from man) that needs protecting, but our species' habitats.

---

29 Jean de La Fontaine (1621–1695) was a French poet who wrote many fables, in addition to other works. 'The Dog and the Wolf' describes an encounter between a starving wolf and a well-fed dog. The dog tries to entice the wolf to take up his lifestyle, pointing out that while the wolf must fight for every meal, the dog merely has to submit to his human masters for food. The wolf, horrified by such a loss of freedom, decides to go back to his hunting lifestyle.

30 Gaia is the Ancient Greek name for the goddess of the Earth. In recent decades, the name has been adopted by ecologists, who use it to depict the combined components of the Earth as a living organism with its different parts acting in symbiosis with one another, rather than as a resource merely intended to be exploited by humans.

Historically, humans, especially Europeans, have sought to dominate and domesticate nature — that is, the Earth's ecosystem. But a good gardener, even when spurred by pride or greed, doesn't do whatever he wants. The proverb *imperat naturam nisi parendo*[31] is well-known. The warming of the planet and the catastrophes it's preparing are already manifesting their harmful effects. That's what comes from not heeding the old Latin precept. **At the planetary level, ecological cataclysms are practically inevitable in the early Twenty-first century — one of the lines in the coming convergence of catastrophes.**

Ecological ruptures are likely to occur in the following realms: rising temperatures, desertification, deforestation, the exhaustion of fishing and agricultural reserves, the spread of viral diseases, pollution of the seas and freshwater sources, etc. Destruction in each of these realms weighs on all the others and compounds their severity.

As to ecologism, it's a pseudo-ecology. It's a front to conceal Trotskyism's cosmopolitan agenda. The Greens oppose nuclear power, which is the least dangerous and least polluting of energy sources. In France and Germany their policies objectively favour the oil lobby. Their principal concern is the Third World repopulation of Europe. These ecologists are nothing but impostors.

Ecology also needs to include biopolitics, social policy, and demography. A real 'ecological society' would obey principles related to maintaining natural equilibriums, the ethno-cultural homogeneity of the population, as well as its public health.

But how is it possible to reconcile ecology and the requirements of economic and industrial power, particularly in Europe? This is the central question. Without productivism, there's no military independence, no industrial creativity, no dynamism. Anti-productivism, ecological fundamentalists refuse to see, is an appendage of speculative capital, for it disfavours the national labour market (in the form of outsourcing, financialisation, etc.), and instead favours the beneficiaries

---

31 Latin: 'one doesn't command but rather obeys nature'.

of various state handouts and other such parasites at the expense of our own producers and entrepreneurs. **There is, however, an ecological productivism.**

Someone truly concerned about ecology doesn't ask, 'How is it possible to produce less in order to pollute less?', but, 'How is it possible to produce better while polluting less?' The answer entails both a rupture with the unified planetary model of 'development' and **an archeofuturist turn to a 'two-tier' economy.**

European economic power is perfectly compatible with environmentalism. On the condition that there's a political will recognising the importance of electronuclear energy (the least polluting energy source), that this will progressively abandons the oil economy, makes use of piggyback trains, electrifies automobiles, introduces canals and other low-polluting forms of transport. Utopia? Yes, within the present framework, which lacks such a will. No, within the scope of a revolutionary project, which might follow the post-catastrophe, the post-chaos. **It's a matter of substituting an 'economy of power'[32] for a 'market economy'.**

(see **convergence of catastrophes; economy, organic; economy, two-tier**)

Economism

The reduction of social and political goals to their economic dimension, characteristic of Western ideologies.

Economism is an offshoot of the classical liberal doctrines of the Seventeenth and Eighteenth centuries and was later extended to socialist doctrines of Marxist inspiration. Its central objective is a policy of 'economic development', quantitative production, pursued without regard to cultural, ecological, ethnic, etc., imperatives. It reduces human happiness to a matter of living standards; it pursues economic

---

32 This was a term first coined by the Belgian political theoriest Jean Thiriart (1922–1992).

'growth' for the sake of short-term interests; and it neglects, among many other things, the conditions necessary for demographic renewal. It believes a country's health is measured solely by its economic performance. From a long-term perspective, **economism actually weakens economic power,** because it ignores the external forces affecting it: such as political independence, resource availability, birth rate, etc.

From the viewpoint of economism, history is explainable solely in terms of economic factors, which are seen as facets of a civilisation's infrastructure, while cultural, demographic, and other factors are ignored or treated as secondary.
(see **society, market**)

Economy, Organic
A 'third way' economic model, which takes the path neither of liberal capitalism nor statist socialism.

An organic economy arises on the precept that the economy ought to function as a living organism, hierarchical and harmonious, subordinated to the political, and not to a cold, lifeless mechanism animated by socialist dogmas or the capitalist logic of short-term profit. An organic economy would put finance in service to production and production in service to the people. It would *organically* integrate entrepreneurial dynamism, social justice, as well as ethnic, cultural, and ecological imperatives in an almost biological way, endeavouring to reconcile the best of the liberal market and the planned economy.

The principal features of an organic economy would:

1. **Refuse globalism's free trade ideology** in favour of the *autarky of great spaces*, i.e., it **centres the economy within a designated civilisational region,** without abolishing world trade and international financial exchanges, but at the same time ensuring that foreign trade is normalised, limited, and subject to quotas and other restrictions.

2. **Refuse statist socialism,** paralysing fiscalism, administrative obesity, and privilege a free competitive market within a self-centred, protected, and regulated market.
3. **Regionalise** production and exchange within Europe.
4. **Respect ecological imperatives**, which are to be understood as being more important than short-term profits.
5. Invest in **great public works.**
6. **Coordinate planning and the market.**
7. Refrain from intervening in the economy except in a **political** manner — to establish the economy's fundamental norms and to consider its general needs, but not to administratively dictate its details.
8. Abandon direct progressive **taxes** for the sake of deducting a small percentage from each income source, whatever it may be, in order to lighten the burden on society's vital forces and improve its overall production.
9. Allow the state, not the hazards of the market, to make **monetary policy**, unlike the present forces affecting the euro.
10. Oblige those receiving **unemployment benefits** to work for the sake of the collective or to accept whatever alternative employment is proposed.
11. **Restrict the employment of foreigners** and deny them welfare.
12. Endeavour, more generally, to eradicate poverty and misery without recourse to centralised, socialist bureaucratic methods that have totally failed, and adopt a policy of social assistance, assumed at local and regional levels, for citizens in need.

An organic economy is imaginable only within a **protected European market.** It would, as such, refuse both reckless globalisation and a statist, taxing socialism, while accepting the market whenever its standards are set by the sovereign authority. It would also subordinate finance to production and production to the political, whereas today the very opposite is the case. Similarly, it would subordinate the currency to political imperatives, not the hazards of speculative markets as it is with the euro.

The organic economy is a doctrine of temperance. It treats the economy as the 'third function', subordinating it to the political, and freeing it thus from both statism and market anarchy. The organic economy reconciles the dynamism and synergy of all social functions, so that one function is not impaired by another.

Paradoxically, the United States, where the state is equipped with a strong political will to pilot a free, dynamic, private economy, is closer to an organic economy than Europe.

(see **autarky of great spaces; economy, two-tier**)

Economy, Two-Tier

The eventual organisation of the world economy into two parallel systems, one of which will take the form of a non-industrial, neo-traditionalist form of economy, while the other retains aspect of the present techno-scientific economy.

Only such a system can preserve the ecosystem and avoid the impending world economic catastrophe, especially given Asia's rapid industrialisation. There is, however, little chance of setting up such a system, since it would clash with the inviolable dogma of 'development'. It's probable, though, that **the revolutionary alternative of a two-tier economy will be imposed by the economic and ecological catastrophes of the early Twenty-first century.**

A two-tier economy presupposes that most of humanity will return to a subsistence economy with low energy needs, while the technological economy continues within certain restricted zones. These two economies would cohabit within a single country. Such a model, however, is something of a 'wager', unthinkable in the present situation — based, as it is, on the hypothesis of the mid-term unviability of the present world economy and its eventual termination in a catastrophic crisis.

(A more extended treatment of this concept is developed in my *Archeofuturism*.)

Egalitarianism

This central dogma of Western ideologies stems from a secularisation of Judaeo-Christian claims that all men are in essence equal, atoms of moral, political, and social equivalence — and that equality needs to be realised in fact.

Egalitarianism is the trunk root of the dominant ideology. It is the source of all modern totalitarianisms, as well as the decadence of so-called liberal, democratic societies. It's based on a pathological refusal to accept the inegalitarian nature of human societies — that is, it's a utopian revolt against life itself. **Egalitarianism derives from Judaeo-Christian individualism — or, said more exactly, it's a perversion and secularisation of this individualism.** We shouldn't forget, though, that the egalitarian virus is also found in non-Christian conceptions of the world and that Medieval Christianity knew how to protect itself from it.

Judaeo-Christianity presupposes that men as individuals are equal before God, that this equality is superior to their differences, to objective inequalities and ethnic attachments. This purely theological and metaphysical view of the world was secularised by the Enlightenment — allegedly 'anti-Christian', but in actuality 'post-Christian'.

In the course of the Nineteenth and Twentieth centuries, egalitarianism evolved from demanding equality of opportunity to demanding equality of results, given the impossibility of actually establishing such a society. Refusing aristocratic principles, which it failed to eliminate, egalitarianism everywhere promotes false elites. It renders natural inequality insupportable, effectively favouring either the law of the jungle or a pervasive bureaucratic tyranny. In refusing an organic, hierarchical vision of society, **egalitarianism gives rise to new inequities and does so in the name of justice.** To affirm that men are unequal by nature is not an injustice, but a recognition of what is. As Aristotle put it, 'Justice is based on the observation of things'.

Egalitarianism stems from the perverted spirit that seeks to transform Judaeo-Christian spiritual equality before God into a forced equality before the contingencies of daily life. Ancient Graeco-Roman conceptions of the world, like those of contemporary India, avoided the illusion that men are equivalent, because they rested on a realistic vision of a polycentric, differentiated, and naturally hierarchical universe. Egalitarianism, on the other hand, makes us believe that hierarchy is inherently unjust, though it can't get rid of it, since it's part of the nature of things; instead, it denies it, creating in its place even more savage forms of inequality. **Egalitarianism is an institutionalised lie.** It's the most humble, paradoxically, who are hurt the most by its imposture, since everywhere the right of excellence is denied and everywhere mediocrities and scoundrels are favoured.

Egalitarianism fails to understand, indeed it despises, the human race, for it privileges a completely abstract conception of man. It leads thus to the astonishing idea that 'everything is to be valued', that the crook has as much right — if not more — than an honourable man, that minor art works are as important as the great works, that the most developed civilisations are no better than savage tribes ('ethnopluralism'), that the citizen has no more rights than the alien, etc. Its days, however, are numbered, for egalitarianism wars on human nature.

In denying differences, as well as individual and collective inequalities — and in treating Man as something almost metaphysical — the West's dominant egalitarian ideology has produced a totally **schizophrenic consciousness.** On the one side, the dogma of natural equality, on the other, the blind reality of the natural inequalities of individuals and peoples. It's perfectly logical, then, that egalitarianism, based on an **anthropological lie**, culminates in social injustice and totalitarianism.

Egalitarianism is the source of all the evils and the illusions of the modern world. Its perverse, metaphysical, anthropocentric core **deifies man and separates him from the animal realm** (*anthropocentrism*). As Spencer[33] and Darwin have shown, the human race is bound like every other animal species to the central fact of existence: inequality. This doesn't mean that religious issues or man's spiritual, cosmic dimensions are out of the question, but, as Evola saw, it does mean that men are unequal and lack an intrinsic metaphysical unity. (see **individualism**)

Elite, elitism

The elite is that social category responsible for society's management, 'chosen' or 'elected', as its etymology suggests. Elitism designates the doctrine promoting the selection of the best, not according to birth, but according to objective capability.

Very close to the notion of 'aristocracy', the notion of 'elite' has likewise degenerated in contemporary society. Elites now lack aristocratic qualities, that is, they don't comprise 'the best', and traditional aristocrats (except for certain exceptions) no longer belong to it, having long ago been neutralised.

Contemporary elites are 'recruited' according to criteria that have nothing to do with excellence or character. These criteria are now nepotism, connection, membership in a lobby, a clique, a mafia, a clan (sociological or ethnic); or else these criteria relate to the ability to make money. **The elites of contemporary society are no longer selected, but recruited on the basis of corporate or market principles.**

---

33 Herbert Spencer (1820–1903) was a theorist of evolution who was a contemporary of Darwin. It was he who coined the phrase 'survival of the fittest' in his 1864 book *Principles of Biology* to describe Darwin's idea of natural selection. Darwin himself later adopted Spencer's term. Spencer also applied Darwin's theories to the social realm, something Darwin never did.

Recruitment is thus no longer on the basis of competitive criteria or of excellence. This blocks the circulation of elites. Two phenomena contribute to this: first, egalitarianism and an educational lack of discipline that no longer allows the best to advance; and second, the dominant ideology's aversion to 'elitism', meritocracy, or selection, all of which have become taboo since May '68. Selection and inequality nevertheless still occurs, it's human nature. The present system of elite-formation is chaotic and unjust. **And anti-elitism leads to the social jungle.**
(see **aristocracy; circulation of elites, meritocracy; selection**)

Empire, imperial federation

The political unification of diverse but related peoples under a common sovereign authority, which leaves each individual people autonomous and free.

A federated empire is united, but not blindly homogenised, like the egalitarian nation-state. It revolves around the function of sovereignty, while preserving the diversity of its other functions. Its existence is legitimated by the power and longevity of its peoples, federated within a **political and historical community.** The empire's vocation is not to become a 'World State', like Islam or the American System, but instead **embraces and guides the destiny of those peoples who historically, culturally, and ethnically feel themselves to be part of the same general community.**

There's also a negative conception — a suicidal conception — of empire. This is the model of the late Roman Empire, following the edicts of Caracalla[34] (who granted Roman citizenship to all the Empire's

---

34 Caracalla (188–217) was the Emperor of Rome from 209 to 217. He granted citizenship to all free men who were subjects of the Empire, and the same rights to all women as Roman women had, in an edict in 212. However, apart from this he is best remembered for his cruelty and his capricious abuses of power He was eventually assassinated.

subjects, whatever their origins); this is the model of Alexander, who sought a single ensemble of Greeks and Orientals; this is also the model of Europe's former colonial empires, which is today colonising Europe itself. **The ethnopluralist, multi-racial model of empire must be rejected,** for it inevitably stirs up internal dissension and, ultimately, ends up destroying the empire's founding stock.

The sole positive conception of Empire is that which doesn't oppose the idea of Nation — in the Roman sense of 'being natives of the same great people'. **Empire is a federation of ethnically related peoples — a Grand Federal Nation, of sorts.** A true **model of empire**. The Empire is not a 'nation-state', both cosmopolitan and centralised, but an ensemble of free nations ethnically, culturally and historically related, federated in a great continental empire. The idea of Empire is not admissible, however, if it's a universalism whose drift is toward a 'World State'.

In this sense, Empire is a decentralised Federation, equipped with a strong central power yet restricted to certain specific domains and regulated according to principles of subsidiarity:[35] as such, this power addresses the domains of foreign policy, border control, general economic and ecological rules, etc. The imperial principle is not one of homogenisation; its various components are autonomous and can be organised in different ways, according to their own internal policies (regarding justice, institutions, fiscal autonomy, education, language, culture, etc.). The Empire maintains the ensemble's unity and the general civilisational project — but it's not to be seen as a fluid, confederated association, totally heterogeneous, open to all the world: a discipline of the whole is necessary, to imbue it with a firm, central,

---

35 Subsidiarity is a principle which emphasises the importance of the people having as much decision-making power as possible in regard to the issues which affect them, while decisions regarding the welfare of the larger community are left to the central government.

clear direction. In this sense, the present European Union, this will-less administrative aggregate, is far from representing the European imperial idea.

The national (or regional) components of the empire would be imbued with a 'probationary freedom' that accepts the 'grand policy' of the ensemble and the sovereignty of its central power, but this power, in exchange, would concede their specific identities, accepting that each nation or region, in conserving its freedom, has the right to leave the Federation at any moment. The notion of Empire presupposes a collective project and longevity in history. Europe would provide an ideal frame in which to constitute an Empire, for it would regroup all Europeans, in their diversity and their unity. To realise a future 'Eurosiberian Empire', including Russia, Europeans will have to decide if the federation is going to be based on the nation-state or the historic region. But whatever their response, **the idea of imperial Federation seems, in the end, the sole way by which Europe will be saved.** (see **Eurosiberia; nation**)

End of History

A historical vision, secular heir to the (teleological and soteriological) salvation religions, according to which the age-old conflicts between peoples will progressively culminate in humanity's regrouping within a single World State, governed by individualistic norms of peace, prosperity, and uniformity.

The end of history is a utopia, formerly professed by Marxists, today by Islam (once its *jihad* has conquered the world), as well as by liberals (notably Francis Fukuyama), who believe the collapse of Communism is leading all the world's peoples to form, in the course of the Twenty-first century, a global liberal society under the auspices of an all-powerful and self-regulating market — a society whose only problems will be minor ones resolvable by the police or existing regulations.

The utopia inherent in the 'end of history' is implicit in all modernist and egalitarian ideologies. Its aim is to eliminate differences and conflicts between peoples for the sake of its peculiar model of humanity (the bourgeois consumer). This utopia hasn't a chance of being realised, but it nevertheless has a detrimental effect on Europeans in challenging their independence, identity, and sovereignty. Linked to notions of 'humanity's global pacification', **the end of history is in essence a profoundly totalitarian utopia.** For history, this river of destiny, whose course is unforeseeable, is far from having dried up.

*

With its impending clashes between large ethnic blocs, the Twenty-first century will, in actuality, be possibly more conflict-ridden and violent than the Twentieth century — because of, not despite, globalisation! On an overpopulated planet, prone to rising perils, it's not the end of history leading to a liberal, democratic world state that we see coming, but **an intensification of history, as the competition between peoples responding to the imperatives of selection and the struggle for life becomes ever more desperate.**
(see **history**)

Enrootment

Attachment to a land, to a hereditary heritage, and to an identity that is the motor of all historical dynamism.

Enrootment opposes cosmopolitanism, cultural mixing, and the ethnic chaos of present-day civilisation.

The concept, however, is 'slippery', because it easily leads to certain misunderstandings. European enrootment is never an attachment to the past or to immobility. Instead, it links the ancestral heritage with creation. It shouldn't be understood, then, in the way a museum has us understand it, which neutralises a people's identity by freezing it in nostalgic memory. The notion of enrootment complements that of 'disinstallation', explained above. **Enrootment is the preservation of roots, based on the knowledge that the tree must continue to grow.** Roots are what live: they engender the tree and permit its growth.

Enrootment is above all based on **loyalty to values and to blood.** The most dangerous form of enrootment, or pseudo-enrootment, occurs in the regionalist and separatist milieu of the Left — in Provence, the Basque country, and Brittany, for example — where the region's linguistic and cultural distinctions are forcibly asserted, but on the basis of a multiracial model. Hence, the frequently heard and astonishing litany, 'Our immigrants are Bretons, Basques, or Occitans like us'. The contradiction is total: in the name of opposing the 'tradition' of Jacobin homogenisation, strangers to our soil and traditions are admitted to the country — in the name of Jacobin universalism!

If limited solely to culture, enrootment becomes a sterile folklorism. For however necessary, in itself cultural enrootment is insufficient.

For Europeans of the future, enrootment ought never to be limited simply to attachment to or defence of one's native country (region or nation); it also needs to be accompanied by an inner revolution that makes them conscious of Europe (perhaps later Eurosiberia) as a community of destiny.

(see **archeofuturism; disinstallation; tradition**)

Ethnocentrism

The mobilising conviction, distinct to all long-living peoples, that they belong to something superior and that they must conserve their ethnic identity, if they are to endure in history.

Whether it's 'objectively' true or false doesn't matter: ethnocentrism is the psychological condition necessary to a people's (or nation's) survival. History is not a field in which intellectually objective principles are worked out, but one conditioned by the will to power, competition, and selection. Scholastic disputes about a people's superiority or inferiority are beside the point. **In the struggle for survival, the feeling of being superior and right is indispensable to acting and succeeding.**

Long-living peoples, the great and the small, whether Chinese or Jews, have always been ethnocentric. But one should be wary of a metaphysical supremacism that becomes demobilising or discourages all effort ('we will always be intrinsically superior, it's futile to worry about it'). It's the fable of the turtle and the hare. History has repeatedly demonstrated that a people imbued with a fierce will and a hardened character can defeat and subjugate more brilliant and gifted populations and civilisations which are overly confident or decadent. This was the case of all those peoples between the Seventh and the Eleventh centuries who were overrun by the eruption of Muslim Bedouins. This is our situation today, for we too risk being overwhelmed by peoples of different cultures and civilisations.

Europeans were powerful when they remained naïvely ethnocentric. Once they starting asking themselves about 'the value of the Other', the decline set in.

America's present dynamism is based on the conviction — whether true or not — that her model is superior to all the others. **History is above all a field of subjectivity, of struggle between subjectivities.**

*

European ethnocentrism was never a matter of hot air. The contribution European civilisation (including its American prodigal) has made to the history of humanity surpasses, in every domain, that of every other people. But one must never rest on one's laurels. In the larger struggle of planetary competition, nothing is ever gained forever. Civilisations in any case don't last if they don't cultivate an **inner pride**, an implicit sentiment of being irreplaceable, a ferocious will 'of identity and continuity'.

(see **competition; consciousness, ethnic**)

Ethnocracy

Ethnocracy[36] (in Greek, *ethnos* means people and *kratos* means power) refers to a political system for which the homogeneity of a people is an unconditional prerequisite for the exercise of the political will of the people. As a consequence, the citizens of an ethnocracy derive all political rights and duties from this ethnic criterion.

The ethnocracy is based on the conservation of the multitude and the differences; in other words, the originality specific to each people and each culture. It is universally applicable for all peoples and cultures, and at the same time constitutes the radical overcoming of all the destructive universalisms of egalitarianism.

It promotes the birth of healthy children (see eugenics) and strives for the conservation of the environment (see ecology), since it prioritises the living before the idols of economy, consumerism and mercantilism. It heals all forms of ethnomasochism and protects the people from self-destruction.

Ethnocracy (also known as genopolitics) will most definitely be the great political challenge of the future.

(see **genopolitics; eugenics; democracy, organic democracy**)

Ethnomasochism

The masochistic tendency to blame and devalue one's ethnicity, one's own people.

Ethnomasochism comes from shame and self-hatred. It's a collective psychopathology, provoked by a concerted propaganda campaign to make Europeans feel guilty about how they've treated other peoples and to make them see themselves as 'oppressors'. They are made, in this way, to repent and pay their alleged debt. A veritable historical

---

36   This entry was written by Pierre Krebs for the German edition.

imposture, their repentance, no less, is urged by the churches and the state.

Ethnomasochism is also at the base of anti-natalist policies that surreptitiously limit the reproduction of the European population. **It's a form of self-racism, in effect.** Tainted with the original sin of his intrinsic racism, European man is guilty of being who he is.

Ethnomasochism promotes a systematic apology for race-mixing and cosmopolitanism. Curiously, it denies Europeans the idea of an ethnic identity, which everyone else is accorded. They are obliged, thus, to mitigate themselves, while others, like Africans for example, are not. Ethnomasochism is the counterpart to xenophilia (the love and overestimation of the stranger, the 'Other'). It's akin to **ethno-suicide.** Ethnomasochism is nothing new in history. It's a symptom of a people too weary to live and perpetuate itself: an ageing people ready to pass the baton to another. European elites have succumbed to this collective disease, which explains their indifference to the present colonisation and their idea that we should welcome it.
(see **homophilia; xenophilia**)

Ethnosphere, ethnic blocs
Those territories ruled by ethnically related peoples.

The notion of an ethnosphere refers to a world based on the laws of life, to one that rejects cosmopolitanism and multi-ethnic nations, whose history is one of ongoing failure. The future of our overpopulated world belongs to homogeneous ethnospheres or **ethnic blocs.** China, India, the Arab world, and Black Africa are ethnospheres. **The Twenty-first century will be one of clashing ethnic blocs and ethnospheres.** It certainly won't belong to the cosmopolitan hodgepodge of a World State! The planet is not going to unite into a global network of exchanges and communications, as peoples and civilisations somehow fuse into a single unity. The very opposite is coming!

At present, Europe alone is trying to mix races and only her elites envisage the spectacle of a motley ethnopluralist society extendable to the whole world. As for the United States, founded on anti-ethnic principles, its racially kaleidoscopic society hasn't a chance of becoming planetary. It's not even certain if it'll endure — for lacking an *ethno-national community*, its existence is likely to be ephemeral. It's far more probable that China or Japan, representing homogeneous ethnospheres, will survive.

The notion of ethnic blocs doesn't necessarily imply a bellicose vision of the future. Conflict, as well as cooperation, are the laws of history. To cooperate in an overpopulated world of disparate peoples, it will be necessary to conserve one's identity. **The world of the future will have to be one of cooperating ethnospheres, though one based on the logic of 'armed peace'.** It will be a world of 'cold war' between ethnic blocs that will best serve us. We should nevertheless have no illusion about it: in an increasingly competitive world, conflict between ethnospheres is inevitable. Islam's present anti-European offensive is a good example of this. As to Europe and Russia, if they don't achieve their destiny by forming a unified ethnic bloc, they will be devoured by other continental civilisations.

(see **autarky of great spaces; identity**)

Eugenics

A technique for improving the genetic quality of a population.

Biotechnologies and genetic engineering today furnish the technical and practical means of improving the human genome, not solely for therapeutic reasons, but for political ones as well. **Biotechnology now makes it possible to practice a positive eugenics** that directly intervenes in the genome to improve heredity, doing so more effectively and rapidly than older techniques based on selection by marriage.

This Promethean challenge posed by eugenics was long anticipated in Europe's archaic pagan imagination. But it evidently poses a terrible problem in offending sensibilities rooted in monotheistic creationism and anthropocentrism.

Not only does man become the creator of himself, self-manipulating, but he finds himself immersed in the living, like a 'biological object', similar to other animals. **Dual revolution, above and below: Man makes himself, being both a demiurge, a rival of the divine, and, in the same stroke, becomes malleable human material to be shaped and moulded.** The combined death of anthropocentrism and metaphysical deism.

Eugenics shocks tender-hearted egalitarians: isn't it a matter of diabolically creating the 'Overman'? Yes, of course. The essential thing is to master the process, to submit it to a political will, and not let it become part of an unregulated eugenic 'market'. To prevent such a development, as the dominant ideology demands, is hardly tenable. The celebrated British physicist Stephen Hawking recently declared that biotechnology will permit 'the creation of a master race' and 'a much improved human being'.[37]

Biotechnology will very soon also make possible artificial, extra-uterine births, in 'incubators' (i.e., without pregnancy), as human and cultural genetic matter are introduced *in vitro*. This procedure could become a powerful means of redressing European natality, now threatened by depopulation ... **It would, of course, be preferable to do this through natural births.** But in tragic situations, half a loaf is better than none ... Between two evils, one chooses the lesser.
(see **archeofuturism; biopolitics; techno-science**)

---

37 Stephen Hawking made these claims during an address in Switzerland, which was reported in *Metro* on 27 November 2000.

Europe

Europe is our real fatherland — culturally, historically, ethnically, civilisationally — embracing and overarching her different nations and native lands.

It's finally time to make Europe a subject of history. It's probably best to begin by defining a European, before determining his formal or legal nationality — simply because a stranger can call himself a Belgian, a German, or a Frenchman, though it's much more difficult to call himself a European (or a Castilian, a Breton, a Bavarian, etc.). Europe needs to think of herself as a community of destiny, one that will replace the nation-state in the Twenty-first century.

*

Besides, most people in the world see us more as Europeans than as Germans, Italians, Frenchmen, etc. The way others look at us is one sign that we're not wrong. In a globalised world, prone to civilisational clashes, Europe — beset by demographic decline, threatened with life-threatening dangers — faces the overriding imperative of regrouping in order to survive, **for the isolated nation-state no longer bears any weight** in a world where an entity with less than 300 million inhabitants lacks the power to assure its independence.[38]

*

The present European Union is a prostrate object, a bastard, devoid of identity.
The irredeemable failings of the EU are well-known: rigid bureaucratism allied with global free-trade, submission to the United States, abandonment of sovereignty, the euro's erratic fluctuations, an overbearing immigrant-supportive multi-racialism, etc. The process is well-known. **The existing EU institutions don't serve the interests of the European peoples.**

---

38   This is also an idea initially formulated by Jean Thiriart.

Returning to a Europe of cloistered nation-states is no longer an option. The French nation-state never sought the preservation of her peoples' identity. Indeed, she herself, spurred by her cosmopolitan ideology, opened the door to the alien colonisers. We face a terrible dilemma: France or Europe? The question, though, is badly posed. What should be asked (to go over rather than under this contradiction) is: *how can Europe be made, the real Europe, without unmaking and denying France?* The answer: it's the French state that's cause for criticism, not France as a historical and cultural entity. **However bad Europe's present organisational form, there's no reason to renounce the prospect of constructing another Europe.**

*

On what general principles can a 'good' European construction take place?

1. Europe must be built according to principles of sovereignty, independence, and power — in the spirit of the best French tradition. Of course, the worst of this tradition should also be avoided — i.e., its levelling centralism that excludes the idea of Europe (depriving her of a sovereign, central state) and resists an overarching, federal authority imbued with a strategic policy and an autonomous economy. 'European construction' needs to be envisioned as having a central executive power and a head of state. The present situation is a complete mess: a single, unregulated currency, an embryonic army, member states dispossessed of 50 percent of their legislation, courts without authority! Two things in one. Either, we return to state sovereignty (with national currencies) and the EU becomes an ensemble of treaties, pacts, accords, and occasional summits (the 'Concert of Nations' established by the 1815 Treaty of Vienna) — the model of Nineteenth-century Europe. **Or else, national sovereignty is abandoned for the sake of a European imperial state worthy of the name.**

2. According to this second hypothesis, **Europe will be federal and imperial or it will not be.** She can't long remain content with the present wobbly assemblage of cooperative but unequal states lacking a common international policy, led by an uncomprehending and uncontrollable technocracy, with everything feebly held together by the rhetorical swish of free trade, democratism, and humanitarian 'values', and undergirded by bureaucratic regulations and financial mechanisms. Europe will exist in the long run only as a large **federation of ethnically related regions.**

3. Western and Central Europe, whose future is now uncertain, needs to ally with Russia to ward off their common enemies.

4. In such a prospective Imperial Federation, every national member would be free, at whatever time, to quit it if it so desires.

That said, the edification of such a Europe would emerge not through the gentle evolution of the present EU, whose present political form is hardly viable, but rather through the dramatic force of already foreseeable circumstances.

(see **convergence of catastrophes; empire; Eurosiberia**)

Eurosiberia

The destined space in which European peoples will finally regroup, from the Atlantic to the Pacific, sealing the historic alliance between the European peninsula, Central Europe, and Russia.

The term is preferable to 'Eurasia'.[39] Europe here reappropriates all of northern Asia for Russian domination. **Beware, though: the concept of Eurosiberia is a 'paradigm', that is, an ideal, a model, an objective, one of whose dimensions is a concrete, agitating, and mobilising myth.**

---

39 Faye is referring to the concept of Eurasianism, one of the tenets of which is that Russia is culturally closer to Asia than to Western Europe.

Eurosiberia will be an 'Empire of the Sun', across whose fourteen time zones the sun will never set. Eurosiberia is the common fortress, the common home, the maximum extension and natural expression of the notion of 'European Empire'. It will be a veritable 'Third Rome', which Russia alone never was.

The notion of Eurosiberia supposes the decoupling of Western Europe from the American West, and Europe's solidarity and alliance with Russia. De Gaulle intuitively sensed the need for this. We have the same enemies, the same ethnic/racial competitors. We — we future Eurosiberians — are a nightmare for the Pentagon, as well as for Islam. **If it should ever be constructed, Eurosiberia would regroup all White, Indo-European peoples in the great regions into which they have spread, becoming — from far off and for long to come — not solely the world's foremost power, but the first hyper-power in history.**

*

The great spatial expanses of Eurosiberia — 'from the land of the steppes to the fjords to the bush' — would be economically independent of North America. It would neither be aggressive nor imperialist, but identitarian. China, India, the Muslim-Arab world, Africa, Southeast Asia, Latin America, even North America, have an interest in managing the Blue Planet (Earth), to cooperate with a future Eurosiberian Federation — on the condition that everyone stays in their own lands.

It will of course be objected that that this is utopian. No. It's only *an idea thrown at history* in the Hegelian sense. The great ideas always find their way. As Pierre Vial says, it's toward a 'self-governed ethnocentric Eurosiberia' that future European elites will turn their energies, once the era of world-changing tragedies arrives.

(see **idea, ideal, historical idealism**)

F

Fatherland, Great Fatherland, native land

The land of one's fathers, ancestors, and lineage. The notion of fatherland (*patrie*) links a 'people' with a 'land'.

The need for a 'native land' (*patrie charnelle*) is ethologically and biologically rooted in the human spirit — and no form of globalisation can abolish it. Identification with a fatherland is one of the pillars of human psychology — **a fatherland in which the crystallisation of the territorial imperative and the ethnic imperative coincide.**

The history of European peoples is so complicated and entangled that the choice of a fatherland is difficult to make in a 'rational' or 'mechanical' manner. Will it be Brittany, Lombardy, or Flanders? Will it be France, Italy, Germany, or some other nation-state? Will it be America, to which European elites continue to emigrate? The French ideology of the nation-state, like the German ideology of Fichte's 'fatherland as language and culture',[40] has diminished the idea of fatherland, basic to all anthropological relations.

In revealing a certain European schizophrenia, this question can only be answered from *above*: **to each European his own fatherland, national or regional (chosen on the basis of intimate, emotive affinities) — and to all Europeans the Great Fatherland, this land of intimately related peoples.** The consciousness of belonging to both a 'small native land' and a 'great fatherland' is very difficult for contemporaries to grasp. The future, though, will likely compel them to

---

40 Johann Gottlieb Fichte (1762–1814) was one of the principal philosophers of German Idealism. He defined the modern conception of the nation as those who belong to a community with a shared linguistic, historical and cultural identity, rather than it being simply a matter of geographic borders. He outlines these ideas in his *Addresses to the German Nation* (Cambridge: Cambridge University Press, 2003).

understand it. **The Great Fatherland organically encompasses and federates the native lands of Europe.** This is what I call the *New Nationalism.*

*

The modern world lives **the assumption of the homeless and the accession of the deracinated.** A nomadic *métis*,[41] modern Western man is a passer-by in a world that has become a Global Village — organised into networks, with universalism and global capitalism constituting its virtual fatherland. This, though, is an illusion, a remnant of a modernism already out of date. There's no doing away with the notion of a fatherland, for it's archaic and atemporal, inscribed in our genes, and, in this sense, it's futurist — *archeofuturist.*

Even the Third World immigrant colonisers of Europe remain attached to their fatherland — to the land from which they came. But for them, especially Muslims, Europe is a new fatherland, a conquered land (*Dar al Islam*).[42] But beware: as a constant feature of human history, resting on the permanent conflict-cooperation dialectic governing the relations between different peoples, there will always be a temptation to **occupy other people's land**. In a rather unique boomerang of history, Europe today is a victim of this alien inversion.

*

Essential to the idea of fatherland is not just an identity with a particular land, but an identity with a particular ethno-spiritual community. **The fatherland is not simply a territory, but a biological lineage,**

---

41   French: 'a person of racially mixed parentage'.

42   In Islam, *Dar al Islam*, Arabic for 'House of Islam', refers to those areas where Islam can be practiced freely, and is usually understood as nations in which Islam is the dominant religion so that Islamic law can be enforced (although not always, particularly according to more liberal Muslim theologians). It stands in contrast to *Dar al Harb*, or the 'House of War', which is applied to nations which are hostile to the practice of Islamic law and which are not in a non-aggression treaty with Muslims.

the place where one's ancestors are buried. Hence the tragedy of the *pieds-noirs*[43] who settled Algeria, where their family tombs have since been profaned — where they once lived and worked and from which they were forcibly expelled. **To survive today, Europeans no longer need to search for other countries to conquer, but to defend the Great Fatherland that comprises all the native lands of which they are the sole rightful occupants.**

At the Continental level, the notion of fatherland must resume a dialectical dynamic. The new horizon of European man — following the failure of European colonisation, the tragedy of the present Third World colonisation, and the fantasy of a 'Western world civilisation' — is now shaped by **the need both to reconstruct their native lands and to construct an imperial Great Fatherland, Eurosiberia, stretching from the Atlantic to the Pacific.**

Words, of course, are always a bit imprecise. They are not mathematical concepts, but things expressive of the spirit's subtleties. The fatherland, as a notion, has a meaning related to that of the 'nation', which etymologically refers to those who are closely related. The essential, however, is that all these notions possess an unshakeable popular basis. Let me give Éric Delcroix[44] the last word here: 'Where is the real native land, in which our contemporaries still recognise themselves as being within Europe, where they can make their life worth living and thus eventually worth sacrificing? There needs to be a people, though, before there can be such a land — however legitimate their attachment to all that they have historically and sentimentally invested.' In his view, this people is the French, who are presently being disfigured by mass immigration, to such a degree that they risk becoming strangers in their own land, given that their new 'compatriots' are non-European.

---

43 Literally 'black foot', this term refers to those of European origin who lived in Algeria during the period of French colonisation (1830–1962). The original meaning of the term has been lost and is still debated today.

44 Éric Delcroix (b. 1944) is a French barrister who has written several radical Right-wing works. He is also known as a prominent advocate of Holocaust revisionism.

The issue here is to define the term 'patriotic' on the basis of ethnic and historical criteria rather than according to the cosmopolitan ideology of the French Revolution. As Corneille wrote in his *Horace*, 'To die for one's country is such a worthy act / Men should contend to gain its glorious prize'.[45] Again, it's necessary that a fatherland corresponds to a single homogeneous people, for in American-style multi-racial society it's even denied that its soldiers are sacrificed for the nation's sake.

(see **enrootment; Eurosiberia, land; nation; people**)

G

Genopolitics

Genopolitics[46] (in Greek, *genos* means race or people), like ethnocracy, is based on the conservation of the *genos*, on the promotion of the healthy, the protection of the environment, and on the overcoming of the *Homo oeconomicus*, the commercial society and all forms of mercantilism.

(see **ethnocracy; eugenics; democracy, democratism, organic democracy**)

---

45 Pierre Corneille (1606–1684) was a French dramatist who has been called 'the father of French tragedy'. This quote appears in his drama *Horace*, in Act II, scene iii.

46 This entry was written by Pierre Krebs for the German edition. See also the extensive explanation in Pierre Chassard, *Idées, Théories, Doctrines: Dictionnaire critique* (Brussels: 2002).

Geopolitics

The study (or practice) associated with the politics of peoples, nations, and states, as they relate to mastering vital geographical spaces of land or water.

Condemned in the aftermath of the Second World War because it was stupidly declared to be 'Nazi' and accused of legitimating the ideology of 'life spaces' (*Lebensraum*), geopolitics (which all nations, including the Chinese and the Americans, practice) has made a forceful return today. Robert Steuckers, a European specialist in the field, writes, 'The most fundamental of geopolitical principles posits that a narrow relationship exists between power and space'. For Steuckers, the American War of Independence, the two World Wars, the expansion of the Russian Empire, and the present (anti-European) policies of the American superpower are (or have been) manifestations of geopolitics in action. He claims, justly, that geopolitical objectives constitute the incontestable historical basis of nations and peoples.

Geopolitics distinguishes between continental powers and maritime powers (thalassocracies). The latter, like Britain in the Nineteenth century and the United States today, endeavours to dominate the land-based powers. Europe, and especially a possible Eurosiberia, is both a continental and a maritime power.

The conquest and domination of vital territorial and maritime spaces (as much for commercial as for military reasons) remains more than ever the centre of world politics. Those who claim that human rights, financial markets, the 'new economy', and globalisation have made geopolitics and the struggle for space obsolete claim the very opposite of the truth. **The Twenty-first century will be a century of peoples struggling for land and sea, more than in any previous century,** because the Earth now is 'full', with no empty spaces left to separate them.

*

Geopolitics displeases globalist ideologues, for it presupposes that a people's struggle for the possession and domination of space (the territorial imperative) takes precedent over the struggle for morality or ideology. Geopolitics challenges the liberal or socialist vision of 'one world': an Earth whose lands are to be unified into a single homeland for a uniformised humanity. Geopolitics helps us rethink human ensembles as **ethno-political territorial blocs**.

In the course of the coming century — and we're already seeing an expansion of struggles for vital spaces — there will be conflicts over petroleum, gas, and mineral resources, over water basins and potable water, over fishing reserves and rare minerals, over control of sea lanes and pipelines, etc.

*

What are the principal geopolitical challenges facing Europe?

1. **The formidable advance and territorial conquest of Islam toward the North and the East, from Gibraltar to India.** Even religion has its geopolitical and territorial imperatives. Islam's present expansion represents another conquering Arab offensive against Indo-Europeans, as it sweeps in to fill the breach created by other Third World peoples.

2. **The American effort to control and subject Western Europe and Russia.** Since the end of Communism, the great fear of the American thalassocracy is Eurosiberia, the union of Russia and Europe, which would be a formidable competitor: hence, the EU's disarmament and NATO's extension into Eastern Europe; the Balkan wars, aimed at dividing Europeans; the Islamo-American pact (encouraging Turkish membership in the EU, etc.) to weaken Europe, etc.

Europe, in a word, is the target of various continentalist designs: occupation by Islam and the Global South, domination by the United States. The former Soviet-American condominium, which divided and occupied Europe during the Cold War, has come to an end. Yalta[47] is no more, but we now face an even more dangerous menace: an Islamo-American condominium. Colonisation from above and from below: this will be the major geopolitical struggle of the early Twenty-first century. If Europeans don't become conscious of it, they will disappear from history.

(see **Europe; Eurosiberia**)

Germen

A people's or civilisation's biological root — the core of ethnicity — upon which everything else rests.

In Latin, *germen* means 'germ', 'seed'. If a culture is lost, recovery is possible. When the biological *germen* is destroyed, nothing is possible. The *germen* is comparable to a tree's roots. If the trunk is damaged or the foliage cut down, the tree can recover. But not if its roots are lost. The comparison holds for civilisations. The *germen* represents a people's ethno-biological roots; the trunk represents the popular culture, the foliage the civilisation. Nothing is lost if the *germen*, the roots, are saved. This metaphor obviously applies to Europe, whose *germen* is now gravely threatened.

Contrary to the dominant ideology, this concept implies that cultures and civilisations rest (not uniquely but mainly) on distinct flesh-and-blood populations, as well as on their physical and cultural heritages — that is, on the real, on *life* — on relatively invariable bio-genetic characteristics To deny these biological factors is as intelligent and effective as denying the Earth's roundness, the circulation of blood, heliocentrism, or the evolution of the species — as the spiritual and intellectual ancestors of the present dominant ideology once did.

---

47 The Yalta Conference in February 1945 was a meeting between Winston Churchill, Franklin D Roosevelt and Joseph Stalin to discuss the post-war organisation and division of Europe. The decisions made here effectively charted the fate of Europe until the end of the Cold War nearly half a century later.

The *germen* is inalienable, it's not the property of some individual fantasy, but is transmitted by every member as he transmits his line. A people can be reborn if its culture is destroyed or if its religion or spirituality are forgotten. It can recover its ancestral heritage and respond to the appeal of traditions preserved in memory, making them live again. But if the *germen* is damaged, no renaissance is possible (or if it is, it's artificial).

That's why the struggle against race-mixing, depopulation, and the alien colonisation of Europe is even more important than mobilising for one's cultural identity and political sovereignty.

All these causes are important, but there's an order of priority based on **absolute necessity.**

(see **consciousness, ethnic; identity; race, racism, anti-racism**)

Globalisation, globalism

The planetary universalisation of exchange, circuits of economic production and finance, along with information; the internationalisation of culture. 'Globalism' is the doctrine advocating the generalisation of these phenomena.

In reality, the process of economic and cultural globalisation began more than two hundred years ago. One speaks today of **globalising** the planetary economy. This phenomenon is not, however, quite as important as generally believed — for economies, along with national or regional cultures, remain everywhere very strong. **Globalist ideology fools itself, for a genuine globalisation would lead to catastrophe, undermining both the world economy and the ecosystem.**

*

Central to the dominant ideology (even to the ideology of the anti-liberal, neo-Trotskyist Left), globalist dogma is no less a part of Islam's universalist ideology.

There are actually **a plurality of globalisms:** that of Islam, the cosmopolitan and pro-immigrant Left, and the liberal, pro-American West. Globalism is a weapon in the war against Europe, her identity, her power, and her economic independence. It gives vent to the utopian illusion of *history's end*. As such, globalist paeans deify the Internet, the 'new economy', the immigrant invasion of Europe, the globalisation of financial networks — without ever seeing that ethnic realities and ancestral religions remain stronger than ever.

Globalisation, in fact, doesn't actually challenge the diversity of cultures and the clash of civilisations, just the opposite. By an ironic dialectic, it stimulates and regenerates them.

*

The more people encounter one another in an overpopulated planet, the greater, in effect, will be the need for identity. This is why **it's very unlikely that Twenty-first century globalisation will be peaceful — or avoid civilisational clashes.**
(see **cosmopolitanism; universalism**)

Grand Politics

Political action in the historical sense, for the *longue durée*, that serves the people and its civilisational objectives.

'Grand Politics', a concept formulated by Nietzsche,[48] opposes the 'petty politics' of politicians and parties, with their short-term career or monetary aspirations. Petty politics results from the domination of the 'third function' (i.e., the reduction of politics and sovereignty

---

[48] 'For when truth steps into battle with the lie of millennia we shall have convulsions, an earthquake spasm, a transposition of valley and mountain such as never been dreamed of. The concept politics has then become completely absorbed into a war of spirits, all the power-structures of the old society have been blown into the air — they one and all reposed on the lie. Only after me will there be *grand politics* on earth.' From Friedrich Nietzsche, *Ecce Homo* in *The Nietzsche Reader* (Oxford: Blackwell Publishers, 2006), p. 515.

to short-term economic interests). Victor Hugo's tragedy, *Ruy Blas*,[49] perfectly depicts the utter opposition between grand and petty politics. Grand politics is not about individual or partisan *tactics* seeking some ephemeral conquest of power, but is a *strategy* — a strategy of great design, based on collective pride, not individual vanity. **Grand Politics belongs to the realm of historical destiny — not the individualistic realm of petty party politics.**

*

The European governments of our day lack any sense of Grand Politics. Their 'petty politics' is actually not even about seeking power, only about appearances or financial advantage or media vanity. This is especially grave considering that other civilisations — those of Muslim-Arab, Indian, Chinese, or American peoples — practice 'Grand Politics', as they project their destiny onto the future.
(see **people, long-living; revolution**)

H

Happiness, 'small pleasures'
A secularised version, converted into social and economic objectives, of the heavenly ideal inspiring the salvation religions.

Small pleasures (*petit bonheur*) for everyone — to satisfy the material demands of one's living standard — has become the formal goal of Western ideology. But happiness, even well-being, is not to be found in this market of dupes. Never have suicide rates been higher.

---

49 *Ruy Blas* is a tragedy about a slave in Seventeenth-century Spain who falls in love with the Queen. An enemy of the Queen disguises him as a nobleman and presents him at court. Following his wise proposals for reforms, he is appointed prime minister and wins the Queen's heart, only to commit suicide after he is exposed.

Defined strictly in terms of economic and materialistic well-being, these small pleasures falsely presume that all human beings aspire to the same ideal of quantitative consumption. This purely passive objective, entailing a **people's domestication**, despises the spiritual, historical, and cultural requirements of an individual's inner sense of well-being. It destroys communal solidarity. It excludes everything that cannot be attained through a certain 'material level of life'. Its massified individual knows, as such, only anguish and insecurity in a society promising heaven on Earth. The frenzied search for material well-being, socially sanctioned but never attained, is leading to what Konrad Lorenz[50] called the 'warm death', which softens and undermines a civilisation.

This narcissistic materialism of small pleasures is accompanied by the simulated pseudo-spirituality of consummate hypocrisy: human-rights humanitarianism and other so-called 'cultural policies' designed to elevate the contemporary soul.

(see **consumerism; domestication; individualism**)

Heredity

Physical and psychological characteristics innate to biological nature — and hence transmittable.

Heredity not only constitutes an individual or familial disposition, but a collective one. A people's hereditary disposition, though not perfectly clear and having thus a fluid character, nevertheless exists.

The dominant ideology now rejects all idea of a people's heredity. Based on the dogmas of assimilation and integration, it holds that identity is not transmitted, but acquired. Any human group can therefore

---

50 Konrad Lorenz (1903-1989) was an Austrian ethologist who won the Nobel Prize in 1973. In his book *Civilized Man's Seven Deadly Sins*, he speculated that the supposed advances of modern life were actually harmful to humanity, since they had removed humans from the biological effects of natural competition and replaced it with the far more brutal competition inherent in relations between individuals in modern societies.

adapt itself to any culture. **The taboo science of ethnopsychology has demonstrated, though, that the behaviour of peoples and nations depends to a significant degree on their collective genetic disposition.** Put in identical circumstances, different peoples produce different results. Those not favoured by their natural environment can often thus produce more than those who are. The Dutch, for example, whose natural environment is atrocious, far out-produce African populations situated in lands that are naturally rich.

We need to finish with the behaviourist dogma, whose origin is Marxist, according to which differences in performance levels and living standards between countries and civilisations are uniquely due to the hazards of history, to the relations of production, and to the exploitation of one people by another. **These differences are atavistic, the fruit of different collective heredities, most of which, of course, are innate.**

Heredity is nevertheless not everything. Or rather it has surprises to reveal. Within every people, **degenerate tendencies** can always surface. Hence the decline of certain civilisations. The Great War of 1914–1918, for example, profoundly damaged the genetic basis of European elites, of her natural aristocrats. Thus, perhaps for this reason, the decline in character and *virtus*[51] so evident today. In addition to genetic factors, harmful ideologies also have the power to deprive human groups of the capacity for resistance and creativity. **No people, except for limited periods, should claim to be hereditarily superior to another.**

History is nothing but the relations of forces — the struggle for life. If Europeans are being colonised by formerly dominated peoples from the South, if they accept every kind of humiliation, it's due, first off, to a weakness within them. Heredity is not eternal. We need to be constantly on guard against superiority complexes. **Heredity is acquired, but it's also conquered and defended.** Every people, by its own hand,

---

51 Latin: 'virtue'.

can lose the hereditary disposition that is its force, for it is actualised only within its own culture; or, in cases of counter-selection, it stupidly squanders its genetic patrimony.

More precisely said — and this remark is totally taboo in Europe today, though not in the rest of the world, which freely acknowledges it — **race-mixing is fatal to a people's heredity and the pursuit of its civilisation.** It's the dialectic of the innate and the acquired, it's also the history of the living. **For the cultural transmission of a tradition and the continuation of a civilisation are impossible without maintaining its biological core, its original stock.** André Lama, for example, has shown that the fall of the Roman Empire was due, in part, to Roman mixing with alien populations.[52]

(see **germen; heritage; miscegenation; race, racism and anti-racism**)

Heritage

The ensemble of capacities and cultural traits transmitted from one generation to another that structures a people's identity.

Heritage has both a cultural and a bio-anthropological nature. A **dual imperative: blood and spirit.** Any rupture in the heritage's transmission, whether popular, artistic, cultural, artisanal, or technoscientific, eradicates a part of a people's memory, preparing the **ethnocide** that will cause it to disappear.

Europeans, especially the French, are now prone to a triple sabotage of their heritage: first, the sabotage of their cultural and historical memory, in which the public schools actively take part; second, the submerging of Europe's cultural patrimony and creative forces under American/Western mass culture and by the neo-primitivism that comes with Africanisation (the 'tom-tom cult' Céline predicted); and third, assaults on their biological *germen*, through race-mixing, a declining birth rate, and the growing weight of alien populations. The

---

52 See his *Des Dieux et des Empereurs* (Paris: Éd. des Écrivans, 2000).

transmission of the biological and cultural heritage is the *sine qua non* for maintaining European peoples in history. Once there's no longer anything of one's own to transmit, one ceases to exist. A people without a heritage is an alienated people and, **if things continue in this way, Europeans will find themselves far more deculturated than the Third World populations they formerly dominated.**

But there's a paradox here. Though the biological heritage hasn't suffered any major changes, the cultural heritage in European history is always in constant metamorphosis, far from being something fixed. The cultural and civilisational heritage is a movement. Like a flame that always remains the same, the substance it burns is ceaselessly being renewed. **The essential is that there exists within the heritage a hard core, a nucleus, of 'fundamental values' — mindful of the historical memory.**

(see **enrootment; heredity; history**)

Heroes

Emblematic figures of mythic or real personage representing the superior values of a people or a nation — who are willing to sacrifice themselves for their people's sake.

European civilisation was founded on the basis of heroic gestures, its 'holy book' being the *Iliad,* then the *Odyssey.* A society is evidently judged by its heroes and anti-heroes. Today, the dominant ideology tends to **reject all notion of heroism.** Strong, virile, conquering societies, like Islam, have always had their cult of hero-martyrs. In the French school system, heroes have been banished and are no longer referenced (Joan of Arc, Bayard,[53] du Guesclin,[54] etc., and by all means

---

[53] Pierre Terrail LeVieux (1473–1524), otherwise known as the Chevalier de Bayard, was a French knight who fought in many battles and came to be seen as the embodiment of the chivalric ideal.

[54] Bertrand du Guesclin (c. 1320–1380) was a French knight and military commander who won many battles during the Hundred Years' War.

let's not speak of Charles Martel, who would probably be accused of 'racism'); even the republican heroes of the Revolution are no longer evoked! There were, though, some residual heroes for the generation of May '68 (Che Guevara, Mao, Castro, Frantz Fanon,[55] etc.), whose dubious stature actually has since diminished.

The post-conciliar[56] Catholic Church, in its rigorous campaign of sabotage, no longer insists on the cult of saints, suspected of latent paganism. Egalitarians reject heroes because they are **superior personalities,** who rise above the mass, providing it with exemplary models and, at the same time, lending themselves to a **dynamic notion of the people — as a historical community of destiny, born from the exemplary standards of its great creative personalities** — a notion, of course, now totally diabolised. Heroes are models, who sacrifice for their people's sake: something completely incomprehensible for today's 'clerks'.

Our decadent, ethnomasochistic society cannot, however, avoid forging pseudo-heroes or sub-heroes: football players, soap opera stars, humanitarian doctors, and *tutti quanti*.[57]

The United States, this society allegedly more decadent than Europe (a view which demands demonstration), is, paradoxically, constantly celebrating in literature and cinema its cult of *patriotic heroes.* This is especially curious in that the United States has created the pseudo-heroes of media and show business, the buffoons fabricated by the 'society of the spectacle'.[58] An analysis of the US situation is thus not

---

55 Frantz Fanon (1925-1961) was a Martiniquan Marxist intellectual and African nationalist whose writings, particularly *The Wretched of the Earth*, have been highly influential upon anti-colonialist movements.

56 Meaning after the Second Vatican Council of 1962-65.

57 Latin: 'everything'.

58 This is a term coined by Guy Debord (1931-1994), a French Marxist philosopher and the founder of the anarchist Situationist International. The spectacle, as described in his principal work, *The Society of the Spectacle,* is one of the means by which the capitalist establishment maintains its authority in the modern world — namely, by reducing all genuine human experiences to representational

so simple. Its popular cult of heroes is unthinkable in Europe, **where patriotic heroism is ridiculed for its 'primitivism'** and cultural elites devote themselves to a blasé negativity. The heroes in French cinema over the last twenty years or so have been for the most part deranged, arm-breaking, psychopathic types. For better or worse, it's been the American cinema that has valorised European heroes. For example, films like *The 300 Spartans, Excalibur, Braveheart,* etc.

Europe's regeneration will include rehabilitating her heroes in popular culture. It's amazing, though, the way the media has stunned the public with their insane cult of millionaire athletes, of talentless but well-paid movie and music stars, and of phony personalities created by opinion polls — all of whose hypocritical 'heroism' is a matter of financial privilege and histrionic vanity.

(see **born leader; personality, creative**)

Heterotelia

The outcome and consequences of an action whose effects are radically contrary to its intended or proclaimed aim (from the Greek *hetero* and *télos* meaning 'other' and 'ends').

In general, heterotelia is the lot of all utopian ideologies and dogmatic religions, particularly those advocating egalitarianism, humanitarianism, and anti-racism.

A few examples: the massacres and wars perpetuated in the name of 'the God of love and the poor'; ideologies of liberation and emancipation which inevitably culminate in totalitarianism; Left-wing socialist programs that create poverty, fiscalism, bureaucratism, and a new class of speculators; academic ideologies of anti-selection that bring about growing inequalities, a 'two-tiered school' system, a bargain-basement curriculum for those of modest income, and a savage or nepotistic admission procedure for professional life (the social jungle); the law

---

images in the mass media, thus allowing the powers-that-be to determine how individuals experience reality.

of the 35-hour work week, which aggravates work routines, penalises enterprises, and, in the long run, harms wage earners;[59] anti-racism and the construction of a multi-racial society, which provokes xenophobia and ethnic tensions; permissiveness and the refusal of strong anti-delinquency measures justified in the name of a libertarianism favouring insecurity and violence; laws against layoffs which end up discouraging hiring; excessive protection of renters that dampens housing construction; growing taxes that narrow the tax base, etc.

The most general and visible expression of heterotelia is **the excessive defence of an individual liberty that ends up restraining it.**

This political heterotelia, distinct to egalitarian ideology, is based on a **refusal of the real** and a profound misunderstanding of human behaviour, economic realities, and social mechanisms.

(see **liberty**)

Hierarchy

The power of command and precedence — established in pyramid fashion at the heart of every society — involving men as well as functions.

The notion of hierarchy highlights the most insupportable contradictions of the dominant egalitarian ideology. Theoretically, hierarchy is rejected, but in practice it's accepted, since no society can do without it and since it's inscribed in the genetic memory. All societies, human and animal, are hierarchical, especially the latter: human societies know extremely complex forms of hierarchy.

Egalitarian ideology, like the Western society that produced it, lives a veritable form of schizophrenia: it ceaselessly attacks hierarchy but can't prevent hierarchies from arising, for every society engenders them. Pathological expressions of anti-hierarchy, for example, are evident in: the attack on 'selection' in the public schools; the dogma

---

59 In February 2000, a coalition of Leftist parties in France lowered the legal duration of the standard working week from 39 to 35 hours.

that all individuals, cultures, and peoples are equal; the doctrine that conceives of information and communication in terms of 'horizontal networks'; and other such illusions...

Anti-hierarchy quite obviously corresponds to no actual reality, since hierarchies spontaneously emerge in every domain. It's nevertheless at the centre of the egalitarian utopia. In Western societies, this rejection of hierarchy has led to the formation of **savage, chaotic hierarchies** without real legitimacy, and to forms of domination that are all the more overbearing and unjust in being hedged and camouflaged in false 'horizontal' relations. In this way, the practice of exclusion and ostracism replaces those of sanction. It's the **reign of hypocritical hierarchy**. This gives rise to the blocked society in which there's no longer a circulation of elites, where privileged castes are established, and where the reign of lawlessness rules. Its mechanisms are perverse; in business, the military, the school, and government one refuses clear and explicit forms of authority for the sake of 'negotiation' and 'dialogue'. In reality, the process leads to networks of influence and corruption — or to **secret hierarchies**. Since no one is any longer obliged to obey, they need to be bought (corrupted).

*

From the European perspective, a hierarchical society is not an oppressive society in the Oriental or Islamic sense. Hierarchy is the disciplined organisation of free men for the sake of their common welfare — this is hierarchy in the sense that rights imply duties and that authority must constantly prove its competence.

Hierarchy is insupportable if it doesn't rest on a transcendental authority; it's insupportable if it rests merely on the forces of money (one no longer orders or commands, but rather buys accomplices) — or else, it rests on nepotism. Hierarchy can only be legitimatised on the basis of a recognised superiority, founded on meritocracy and talent, on character and sound judgement.

A society that refuses a clear meritocratic hierarchy, established on the basis of just legal sanctions, inevitably falls into the hands of **anarchic, tyrannical hierarchies**: like mafias, ethnic gangs, pressure groups, financial powers, etc. It's no less necessary to oppose the latest illusion, very fashionable among sociologists (our contemporary counterparts to Nineteenth-century socialist utopians): that a 'new society' is being organised as 'networks' and 'tribes', which will, supposedly, bring about an era of communication and non-hierarchical cooperation — networks and tribes, moreover, founded solely on the individual will of those comprising them. In separating roles, hierarchical society foregoes, in contrast, the very possibility that the sovereign function will fall into the hands of others — just as it evolves in ways that are as positive as they are inescapable.

*

From a spiritual perspective, the abolition of the sovereign function can only culminate in the brutal domination of the market, not in the installation of horizontal networks; network societies innervated by this miraculous extravaganza called 'communications' reproduce the most savage and unregulated hierarchies, against which the individual remains utterly defenceless. The one certain thing: the rejection of natural hierarchies gives rise to a chaotic society with the most brutal and rigid forms of hierarchy — i.e., authoritarianism.

The question, thus, is not for or against hierarchy (for or against selection), since it's an unavoidable sociobiological given; the question is to know **what type of hierarchy** to choose.

*

Hierarchy can only be envisaged in terms of a holistic ensemble (i.e., as a harmonious, organic totality), **in which the rules of the game are clear, rights and duties are progressive and unequal, and the superior echelons possess competence, authority, and an indisputable honesty.**

(see **aristocracy; egalitarianism; elite; meritocracy; selection**)

History, conceptions of history

The consciousness, evident in European and several other civilisations, of the emergence and continuity of a people's collective destiny in time.

History is profoundly tragic. This is why both bourgeois and egalitarian spirits reject it. Whether Marxist or, today, liberal-cosmopolitan, these spirits have always sought **the end of history,** synonymous with the valley of tears. Since the fall of Communism, the present Western/American ideology implicitly strives for the end of history, seeking to establish a 'New World Order', a unified planet. **History, though, is making a thunderous comeback, with the inevitable confrontations that come from an increasingly multipolar world.**

There are three great, opposed conceptions of history: **the cyclical conception; the linear, finalist conception; and the spherical conception.**

1. The cyclical conception found in primitive or ancient societies holds that everything is eternally repeated, and nothing ever changes. History is a loop, a recommencement, a succession of 'ages' that returns again and again.

2. The linear and finalist conception (teleonomic and soteriological) was introduced by Judaeo-Christianity: history's dynamic inevitably culminates in the Last Judgement. This conception was adopted by Western ideologies, elaborated in the thought of Hegel and Marx (as well as cosmopolitan liberals), and secularised the Judaeo-Christian vision of heaven. Such a notion of Salvation, naïve and sullied by a belief in Progress distinct to an exhausted modernity, continues to dominate the prevailing ideology, like an exorcism, though everything suggests that the Twenty-first century will refute its infantile optimism.

3. The 'spherical' conception of history, formulated by Nietzsche and developed by Giorgio Locchi,[60] is this tragic, superhuman, and Faustian philosophy whose dynamic is no longer based on an eternally recurring cycle or a predetermined linear movement ('the meaning of history'), but by the 'eternal return of the identical' (not the 'same'). The past can be reappropriated. even transformed, at any moment by a project of renewal. This position is spherical, like a ball that rolls across a flat surface, with its different points touching the same phases of ascension, decadence, war, peace, crisis, etc., that constantly return, but in different situations and modalities. The present in this way fuses the immemorial past with a desired future. **Tradition and futurism become here the same willed energy. The future remains open,** unlike archaic pagan cyclicalism or Judaeo-Christian linearity — both of which are deterministic.

*

Europeans would do well to take inspiration from this Nietzschean-Locchian notion in order to **regenerate their history,** for they have left history — they are no longer its master, having abdicated their destiny to foreigners. The spherical conception of history is **anti-fatalistic,** accepting that an unwanted decadence or an unforeseen regeneration is always a possibility. **Europe's present decline** (especially demographically, ethnically, and spiritually) **is not irreversible.** Anything can happen: divine as well as evil surprises are the lot of history, this torrent whose course no one can foresee. But if the torrent is a succession of metamorphoses that are slow or brutal, painful or bearable, usually unforeseeable, it's nevertheless important to realise that Europe's

---

60 Giorgio Locchi (1923–1992) was an Italian journalist who was a founding member of GRECE and an occasional collaborator with Alain de Benoist. He also wrote on Wagner and Nietzsche. Arktos has published *Definitions* (2025), an English translation of a collection of Locchi's essays.

historical regeneration will be 'a leap into the unknown' — anything but peaceful.
(see **archeofuturism; destiny, becoming; end of history**)

Homo Oeconomicus
Man reduced solely to his economic function as a consumer and producer.

Whatever its project, egalitarian and humanitarian ideology, in either its liberal or socialist versions, sees men as interchangeable economic atoms. The only thing that counts in this ideology are differences in productive performance or the capacity for consumption — i.e., the only thing that counts is money. **Reduced thus to his market or monetary dimension, man loses his personal, cultural, and ethnic value.** For both Marxist socialists and liberals, man is *preeminently* a producer and a consumer. The West is economist, in essence, unlike, say, Islam, whose main ambition is to conquer for the sake of its military and religious aims. The latter ideology is far sounder than the first.

The catastrophic colonising immigration we've known since the '60s was motivated by economic concerns. The sole thing that mattered was the docility and cheapness of labour. Its ethnic disfigurement of Europe never entered the mind of employers or unions. Such a strictly economic conception, oriented to production and consumption, is one of egalitarianism's great dogmas.

Today, however, the *Homo oeconomicus* born of Eighteenth- and Nineteenth-century utopianism has fallen into crisis at the very moment 'he' seemed triumphant. His failing stems from the supposition that man is a 'citizen of the world', uniquely motivated by his economic needs. But we are now witnessing a planetary return of the 'needs of identity' (culturally, ethnically, religiously), as well as the 'needs of the will to power'. The economy can never meet or master these needs. The principal aim of contemporary politics is to make man happy through economics, as if his well-being were strictly a matter of wealth.

*

In a word, the notion of *Homo oeconomicus* is founded on a **totally erroneous interpretation of human motivation.** Apart from the historical parenthesis of the last two centuries, the most profound human motivations have never been about economics or consumption. Human nature is more about sentiment than matter; its most profound impulses carry man far beyond economic concerns — toward immaterial satisfactions (feelings, faith, patriotism, etc.).

*

Homo oeconomicus represents a diminished man, domesticated, and deprived, above all, of his natural traits. Europeans have succumbed to such a domestication. But this won't last forever; human nature will eventually reclaim its rights. And besides, **this type of man is miserable:** in the wealthiest, most economically successful market societies of the West, suicide rates are significantly higher than in poor societies, past or present.

Western civilisation has a totally mistaken view of human nature. Man isn't primarily a *Homo oeconomicus,* but, more generally, in the larger view of the Greek philosophers, a *zôon politikon,* a 'political animal'. The repercussions of such an error will not be long in coming. (see **bourgeoisism; economism; society, market**)

Homophilia

The justification of homosexuality, considered not only as a normal form of behaviour, but as something worthy of protection and admiration.

After having long sought recognition as a marginal social element, the homosexual lobby now demands a sort of superiority, with heterosexuality treated as something inferior or mutilated. First equal rights, then privileges. 'Homophobia' (the critique of homosexuality) is accordingly prosecuted as if it were a form of racism or anti-Semitism. The lavender mafia doesn't merely want to exist in peace, but to dominate.

*

Homophilia is one of the crudest symptoms of the decadence and dissolution of society's sense of meaning. A people that treats homosexuality as one of the fine arts is a people that lives in contradiction to the rules of biology and ethology, and in contradiction to the 'natural law' of which Robert Ardrey spoke. It endangers a people's reproduction and existence: it belongs to the anti-vitalist doctrine of the Masonic gnosis and, along with race-mixing, xenophilia, anti-natalism, and feminism, endeavours to destroy the vitalist forces, the European *germen*, prelude to the European's programmed eradication. (see **devirilisation**)

Human Rights, human rightism

The cornerstone of the modern ideology of progress and individualistic egalitarianism — and the basis upon which the thought police have been set up to destroy the people's rights to exist as a people.

As a synthesis of Eighteenth-century political philosophy (often badly understood), human rights[61] is the inescapable horizon of the dominant ideology. With anti-racism, it becomes the central reference point for all collective forms of mental conditioning, for ready-made thought, and for the paralysis of all revolt. Profoundly hypocritical, human rights ideology accommodates every form of social misery and justifies every form of oppression. It functions as a veritable secular religion. The 'human' in human rights is nothing but an abstraction, a consumer-client, an atom. It says everything that human

---

61 In French, literally, 'rights of man'.

rights ideology originated with the Conventionnels of the French Revolution,[62] in imitation of American Puritans.

Human rights ideology has succeeded in legitimating itself on the basis of two historical impostures: that of charity and philanthropy — and that of freedom.

'Humans' (already a vague notion) possess no fixed or universal rights, only those bequeathed by their civilisation, by their tradition. Against human rights, it's necessary to oppose two key ideas: that of the rights of a people to an identity and that of justice (which varies according to culture and presumes that all individuals are not equally praiseworthy). These two notions do not rest on the presumption of an abstract universal man, but rather on actual men, localised within their specific culture.

To criticise the secular religion of human rights is obviously no apology for savage behaviour, though on numerous occasions human rights have been used to justify barbarism and oppression (the genocidal repression of the Vendée during the French Revolution[63] or the extermination of Amerindians). **Human rights ideology has often been the pretext for persecutions: in the name of the 'Good'.** It no more protects the rights of individuals than did Communism. Just the opposite, for it has imposed a new system of oppression, based on purely formalistic freedoms. Under its auspices and in contempt of all

---

62 This was the National Convention that was held between 1792 and 1795 in order to draw up a new constitution following the Revolution.

63 This is a reference to an episode during the Reign of Terror when, in 1793, the citizens of the Vendée region of coastal France, who were supportive of both the clergy and the monarchy, began an uprising against the revolutionary Republican government. Following the defeat of the uprising in February 1794, the Committee of Public Safety ordered the Republican forces to conduct a scorched-earth razing of the area and the mass execution of its residents, including noncombatants, women and children. Several hundred thousand people are estimated to have been killed out of a population of 800,000. Some historians, especially on the Right, have classified this incident as a genocide, although this has been disputed.

democracy, it legitimises the Third World's colonisation of Europe, tolerating freedom-killing delinquencies, supporting wars of aggression carried out in the name of humanitarianism, and refusing to deport illegal immigrants; this ideology never speaks out against the environmental pollution it causes or the social savagery of its globalised economy.

The ideology of human rights is above all strategically used to **disarm European peoples,** by making them feel guilty about almost everything. It thus authorises their disarmament and paralysis. It's a sort of corruption of Christian charity and its egalitarian dogma that all individuals should be valued equally before God and Man.

The ideology of human rights is the principal weapon being used today to destroy Europe's identity and to advance the interests of her alien colonisers.

(see **egalitarianism; ideology, Western ideology**)

Humanism, superhumanism

The philosophical and political attitude inherited from Graeco-Roman civilisation, which advocates the ideal of the free man — liberated from dogmas and from barbarism, part of a civil order, and cognisant of the diversity of nations.

In no case should humanism be associated with humanitarianism, as Yvan Blot (President of the Club de l'Horloge)[64] explains, 'The humanist ideal is a synthesis of the ideal of liberty and the ideal of enrootment. To values of free speech, competitiveness, the striving for excellence, the desire to be first, there corresponds Greek values

---

64 Yvan Blot (1948–2018) served as a Member of the European Parliament for the French National Front from 1989 to 1999. He was a founding member and the first president (1974–1985) of the Club de l'Horloge, a Right-wing national-liberal think tank established in 1974, which initially had close ties to GRECE and the Nouvelle Droite. The organisation was renamed Carrefour de l'Horloge in 2015 and has been led by Henry de Lesquen since 1985.

of honour, justice, equity, family loyalty, patriotism, religion — and of "philanthropy", in the sense of that which is human'.

Humanism is a 'school of realism' that sees man, without utopian or optimistic expectations, as he is. It advocates both wisdom and ambition, respects differences and rejects unwarranted hatreds — but at the same time it recognises the existence of different ethnic and cultural identities.

The humanist attitude is the opposite of the desert's fanatical monotheistic religions, particularly Islam. But it's **not a form of absolute tolerance nor, above all, is it an egalitarianism**. Humanism — an anti-chaos attitude *par excellence*, a doctrine of equilibrium — rejects brutal dictatorship and totalitarian regimes, just as it rejects social permissiveness. It defends justice, the City's holistic hierarchy, and patriotic duty. **It similarly rejects cosmopolitanism and every vision of a 'united, uniform humanity'** (the utopia of the 'World State'), since the idea of ethnic distinction and civic equity are central to its conception of the political. A doctrine of wisdom and balance, a school of will and a subject of the real, humanism is the basis of the 'state of law' — today completely abused by its 'democratic' defenders.

The basis of humanism, a central tenet of the European tradition and its Graeco-Roman heritage, is thus **the recognition and fusion of justice, positive law, citizenship, and ethnic identity.**

*

Superhumanism, a Nietzschean notion conceptually developed by Giorgio Locchi, is a **humanism for an age of crisis and transcendence. It's a positive and tragic transgression of humanism in a state of emergency.** Faced with great dangers, the authentic European needs to surpass and transgress certain principles. For the dangers threatening his *people* demand solutions that are as unthinkable as they are indispensable. As such, he transgresses not for the sake of pleasing a dictator or obeying such and such a dogma, but of serving his people's survival, that is, in defending its future lineage and ancestral heritage.

Over 2,400 years ago, Xenophon wrote in his *Anabasis*,[65] 'A day will come when Zeus' eagle serenely and mercilessly extends its claws.' This is what superhumanism means.

In moments of supreme tragedy, man grants himself divine powers, attending to that which inspires and exceeds him. According to the Pythagorean tradition, he becomes 'the ear of the gods'.
(see **liberty**; **Promethean**; **techno-science**)

Humanitarianism

The professed love of all humans regardless of distinction — and the affirmation of our alleged duty to assist the oppressed, hungry, or ill, etc.

Humanitarianism is a delinquent and disfigured humanism. It comes from a sort of systematic pity for the 'Other' and an indifference to the 'Next'. It's an exacerbation of what was formerly called 'philanthropy' and a hypocritical secularisation of Christian 'charity'. In this sense, it comes from xenophilia and legitimises, as such, 'foreign preferences' that discriminate in favour of aliens.

Humanitarianism demonstrates mass support for illegal immigrants and assists victims of massacres and civil wars in faraway places (for which it feels responsible), yet at the same time it's utterly indifferent to the poverty and precariousness of native Europeans. It's scandalised by the deportation of Albanians, but not the deportation of Serbs. It condemns Russia's war against the Chechens, but not the Chechen war against Russia or the Anglo-American bombing of Iraq, etc.

Modern humanitarianism began with Twentieth-century campaigns against 'world hunger' and with the hypocritical ideology of Third World assistance. **Humanitarianism corrupts the Graeco-Roman notion of humanism,** for the latter advocates no *indiscriminate*

---

65 Xenophon (c. 430 BCE-354 BCE) was a Greek historian and soldier. His *Anabasis* is the record of an expedition by the Greeks to capture the throne of Persia.

love of humanity. Concretely, humanitarian movements don't actually come to the assistance of the larger world. Behind their humanitarian enterprise, there's the *charity business*, which is very profitable and gives the personalities of the cosmopolitan Left a good deal of media exposure. Humanitarianism has indeed been commercialised — a phony distillation of Enlightenment 'philanthropy'. Though hardly effective in practice, its noxious ideology negatively affects Europeans, for its frantic egalitarianism implies that all men, and all peoples, are of equal worth and that the metaphysical unity of the human race imposes an obligation to help the 'Other', rather than one's own kind. (see **ethnomasochism; human rights; preference, European; xenophilia**)

I

Idea, ideal, historic idealism

Historical idealism, theorised by Hegel, holds that a great Idea is necessarily incarnated in history, though with no advanced knowledge of how it is to be realised.

Hegel's position has often been misunderstood, especially by Marxists, who have inverted its meaning. When Hegel invoked the 'appearance of Reason in history', he didn't mean that it was some sort of automata of fate, but rather an irruption of an Idea (embodying a will to power) that could just as well become the counter-current to the 'inevitable'.

Curiously, historical idealism is both fatalistic and anti-fatalistic. It's fatalistic whenever it expects that certain ideas will be realised, of necessity, by some sort of pre-programmed metaphysics (classless society, Marx's universalistic Communism, liberalism's myth of an indefinite Progress).

It's *anti-fatalistic* whenever it poses **a dissident or apparently unrealisable Idea that might be manifested in history through**

the power of will: the Spanish *Reconquista* that took centuries,[66] De Gaulle's affirmation of German defeat in 1940, Algerian independence, Kohl's reunification of divided Germany, etc.

*

Historical idealism is the opposite of that *negative historical fatalism* distinct to our myopic experts. Today, for example, these experts claim that Islam and non-European aliens are now an established part of Europe. Against such claims, we wilfully affirm and inculcate the idea of *reconquest*, even if its exact modalities are still unknown.

Similarly, the concept of *Eurosiberia* stems from a will to be realised in history, even if it's too early at this point to determine how.

*

This **positive historical idealism** opposes the mechanistic view of history, in which everything is foreseen, in which every surprise or wrong turn is dismissed in advance. In contrast, positive idealism presupposes that an Idea — conceived by **an unwavering will** and transmitted by conscious, capable elites to successive generations — has a chance one day of being realised, despite the claims of fatalists. Nothing is ever totally lost and **it's always been minorities imbued with an idea-force that have reversed the expected course of historical events.**

We obviously need to be patient, to adopt a long-term perspective, and stop believing that Rome is to be built in a day. The current acceleration of history and the rising stakes of the new century could divulge divine surprises...

(see **history; resistance and reconquest**)

---

66 *Reconquista* is a Spanish word meaning reconquering or recapturing. Historically, it refers to the struggle of the Christian Spaniards against the occupation of Spain by the Muslims during the Middle Ages, lasting for nearly eight centuries from 718 until they were finally driven out completely in 1492.

Identity

Etymologically: 'That which makes singular'. A people's identity s what makes it incomparable and irreplaceable.

Characteristic of humanity is the diversity and singularity of its many peoples and cultures. Every form of its homogenisation is synonymous with death, as well as with sclerosis and entropy. Universalism always seeks to marginalise identity in the name of a single, unique anthropological model. But **ethnic and cultural identities form a bloc: maintaining and developing the cultural heritage presupposes a people's ethnic commonality.**

Humanity will not survive the challenges it's generating if it remains a *pluriversum,* that is, if it remains a fractious aggravation of profoundly different ethnocentric peoples.

Look: **identity's basis is biological; without it, the realms of culture and civilisation are unsustainable.** Said differently: a people's identity, memory, and projects come from a specific hereditary disposition.

*

The Jacobin and universalist republicans — who allegedly defend the 'identity of France' and her 'cultural exceptionalism', believing they can integrate ethnically alien masses — are in the grips of a total contradiction.

The notion of identity obviously refers to **ethnocentrism** and remains incompatible with 'ethnopluralist' cohabitation. In this respect, Pierre Vial writes (in *Une Terre, un Peuple*) that: 'Identity, for an individual or a people, stems from three basic elements: race, culture, and will'. The implication here is that no one of these elements suffices to form an identity: without a relatively homogeneous biological base, no culture prospers; but **biology alone will not ensure a culture's longevity, if the will of the people and its elites are lacking.** A culture neither survives nor prospers with decapitated elites.

*

The idea of identity is a thorn in the side of the dominant universal and egalitarian ideology. On the one hand, it finds it terribly shocking, suspecting (rightly) that identity always has an ethnic scent. On the other hand, one can't — or rather can no longer for political reasons — openly counter a 'Corsican identity' or a 'Breton identity'. Not to mention a 'Jewish identity', which no one would think of contesting, though in the Nineteenth century secular and universalist Jews, beginning with Marx, advocated eradicating Jewish identity — eradicating Jewish customs, religion, and endogamous prescriptions. How are such flagrant contradictions overcome? Only through ideological contortions:

1. The identity of the peoples constituent of Europe is not openly denied, but neutralised, emptied of substance, and relegated to academic study or folklore (in the worse sense of the term), stripped in this way of every ethnic reference. Only linguistic identity is paid lip service and then only with a good deal of reticence. As the Left-wing leaders of the Breton independence movement insist, a non-European settled in Brittany is automatically a Breton. (Here the term 'Breton' assumes the universalist sense that 'American' has.)

2. **It's understood, of course, that identity is acceptable for alien populations, but abhorrent whenever demanded by Europeans — because it's 'racist'.** African, West Indian, and Arab-Muslim identities are encouraged, while any profession of ethnic identity by native Europeans is automatically subjected to a hermeneutic of suspicion. In this spirit Europeans are urged to shed all trace of identity (or else relegate it to the museum). It's simply too dangerous.

*

The notion of identity is not at all endangered by the world that is coming, for despite — or because of — globalisation and Westernisation, we're going to see identity massively enhanced by the formation of great ethnic blocs in the Global South. **The only threatened identity is that of the dangerous peoples (analogous to the 'dangerous classes' of Nineteenth-century Paris):**[67] the 'dangerous peoples' being native Europeans, who are now prohibited from having an identity, at least an identity that is anything other than a museum piece.

*

Finally, **the idea of identity has to be linked to the notion of continuity** (in Robert Steuckers' formulation). Identity is never fixed or frozen. It remains itself in changing, reconciling being and becoming. Identity is dynamic, never static or purely conservative. Identity should be seen as the foundation of a movement that endures through history — the generational continuity of a people. Dialectical notions associating identity and continuity permits a people to be **the producer of its own history.**
(see **enrootment; ethnocentrism; ethnosphere; fatherland, native land**)

Ideology, hegemonic ideology, Western ideology, European ideology

An ideology is an explicitly or implicitly organised system of ideas that is both a conception-of-the-world and the bearer of a specific political, social, economic, and cultural project.

Europe today is the victim of an ideology that she herself created — one that began with the Eighteenth-century philosophy of the Enlightenment and culminates in what one calls 'Western ideology' or 'globalist ideology'. **Western ideology has boomeranged against**

---

67 The 'dangerous classes' was a term applied by the Parisian bourgeoisie during the early part of the Nineteenth century to the poor classes.

Europeans. This ideology (which Communism shared in large part until its collapse) is based on the following presuppositions:

1. An absolute individualism and the pursuit of pleasure through economic materialism.
2. An interpretation of technology as a kind of divinity capable of bestowing happiness and serving as a substitute for spirituality — technology seen here not as an instrument of power and sovereignty, but simply as a means of comfort — a domination by *gadgets*.
3. The hypocritical affirmation of the equality of all human beings and, on this basis, the implicit negation of the idea of a people (in the ethnic sense).
4. A rejection of the divine and the ancestral heritage and their substitution with a presentism, contemptuous of both past and future.
5. The belief in the infinite economic 'development' of humanity, as the supreme form of collective and individual happiness — a development without any regard to physical or ecological limits.
6. The cult of endless progress.
7. The struggle against Europe's ethnic identities.

*

Founded on Reason (a self-sufficient rationality), **Western ideology is but a degenerated form of metaphysics, for it claims to represent all human aspirations, serving as it does as a universal ethical norm, in lieu of religion.** Its postulates, though, are unrealistic and anti-vitalistic, disdaining the real — that is, the observable reality of human societies. While criticising the absolute materialism of Western ideology and society, certain unseeing philosophers (on the intellectual Right) imagine that a 'spiritual' alliance with Islam is desirable. That would be like falling between Charybdis and Scylla.[68] In themselves alone — in their own traditions — will Europeans succeed in finding and reviving their people.

*

The philosophy of 'human rights' and the idolatry of technology as sources of well-being make up the résumé of Western ideology. Today it is hegemonic, totalitarian. It tolerates no challenges. Rather than being rivals, the different Right and Left versions of Western ideology pursue the same general civilisational project. However triumphant this ideology may be at the moment, it is inherently destructuring. For the world doesn't conform to its postulates, none of which have ever been realised. Its present triumph will be ephemeral.

Western ideology beckons a revival: a real *European ideology*. (see **belief in miracles; egalitarianism; human rights; modernity; progress, progressivism**)

Immigration

The influx of alien populations into a territory whose native people risks being submerged.

The immigration of non-Europeans into Europe has led to a veritable colonisation. **The term 'immigration' ought to be criticised as insufficient and replaced with the term 'colonisation'** — this colonisation which is the gravest historical phenomenon to beset Europeans since the fall of the Roman Empire. In political and ideological struggle, we ought not to rely on the words of our adversary, but instead impose

---

68 In Greek mythology, Scylla and Charybdis were two monsters who lived on either side of a narrow strait. Sailors who attempted to pass through the strait were always in danger of being eaten by one while attempting to keep away from the other. It is considered the origin of the expression 'between a rock and a hard place'. Scylla and Charybdis appear most notably in Homer's *Odyssey* and Ovid's *Metamorphoses*.

our own concepts. **We don't welcome alien immigrants, we are being colonised by them.**
(see **colonisation** and also my *La Colonisation de l'Europe* [Paris: L'Æncre, 2001])

Individualism
The ideology and cultural tendency to affirm the primacy of the individual and his interests over the group to which he belongs.

This is an ambiguous notion. For there exists a positive individualism, that of the Hellenic, Celtic, and Germanic traditions, and a negative individualism, which is a tragic distortion of the first, and stems from a bourgeois mentality hostile to one's own community or people. It also stems from religions of individual salvation (soteriological ones), in which man speaks directly to God, without an intermediary.

*

Positively, European individualism is typically linked to notions of liberty and responsibility, and accepts the cause of patriotism, as well as the spirit of sacrifice. This is the individualism of the creative personality, artist, or aristocrat. **The negative individualism of consumer society, in contrast, comes from the massification and domestication of the isolated individual.** This is the individualism of conditioned masses, of men who are nothing but consuming atoms, detached from their community and people. It's thus necessary to distinguish between **aristocratic individualism** and **bourgeois individualism.** The latter is narcissistic and nihilistic, susceptible to forms of slavery or robotisation that are usually introduced in the name of emancipation. Despite its appearances and simulacra, Left-wing socialism, like market society, upholds a flattened individualism — irresponsible and in need of assistance — that rejects solidarity and culminates in corporate or egoistic reflexes.

Contemporary individualism pursues the following paradox: it exalts the narcissistic individual but in the long run oppresses the individual by isolating him from natural solidarities. Individualism is positive if it values the creative personality, within the community-of-the-people. (see **community; personality, creative**)

Inegalitarianism

Recognition of the diversity and inequality of all life forms, biological or social.

According to the philosopher Giorgio Locchi, the difference between 'egalitarianism' and 'inegalitarianism' amounts to a veritable **war between conceptions of the world,** as Nietzsche first noted.

Inegalitarianism ought not to be confused with injustice, social oppression, or the establishment of caste privileges. Its vision of the world stems from the principle that humans are neither equivalent nor comparable (collectively or individually), that they are **unequal by nature,** whether by temperament or virtue. Solutions and morals cannot, therefore, be the same everywhere. Similarly, this implies that **human beings and civilisations are not and cannot be equally capable or estimable.**

*

The inegalitarian vision of the world is the basis of all justice and social harmony, because it respects the organic character of *life*. For Nietzsche, egalitarianism represented a 'hatred of life' and led to tyrannical efforts to create an artificial social universe. The democratic despotisms of the Twentieth century are excellent examples of this.

Inegalitarianism is a recognition of life's diversity, it's the basic logic of competition dominating the different life forms. Without this recognition, the results would lead to savagery — to the very opposite of order, equilibrium, and justice. There's no need to limit inegalitarianism to *diversity* (as do our 'ethnopluralist' intellectuals, who are, actually, profoundly egalitarian), but to understand that **unequal life forms imply notions of superiority and quality.**

*

This raises the question as to how criteria of inequality or superiority (of men or civilisations) are to be judged. Is it a matter of wealth? Of force? Of power? No, it's **the capacity to endure and survive, which is the basis of domination.**
(see **egalitarianism**)

Interregnum

A concept of Giorgio Locchi, in which historical time culminates both in a civilisation's end and in the possible birth of a new civilisation.

We are currently living through an interregnum, a tragic historical moment when everything is in flames and everything, like a phoenix, might rise reborn from the ashes. This is the dark night, the 'midnight of the world' evoked by Hölderlin, between dusk and dawn.[69] The interregnum is the period of regeneration between chaos and post-chaos, the moment of tragedy, when everything is again possible. European peoples are presently living through an interregnum. Metamorphic in essence, **European civilisation has known three distinct ages:** Antiquity, the Middle Ages which rose from the ruins of Antiquity, and, beginning in the Sixteenth century, a Third Age of expansion, that of 'modernity', which is now coming to an end, following the

---

69 The author is here most likely referring to Hölderlin's poem 'Bread and Wine'. The night is used to symbolically represent our age, when the ancient gods of Greece and Christ have left the world and it is only the poets who attempt to keep their memory alive until their return. Many translations exist. Martin Heidegger discusses this poem at length in his famous essay 'Why Poets?', translated in *Off the Beaten Path* (Cambridge: Cambridge University Press, 2002).

terrible decline inaugurated by the First World War. Colonised by alien peoples, our civilisation faces death in the first twenty years of the new millennium. **The interregnum through which we are presently living is the most crucial and decisive period since the Persian and Punic wars.**[70] Either Europeans will unite in self-defence, expel the colonisers, throw off the American yoke, and regenerate themselves biologically and morally — or else their civilisation will disappear — forever. Never have the stakes been so high. **The interregnum will give birth to the Fourth Age of European Civilisation** — or else Europe will die, purely and simply. Everything is to be decided in the decisive period now beginning. And birth, if it occurs, will be painful, full of blood and tears — the fuels of history. For our civilisation, the Twenty-first century is to be a trial of life or death, with no possibility of appeal. (see **chaos, Eurosiberia, history**)

Involution

The regression of a civilisation or species to moladaptive forms that lead to the diminishment of its vital forces.

We are presently endangered by a grave involution, particularly in culture. This is due not simply to the spread of pop culture, of which America is the principal distributor, but also to the Africanisation of European culture and to the Islamic invasion. Cultural involution has also been stimulated by the decline of National Education (40% of adolescents are now partially or completely illiterate), the regression of knowledge, the collapse of social norms, the immersion of youth in a world of audio/visual play, the progression of neo-primitivism, the loss of defensive reflexes, etc.

---

70 The Persian Wars were fought between the Persian Empire and the Greek city-states in the Fifth century BC, when the Greeks successfully repelled multiple invasion attempts. The Punic Wars were fought between the Roman Republic and the Carthaginian Empire. The Roman victory in these wars secured their dominance in the coming centuries. Both wars could be seen as the triumph of Western civilisation under the threat of foreign invasion.

Involution has biological roots, as well: devirilisation provoked by the ideologies and lifestyles of urban market societies and by culpatory ideologies of dropping birth rates, anti-selection, etc.

Undoubtedly, our leaders will tell us that they see no signs of involution. No sign because the market continues to expand. Involution, though, is like a virus, whose appearance at first goes unnoticed. For those who see, however, it's already busily at work. Involution starts with the spirit and then with individual behaviour, before its gangrene spreads to social and economic institutions.

(see **chaos, decadence, neo-primitivism**)

J

Judaeo-Christianity

The conception of the world distinct to Judaism and Christianity, to which the latter confers its major forms, first as religion, then, with the advent of modernity, as ideology.

The implantation of Judaeo-Christianity constituted an alien addition to pantheistic and polytheistic Europe. Hence, her cultural and mental schizophrenia: on the one hand, an egalitarian and universalistic Christian consciousness; on the other, a pagan, particularistic consciousness. The scientific mentality developed in opposition to Judaeo-Christianity, in accord with her pagan spirit, but her political ideologies (egalitarian, cosmopolitan, progressive, and individualistic) have taken a Judaeo-Christian turn. The Marxist postulates animating the Left (even after the fall of Communism) are, for example, a direct secularisation of Judaeo-Christian doctrines of salvation. Similarly, American hegemony and its 'humanitarian' interventionism, like its market model of society, express a Protestant version of Judaeo-Christianity. It's important, though, to note that Judaism (which escaped Christianity's Pauline schism) has never been universalistic and cosmopolitan in this sense, given the communitarian imperatives of the 'chosen people' to privilege other spiritual considerations.

Traditional Catholicism, elaborated in the course of the Middle Ages, was marked by a certain 'paganisation of Judaeo-Christianity'; in this sense it's part of the integral European tradition, though it holds no monopoly over it.

In the arts, culture, philosophy, mentality, and popular rites, paganism is present and still vital. Similarly, there's no comparison between the Christianisation of Europe and Islam's present installation. Christianity was developed and elaborated by Europeans themselves — if on the basis of certain alien sources — while **Islam — which ought to be seen as a greater danger to Europe than Americanism — has simply been imposed,** without any acclimation, as a conception of the world and society radically alien to the European mentality and tradition.

*

The Christianity of Vatican II, in returning to the Biblical sources of primitive Christianity, constituted a compromising rupture with the pagan-Christian sense of the sacred. It inaugurated a profanation of Christian religious doctrines, a politicisation of its spiritual principles, and, similarly, the collapse of Catholic religious practices. Having abandoned its sacred language, Latin (while Islam retains its classical Arabic), and having succumbed to modernity's sirens, the neo-Christianity born at Vatican II (this palaeo-Christianity which returns to the ultra-egalitarian sources of primitive Christianity) has thrown off the sacred sense rooted in the ancestral tradition (however subterranean and unconscious), and fallen into a pure and simple atheism, as evident in the works of contemporary Catholic theologians.

Contemporary churches resemble post offices, having retained nothing of the cathedral. The discourse of its official prelates is virtually identical to that of a trade union official. **In dismissing pagan sacrality, the cult of the saints, and the Virgin Mary, the official neo-Christianity of Vatican II has destroyed the Church as a religious**

institution and become an ideology objectively opposed to the destiny of European peoples. It's tempting to compare it to primitive Christianity, which contested Roman patriotism before the *aggiornamento* of the Fourth century.[71]

Hence: the Church's 'ecumenical' tolerance of the Islamic offensive, the systematic alignment of its prelates along neo-Trotskyist lines, its encouragement of *ethnomasochism*, its almost perfect accord with the politically correct intellectual-media classes — all centred on the hypocritical religion of human rights. In the East, fortunately, the Orthodox Church has better resisted these siren songs. **The official Catholic Church is in the process of committing suicide; but in dying it hasn't killed off the real soul of Europe's peoples.**

Why? Because — and this can be seen in the massive defections it's wrought — the post-conciliar Church has cut itself off from the sacrality distinct to Europeans. Its 'marketing' ploys (like World Youth Day) change nothing. The Church has condemned itself to being just another sect swept along by the cold wind that comes with Islam.

*

For the resistance: what is to be done?

A historic compromise is evidently possible between authentic pagans and those Catholics and Orthodox Christians who continue to practice traditional European Christianity. But no resistance to the present offensive can be waged without appealing to the 'pagan soul', associated with the spirit of the two invincible pagan divinities, Apollo and Dionysus. Pierre Vial writes in *Une Terre, un Peuple*, 'During two thousand years of Christianity, Europeans somehow or other never forgot these ancient divinities: they are part of our heritage

---

71 *Aggiornamento* is Italian for 'bringing up to date', and was applied to the Second Vatican Council of the 1960s. By the *aggiornamento* of the Fourth century, Faye is referring to the First Council of Nicaea, which was called by Constantine after becoming the first Roman Emperor to convert to Christianity. It was the first attempt to standardise Christian doctrine and laid the foundations for the modern-day Catholic Church.

and are to be assumed, like other of its parts, whether they please others or not'.

Said differently: an **authentic pagan will always oppose a church transformed into a mosque, a bell tower into a minaret — even if an official prelate of the Church sanctions such a transformation...** (see **paganism**)

L

Land, territory

The geographical space of a people's existence and survival — and its incarnation in a 'place'.

The notion of people, like that of blood or identity, is incomprehensible without a notion of 'land' (*terre*). **A territorial appropriation is an ethological imperative of the living.** The only people — the Jewish people — having existed for a certain period in diaspora without a land, being as such a blood and spirit without a soil — always sought to recover their territorial roots: the state of Israel has since become the concretisation of its Promised Land. Similarly, the Chinese diaspora always refers to its original homeland, to which it feels bound.

*

Even Muslim peoples, Arabs and Turks haunted by their nomadic past, have 'the land of Islam', which they are always trying to expand. Sedentism[72] and nomadism are linked. Purely nomadic peoples, like Gypsies, have never been historically creative. Land is the place one leaves to conquer, the place one inhabits and loves — and where one is to be buried.

---

72 Sedentism is a term used in anthropology to refer to the process by which a nomadic people decide to stop circulating and set up permanent settlements.

The conquest of space, as formulated by Wernher von Braun and Jules Verne, its principal theoreticians, has never been understood as a nomadism or an abandonment of Mother Earth, but rather as an extension. The astronomer Hubert Reeves could write, 'When humanity begins conquering the planet Mars, it will inevitably be divided into territories'.

A people cannot exist without a land. It's often said that the Twenty-first century will be a century without frontiers — a century of networks, flux, an age in which zones replace clearly bounded lands. This nomadic vision, however, corresponds in no way to what is coming. **Globalisation provokes not a weakening of the territorial idea, but rather, as an indirect consequence, its reinforcement.** Notions of homelands and territory will never be obsolete, for they are inscribed in the genetic memory. The seas, like airspace, are extensions of national territory.

*

Man is a territorial animal — one who defends his land or conquers another. Today, European lands are threatened by Islam, which is trying to turn Europe into a 'land of Islam' (*Dar al Islam*), and by Americans, who are trying to turn the Continent into one of their geostrategically dominated spaces. The defence of European lands, and beyond that, the Eurosiberian space, is inseparable from their defence as a people. (see **enrootment; Eurosiberia; fatherland; geopolitics; people**)

Legitimation (positive or negative)

That set of media discourses, ideological and educational systems, and legislated arsenal of laws, which endeavours to justify the domination of a particular governmental regime and political system — through consent and legitimacy.

Positive legitimation designates a discourse in which the dominant system justifies itself through its positive acts, through its successes, and through the prosperity and civil peace it ensures. This sort of positive legitimation is no longer possible today: faced with unemployment, growing poverty, the effects of mass immigration, the explosion of insecurity, and the general imperiousness of the political class to finding workable solutions, **the system now depends on negative legitimation.** This sort of legitimation rests on the precept that 'without us, things will get worse, they'd be fascist'. **Power here no longer legitimises itself on the basis of its achievements, but in a virtualist manner, by invoking the spectre of the Great Threat — the spectre of racism, anti-democracy, dictatorship, etc.**

After a period of failed promises comes thus the blackmail — in the form of protecting the population from evil phantoms. A political system resting on this sort of negative legitimation hasn't long to live. (see **democracy**)

Liberalism, managerial liberalism

Economic doctrines and practices advocating the maximisation of freedom for private actors in the market — and the minimisation of socioeconomic rules and interventions by political authorities.

In the United States, the term 'liberal' implies 'political liberalism' and thus ought to be translated as 'progressivism'. The concept of economic liberalism, in contrast, is ambiguous. Let us simply say that **economic liberalism is preferable to a paralysing social-statism, but in itself is positive only when serving a higher political will and operating within a protected, self-centred economic space.**

To designate liberalism as the *enemy* often reveals a badly understood para-Marxism — a tendency which also touches the ideologues of the romantic Right, ignorant of economics and imitative of the Left. Nothing is ever black or white, and liberalism doesn't comprise a single bloc. Properly speaking, it's not even an ideology but rather a method, a practical economic technique. To its credit, liberalism brings to the economic realm the spirit of initiative, of competition, responsibility, efficacy, and selection. Negatively, it fosters a cult of the short-term, is indifferent to ecology, to biopolitics, and to the people's destiny, etc.

The error of dogmatic anti-liberalism is to demand everything of it. But liberalism cannot be more than a limited doctrine, in need of correction and completion. Applied to a European autarkic space, **liberalism ought to be, domestically, subject to the general political economy and, internationally, protected from global free trade.**

Liberalism arises from the realm of means, not ends. It's necessary to respect its practical efficacy but at the same time to balance it with social and economic policies subject to larger political objectives. The intervention of sovereign power in the liberal economy must not be directly economic, administrative, or fiscal — but political. It ought to be a matter of laying down general rules, establishing the major aims of industrial policy, ensuring market freedom, favouring dynamic enterprises, protecting the domestic economy — without paralysing economic actors with excessive regulation and taxation.

In this sense, we can talk of **managed liberalism**, which is a far cry from the EU's bureaucratic, regulatory free-trade globalism, combining, as it does, the negative aspects of both unregulated transnational capitalism, on the one hand, and a technocratic, corporatist socialism, on the other.

(see **autarky of great spaces; economy, organic**)

Liberty, liberties

An individual's or a people's capacity to act according to their own will — a capacity gained by discipline and founded on the multiplication of competence and freedom.

The 'free man' has long been a model for European society, in opposition to the barbarians and slaves of Greek thought. Today, the concept of 'liberty' has suffered a veritable inversion of meaning, as has the term 'democracy'. **Liberty nowadays signifies what was once called 'slavery', since it's confused with a permissiveness that leads**

to a certain kind of servitude. In contrast, real liberty is the faculty of augmenting one's power, of multiplying one's capacity to affect the real, and, through autonomy, of overcoming determinism. This conception opposes individualistic and egalitarian notions of liberty — conceived as forms of **passive license** or the **absence of constraints.** The slavery — that comes from the dominant ready-to-think ideology and prevents the people and its defenders from openly expressing their convictions and demands — is enforced by a thought police, an obligatory xenophilia, the interdiction of direct democracy, and the power of judges.

Defined as a global, abstract concept during the French Revolution of 1789, **Liberty opposes liberties.** Taken in this way, as an absolute, freedom becomes a cold, totalitarian concept. Western society no more defends liberty than did Communist society, for it fosters a general conformity in which the permissiveness toward various delinquencies goes hand-in-hand with the repression of all legitimate opposition.

The exercise of liberty presupposes discipline and order, authority and the rule of law. The *laissez-faire* of today's school system, which leaves young minds completely uncultivated, is preparing the way for future barbarians and slaves. Above all, the free man is master of himself — thanks to the discipline enhancing his possibilities.

*

A free people decides its destiny for the *longue durée*. Today, for example, **the population-replacing colonisation of Islam and the South is a symbol of Europe's loss of liberty.** It's part of the same process that subjects Europe to America's sphere of influence and diminishes her political and economic independence. Even individual liberty, gnawed at by the demission of the public powers before the **social jungle**, is affected: laxity toward delinquency, indifference to the social-economic exclusion of native Europeans, etc. In these and other domains, the singular dogma of 'Liberty' undermines the people's liberties. One might paraphrase Big Brother here, with his formula: 'Freedom is slavery'. And vice versa.

We are living through a strange, paradoxical situation — a situation of regime end: the public powers never cease regulating, monitoring, oppressing, taxing — gently and skilfully ostracising those who create and work — as it dispenses tolerance and advantage to delinquents, illegals, and lowlifes. **For the regnant ideology, everything that is 'Other' has every right and no duty.** Everything that is native and follows the natural law has only duties and is always suspect. The system endeavours to make free men slaves, and helots[73] free men. The Roman Empire died from this.

Given the demission of the public authorities before delinquencies of every kind, **public freedoms have receded** for authentic citizens, now deprived not just of the right to security, but victimised by arbitrary taxes and regulatory infringements. For the sake of legitimating itself, the state creates a **simulacrum of new freedoms** (PACs,[74] racial quotas, vaguely-designated 'rights' for vaguely-designated subjects, feminist laws, homophile and xenophile laws, etc.), while in the real world it's increasingly restrictive, regulative, spying, overtaxing — discouraging every initiative, and indifferent to the collapse of public safety and the civil spirit. **Globally speaking, everything that is deviant and delinquent is the object of benevolent tolerance, everything that is creative, inventive, productive, and identitarian is suspect and repressed.** Even freedom of thought is no longer assured, since the politically correct (whose principal dogmas are anti-racism and the prohibition of identitarian reflexes) controls every social sphere. Freedom to think and express oneself is restricted to secondary

---

73 PACS, or *pacte civil de solidarité*, is a type of civil union in France which is available to same-sex couples as well as traditional couples, although it gives fewer rights than does marriage.

74 Helots were a group in some of the ancient Greek city-states which fell somewhere in the hierarchy between slaves and free men.

spheres, affecting mainly those on the margins of society and deviants, particularly in respect to sexual matters.

All this is quite normal and has occurred before in history. To what conception of liberty and liberties, then, should we attach ourselves? The first rule must be a **people's ethnic freedom** to determine its own destiny. The people's will ought to transcend the authority of judges, censors, and experts. **Disembodied and abstract moral principles are not to be imposed on the popular will, just as the popular will must be allowed to determine its own distinct principles.**

The second rule is that the sovereign function, the public power, must guarantee social order and civic discipline, with the aim of preserving both individual and communal freedoms. **There is no freedom without a legal order conforming to the natural law: there's no freedom without authority.**

(see **democracy, organic**)

M

Mass, massification

The transformation of a people into a mass of undifferentiated, uniform individuals.

It comes with modern egalitarianism. 'The masses': this concept shared by both Marxism and capitalism is alien to every organic notion of an ethnically-created people. Massification implies cultural uniformity and race-mixing (*métissage*), consumerism and the cult of commodities. The 'atomised masses' oppose both the free individual and the people as an organic ensemble organised in communal hierarchies. **This enterprise of massification and homogenisation has, however, failed everywhere, except unfortunately among native Europeans, who have been emasculated by it.** But despite its will to 'reduce everything to the same', despite socioeconomic standardisation, egalitarian market society has failed to neutralise ethnic nationalism or the resurgence of identities.

(see **individualism; neo-primitivism**)

Memory, collective memory

The mental integration and appropriation of one's own past.

Just as an individual can't act if he's forgotten his past, **a people becomes impotent and defenceless if it loses the collective memory of its history.** What is memory? It's a reserve of information about oneself that structures one's experience and permits activities in the present to anticipate those of the future.

The dominant ideology aims today at making Frenchmen and Europeans amnesic. This is done in several ways: by deculturation, by the slow destruction of historical learning (or, similarly, by making Europeans feel guilty for being who they are or by systematically negating their genius), by fabricating a 'false memory' based on the memories of other peoples, by the cult of presentism, etc. If one speaks of the 'work of memory' today, it's to make **Europeans repent for what they have allegedly done to others**: not only is our memory lost in this way, but whatever of it we do conserve is for the sake of self-flagellation. All strong, ambitious, vivacious peoples and civilisations exalt in their historical memory.

*

Long-living peoples never forget their past and possess tenacious memories. Muslim peoples haven't lost the memory of their *Qur'an* and from this comes their force. Marxism never succeeded in eradicating the historical memory of Serbs, Russians, or Chinese. A people deprived of its history is a people debilitated.

'The man of the future is the man with the longest memory':[75] this *archeofuturist* formula of Nietzsche suggests that it's necessary to project one's memory into the future as will and project. An amnesic civilisation condemns itself to a short life. To dominate space, it's necessary also to dominate time — to pursue one's future destiny, one has to **proudly** take hold of one's past.
(see **archeofuturism; identity; people, long-living; tradition**)

Mental AIDS
The collapse of a people's immune system in the face of its decadence and its enemies.

Louis Pauwels[76] coined the term in the 1980s and it set off a media scandal — for it pointed at a painful truth (in general, the more the neo-totalitarian system is scandalised by an idea and demonises it, the more likely it's true).

AIDS comes from a retrovirus that destroys an organism's immune system. 'Mental AIDS' is an infection of a psychological nature that affects virtually all the 'elites' — the political class, the media class, show business, the 'cultural' community, 'artists', filmmakers — inclining them to oppose the interests of their own people and to **advocate degenerate values as if they were actually ones of regeneration.** A people, a nation, a civilisation — at the most complex, holistic level — is a living organism. European societies today are menaced by

---

75 This quote is the motto of Terre et Peuple, a group composed of intellectuals who have broken away from GRECE or the National Front. Faye has contributed to their journal.

76 Louis Pauwels (1920–1997) was a French author and journalist, and a follower of Gurdjieff, who became known in the 1960s as a writer and publisher of popular writings on occult matters and science fiction, particularly through his book *The Morning of the Magicians*, which remains one of the most popular (if highly inaccurate) accounts of the supposed 'occult' origins of National Socialism. In 1978 he began publishing the *Figaro Magazine,* which became a forum for New Right thinkers.

the collapse of their immunological defences: aggressions in this vein are not combated but encouraged. Faced with an evident danger, we're witnessing a morbid case of *anti-opportunity*: that is, **at the very moment when measures of anti-pathological defence are most needed, exactly the opposite is being called for** — which, of course, simply **reinforces the pathology's progression.**

Some examples: where the educational system produces illiteracy and violence, the reinforcement of the 'anti-authoritarian' methods responsible for these conditions are further encouraged; at the point when greenhouse gases have provoked a catastrophic global warming and need to be reduced, nuclear power, the least polluting of energy sources, is abandoned; as civil violence, delinquency, and insecurity explode everywhere, not only are their reality denied in the name of certain intellectualist sophisms, police and judicial measures that might curb them are at the same time undermined; the more Third World colonisation damages European peoples, the more measures are taken to continue it, to prevent the immunological reactions ethnic Europeans might have to it, and to denounce as 'racist' anyone who dares to resist it. Similarly, just as Europe is threatened with demographic collapse, policies which might increase the birth rate are denounced and homosexuality idealised. At the very moment, then, when corrective measures are required, the very opposite is advocated — which simply reinforces the malady's progression.

There are other examples of mental AIDS: worthless, vacuous forms of 'art', like *tags*,[77] are characterised as 'works of genius'; degenerate or deviant human types are turned into social models, etc.

*

The mental AIDS afflicting European 'elites' is spreading through a process of **intellectual bewilderment**: its pathology arises from the

---

77 Tags are a type of graffiti, usually used to mark a particular gang's territory or the identity of its creator.

'false spirit' that despises 'vulgar common sense' (claiming that black is white) and relies thus on a **forced optimism** ('everything is going great', even though it's not). Mental AIDS is based on a misrepresentation of reality — as well as an inability to detect viral attacks.

With biological AIDS, T4 lymphocytes, which are supposed to defend the organism, fail to react to the HIV virus as a threat, and instead treat it as a 'friend', helping it in this way to reproduce. The same holds true for mental AIDS. Catholic prelates, like secular republicans argue with great conviction that 'Islam and immigration are an enrichment', even though it clearly threatens to destroy them. Most of the time, this is not a matter of the 'elites" cynical *betrayal*, but something worse: the loss of inner reference and sound judgement. Mental AIDS is an intellectualist pathology which must be ceaselessly denounced — for its watchword seems to be: 'Why do something simply when instead it can be made complicated?' **Mental AIDS confuses, in effect, the enemy with the friend.**
(see **ethnomasochism; xenophilia**)

Mercantilism

The theory according to which the market is the sole basis of order and prosperity.

International mercantilism is the official doctrine of contemporary economic thought — the official doctrine of the corporations, the banks, and the European Commission. The exchanges and profits it generates take precedence over notions of production, full employment, independence, or supply. Hence, outsourcing and the abolition of tariff barriers. Mercantilism works against the European economy, against its independence and power — to the benefit of the United States and the 'emerging economies'.

Mercantilism is the basis of free trade, which negates any idea of economic independence. It rests on the false assumption that humanity is an ensemble of homogeneous economies, each nation responsive

to the same relations of production, each specialising in a particular area in which it excels.
(see **economy, organic; society, market**)

* * *

Meritocracy

Power to the most capable and meritorious, independent of their social origin or communal membership.

Meritocracy is inspired by the 'social Darwinist' theory of natural selection and is rationally organised by the state. It's long been one of the principles of the French Republic (competitive exams, free public schooling, scholarships, etc.). It seeks to abolish the privileges of birth by selecting the best from the different social classes of the people. Today, though, with the combination of anti-selection principles in the schools, affirmative action (racial quotas and preferences for aliens), and the destruction of public education, meritocracy has given way to **social chaos**. There is no longer a circulation of elites, nor are the most capable socially promoted. As usual with egalitarian doctrines, illegitimate castes are created. Only aristocratic principles allow the best elements from the people to develop their innate capacities. **Meritocracy is an aristocratic socialism.**
(see **aristocracy; democracy; elite; selection**)

* * *

Metapolitics

The social diffusion of ideas and cultural values for the sake of provoking a profound, long-term, political transformation.

Metapolitics is an effort of propaganda — not necessarily that of a specific party — that diffuses an ideological body of ideas representing a global political project. **Metapolitics is the indispensable complement to every direct form of political action, though in no case can it or should it replace such action.**

From the 'societies of thought' (and 'clubs') that prepared the French Revolution to today's pressure groups and associations, metapolitical practice constitutes **a requisite not just to every political or revolutionary action, but to the maintenance of the powers-that-be.**

Situated beyond partisan politics, metapolitics has the advantage of a non-electoral or disinterested 'neutrality', which enhances its persuasive powers. Possible in every kind of media, metapolitics diffuses a conception-of-the-world applicable to the long term. It was through a long, exhaustive metapolitical effort that egalitarianism came to dominate not just the political scene, but the mentality of those supposedly opposing it. **Metapolitics is the occupation of culture, politics is the occupation of a territory.**

*

A multifaceted metapolitics addresses the movers and shakers, as well as the general population; it aims at ideologically forming an active elite, as well as influencing the populace. Finally, metapolitics has to **avoid excessive culturalism,** which risks becoming an empty intellectualism, a boastful erudition, or a philosophy of amateurs — instead, it needs to pursue the political objective of positively affirming the principal lines and central concepts of its particular social/civilisational project.
(see **politics, Grand Politics**)

Miscegenation
The mixing of races or different ethnic groups.

In the name of anti-racism, the dominant ideology insists that miscegenation (*métissage*) is the planet's fate. **It's only Europeans, however,**

who actually believe it, not the world's other peoples, who are now organising themselves into **ethnic blocs** to preserve their identity.

With the replacement population that comes with Third World colonisation, miscegenation threatens to destroy our *germen*, i.e., the roots of European civilisation. Ethno-racially mixed populations, similarly, foster instability and rarely carry out great historical creations. Inevitably they succumb to racial supremacism, which weakens national solidarity. The example of Latin America is especially eloquent: the social hierarchy there is organised, whether admitted or not, according to an implied criterion of 'more or less White blood'. **The ideology of miscegenation culminates, as such, in an implicit and generalised racism.**

The constant, repetitive justification of **miscegenation as a social imperative** is pre-eminently an ethnomasochistic trait of European elites; but it also comes from a utopian optimism that sees a future racially-mixed Europe as necessary to her larger welfare. This dogma rests on certain pseudo-scientific tenets of *la pensée unique*[78] — the reigning one-track thought (as represented by Jacquard,[79] Coppens,[80] Le Bras,[81] etc.), which holds that 'pure races' are degenerate and that ethnic homogeneity is a historical handicap. This dogma just happens

---

78   French: 'single thought'. Since it was first coined in the French magazine *Le Monde diplomatique* in 1995, it has become a common way in France to refer to the unquestioning manner in which the assumptions of liberal ideology are accepted.

79   Albert Jacquard (1925–2013) was a French geneticist who frequently opposed racism in his scientific writings and was also active in protecting the rights of illegal immigrants.

80   Yves Coppens (1934–2022) was a French anthropologist who is best-known for postulating what he termed the 'East side story,' in which he claimed that all humans are descended from hominids who originally lived in East Africa, but were driven out as the result of a massive drought and began the process of outward expansion which continues to this day.

81   Hervé Le Bras (b. 1943) is a demographer and is the Director of the National Institute of Demographic Studies (INED) in France, and has held some government-appointed posts. In 1991 he published a book in which he claimed

to be based on a flagrant contradiction: for the partisans of miscegenation (partisans, similarly, of 'anti-racism') claim that it's biologically necessary to 'mix the races' — though at the same time they claim that 'races don't exist' and that biological determinants have no significance...

*

The dogma of the *métis* (miscegenated man), this figure of the future, is also part of the universalist dream of *l'homme unique* — a uniform humanity — the unattached man. **The ideology of miscegenation has, as such, a totalitarian component — that of the world state and that of a new man, who is to be the same everywhere — an idea shared by both Trotskyists and ultra-liberals.**

Miscegenation is tolerable only in exceptional cases, not on a mass scale, and especially not when it's obligatory or systematic.

*

In the same spirit, 'cultural miscegenation' is called for — a miscegenation that leads not to the expected formation of a universalist culture, but to the destruction (the Afro-Americanisation) of European culture — alone subject to the **race-mixing imperative.** Decked out in the most elaborate phraseology, this imperative dominates virtually every contemporary realm of European discourse.

*

In biological and cultural matters, it would be stupid to categorically reject all miscegenation in the name of biological purity. **To be fertile, though, such melanges need to occur between closely related peoples.** It's a general law of life. Overly close unions, like overly disparate unions, fail: the first leads to sterility, the second to chaos. In any case,

---

that fears of falling birth rates among the native French were based upon biased studies produced by pro-natalist partisans within the INED.

the facts hardly suggest that humanity is evolving toward a general mixing of races; only declining societies succumb to such an illusion. (see **chaos, ethnic; ethnosphere; identity; race, racism**)

Modernity, modernism
Cult of the present, alleged to be intrinsically superior to that which is past.

As a notion, modernity is ambiguous; at first positive, it became negative. Originally conceived in terms of the European's capacity for innovation and transcendence, by the Twentieth century modernity has ended up being confused with a naïve progressivism and anti-traditionalism — in the name of the **present,** treated as if it's intrinsically superior to the past. **Modernism is now nothing but a fashionable academicism.**

Modernity has never fulfilled its promises, because these promises were impossible, given their roots in utopianism and their denial of the real. Modernity promised to: first, ensure happiness, peace, and prosperity through economic and technological domination; second, replace aesthetics and traditional philosophies with radical new aesthetics and philosophies lacking continuity; and third, do away with peoples, religions, and customs for the sake of a homogeneous humanity and an atomised individual. Formulated in the late Seventeenth century, such objectives have since been taken up by globalist mercantilism, Marxism, and the myth of *progress*.

*

Modernity has been a total failure, commensurate with the conceit of its pretensions. After three and a half modern centuries, the Twenty-first century is heading now toward a **convergence of catastrophes.** Its failure, however, is no reason to embrace a contemplative 'traditionalism'. Just the opposite.

*

Modernity is old-fashioned, the very opposite of futurism. In condemning a despised ancestry, that is, the formative vitalistic traditions, modernity condemns itself to the ephemeral. (On this point, see my *Archeofuturism*.) In accord with my theses, Rodolphe Badinand and Georges Feltin-Tracol write, 'Post-modernity (or archeofuturism, or paganism, the term doesn't matter) senses the imperative of re-establishing that ancient spherical coherence between present, past, and future. Contrary to **the traditionalist attitude, vehemently voluntarist, coming ultimately from modernity** in its refusal of modernism, it doesn't take refuge in a long-gone past, impossible to recover — but **affirms the possibility of another future,** to which it opens the way'.[82] Traditionalism might be seen as a 'shallow modernism'. Not so much 'anti-modern', as 'non-modern'. The alternative to modernity is not traditionalism and antiquarianism, since they share the same linear vision of time as modernity (except in seeking a regression rather than a progression); traditionalism and modernism are both equally opposed to the spherical, dynamic vision of time.

*

Exhausted at the height of its influence, at the very moment when it's everywhere acclaimed with thunderous praise, modernity is dying. The word 'modern' has even lost its meaning. It was already employed in the Seventeenth century (during 'the quarrel between the Ancients and Moderns').[83] The deepest sense of the concept implies 'everything opposed to the past' — and this for the last three centuries. This makes

---

82   From *Roquefavour*, no. 14.

83   This famous quarrel began in literary circles in Paris in the 1690s. The Ancients believed that it was not possible to produce literature greater than what the Greeks and Romans of antiquity had produced, and that contemporary authors should simply aspire to imitate their example. The Moderns upheld that knowledge was progressive and that new discoveries could open up possibilities that were much greater than what was known in the ancient world.

the term now doubly stupid, since it opposes what was considered modern a hundred years ago (in a period when the term had a far greater resonance than it has today), but above all, it deprives itself of a future by 'making the past a *tabula rasa*'. The concept of 'modernity' is inherently suicidal, since, from the beginning, it denies a people and civilisation longevity, it denies the **unity of past and future.**

Pierre-Émile Blairon writes, 'Modernity is a totalitarianism of nothingness: globalisation, indifferentiation, homogenisation… Modernity isn't in crisis, modernity is a crisis'.[84]

*

In every realm, the present system endlessly reassures itself, legitimising itself, forgetting its failures and imperiousness. In its view, everything is to be modernised — *'to modernise democracy'* being one of its favourite expressions: human relations, communications, morals, institutions, justice, sexuality, social behaviour, immigrant policy, etc., all are constantly to be 'modernised'. And we've seen the results. The most pitiful of these are evident in the modernisation of art, which has come to mean **decadence and primitiveness — the new barbarism.**

*

Similarly, 'modern' (or 'contemporary') art has become the worst sort of academic nostalgia; for fifty years it's gone in circles, a subsidised nonentity. **Paradox: seeing itself as permanent innovation, modernity ends up being an insistent repetition, powerless to advance or create. Once an avant-garde, modernity has since become a rearguard, stymied by its own insolence.** It is now a cult — sign of an ageing people that has persuaded itself that it's eternally young.

*

---

84 From *Roquefavour*, no. 14.

With Vatican II, the Church also sought to modernise itself: the result, a seventy percent loss of parishioners. In triumphing, Islam has never for a second thought of 'modernising'! Indeed, **everything decadent and declining assumes the guise of the 'modern'**. It thus adorns itself with the degradation of mores, the confusion of sexual roles, social permissiveness, the abdication of discipline, cosmopolitanism, unbridled free trade (after having made the proper sacrifice to the Marxist god), etc., portraying these pathological trends as 'novelties', in the sense that 'everything new is positive', even the nothing, the regressive, anything. It has indeed succumbed to historical fatalism, without the slightest understanding that history is no longer following it.

*

Against modernity, we oppose not traditionalism or reactionism, which are also forms of the 'modern', but the tradition and spirit of continuity. As for techno-science, there's nothing 'modern' about it, since it comes from Greek Antiquity; it's a perfectly neutral instrument in service to the will.

(see **archeofuturism; convergence of catastrophes; interregnum; progress**)

Museologicalisation

The transformation of a living tradition into a museum piece, which deprives it of an active meaning or significance.

We are living a paradox: **everywhere it's claimed that 'patrimony' is a matter of utmost concern, but all the while it is being passionately destroyed.** In making museum pieces out of traditions, in petrifying them, killing them, freezing them, their character as 'tradition' (as something transmitted and evolving) is eliminated, as they are rendered into objects of erudition or curiosity.

There's no question that preserving the patrimony is fundamental, but in itself this is insufficient, because **a patrimony is constructed every day and can't, thus, be conserved in a museum.**

*

Modern society is paradoxically ultra-conservative and museological, on the one hand, and, at the same time, hostile to the living traditions of identity; Western modernity has proven itself similarly incapable (especially in the arts) of producing new works in continuity with tradition. So-called 'modern' art or architecture hasn't been modern for at least fifty years, it simply recycles the official academicism, which is nihilistic.
(see **tradition**)

N

Nation, nationalism, new nationalism

Etymologically, a 'nation' is a popular and political community made up of those of the same ethnic origins, of the same 'birth'.

The nation ought not to be confused with the nation-state. 'Nation' and 'ethnos' are the same word, designating a community whose members are of the same origin. To oppose the nation to the Empire is, semantically, to misunderstand it. An Empire, in the positive sense, is a federation, an ensemble of similar, closely-related nations — a 'federal nation'.

Nationalism ought not to be associated with a defence of the Jacobin and cosmopolitan nation-state. As a concept, nationalism needs to change its meaning: first, it needs to acquire **an ethnic association and no longer a strictly abstract political one.** It should return to its original etymological sense. Second, henceforth, nationalism ought to be understood in an enlarged European sense — in a visionary, future-oriented way — to include all the Continent's Indo-European peoples. In this vein, regional patriotism becomes an organic component of an **imperial Great-European nationalism** — what I call the **New Nationalism.**

*

In respect to France, the situation is especially delicate and complex. In no case should French nationalism identify with the tradition of Jacobin nationalism, since the latter is cosmopolitan, anti-ethnic, and, paradoxically, destroys the 'France' it claims to love (this is the 'French paradox'). The same holds for the present institutions of the European Union, whose principal concern seems to be the destruction of Europe's peoples and nations. **Another path is possible, an imperial one, with three dimensions: first, the ethnically based region; second, citizenship based on the historical nation; and third, a global, ethnic, historical nationality embracing the whole Continent.**

*

The relationship between these three levels is too complex to be rationally resolved in a single blow. Only history will solve it. Europe's problem dictates a **top-down solution** that transcends existing divisions, a solution that doesn't destroy attachment to the ethnically-based region, that doesn't destroy loyalty to the historical concepts of Spain, France, Germany, etc. (to their languages, their cultures), that doesn't close off a *futuristic* construction of the **Great European Nation.** We need to privilege the idea of exclusion and not that of inclusion. (see **empire; Europe; Eurosiberia**)

Neo-primitivism

The present process of observable cultural involution toward primitive mass behaviour, a weakening of the cultural memory, and the advent of social savagery.

The signs of this new primitivism are multiple: the rise of illiteracy in the schools, the explosion of drug use, the Afro-Americanisation of popular music, the collapse of social codes, the decline of general culture, knowledge, and historical memory among the young, the dissolution of contemporary art into a brutal, vacuous nihilism, the mass coarsening and deculturation fostered by audio/visual media (the 'cathodic religion'), the increase of criminality and uncivil behaviour, the decline of civic duty, the accelerated crumbling of social norms and collective disciplines, the deterioration of the language, etc.

The generation of 'Beur-Black' youth offers a remarkable example of this neo-primitivism, but they are not the only ones touched by it.

*

The paradox of this new primitivism, veritable process of 'decivilisation', is its association with the dominant devirilised ideology, which advocates civility, the rule of law, altruism, humanitarianism, citizenship, and 'culture'. But this is eyewash. Neo-primitivism perfectly accommodates social control, domestication by consumerism, and the collective loss of civic spirit. It's **the counterpart of neo-totalitarianism.** It serves the short term strategy of the political class, the intellectual-media class, and, above all, the transnational financial powers. If one reasons dialectically, this neo-primitivism could well turn against the civilisation engendering it — to the degree that the present generation of youth will be technologically incapable of performing the functions that make such a civilisation possible.

*

This generation will offer but the most minimal resistance to active minorities, whoever they may be. What could such a mass of slaves — these 'last men' of whom Nietzsche spoke[85] — do in face of a resolute aristocratic minority?
(see **deculturation; involution; mass, massification**)

Nihilism

A profound belief in the absence of all 'meaning in life': the annihilation of superior values; a cynical, dispirited tendency to despise the principles of action, even to believe that they no longer exist.

Nihilism (from the Latin *nihil*, 'nothing') characterises an era when everything has become equivalent, when all authentic sense of the sacred has gone, when the principal preoccupation is consumerism and immediate materialism. Vitalist values (related to the conservation of a line, the defence of a land, the communal spirit, concern for future generations, the perpetuation of traditions, aesthetics, etc.) collapse for the sake of **a dissimulating ethic of false values** (the humanitarian, anti-racist, democratic vulgate, pseudo-social or ecological discourses at odds with the facts, etc.). Nihilism is the direct offshoot of the bourgeois spirit — obsessional, egoistic, and calculating. The system's dominant preoccupations, similarly, are short-term financial gain, the maximisation of profit, and the exclusion of every other consideration, even those of health.

---

85 'Alas, the time is coming when man will no longer give birth to a star. Alas, the time of the most despicable man is coming, he that is no longer able to despise himself. Behold, I show you the last man. "What is love? What is creation? What is longing? What is a star?" thus asks the last man, and he blinks. The earth has become small, and on it hops the last man, who makes everything small. His race is as ineradicable as the flea-beetle; the last man lives longest.' From Friedrich Nietzsche, *Thus Spoke Zarathustra* (New York: Penguin Books, 1978), p. 5.

This attitude is fundamentally nihilist because it holds that *nothing* is of value except immediate materialist concerns. It represents the collapse of all historical consciousness and a refusal of every transcendence beyond individual materialist egoism. We are living today the apotheosis of nihilism: individual uprootment, the triumph of the market for the market's sake, and the dissolution of authentic meaning in life. The pursued 'happiness', though, is obviously no rendezvous, but the reverse, something even worse: despair. This is evident, for example, in the suicide rate, but also in the morbid, noxious forms of contemporary art, in the lowering of comedy to the rank of derision, the replacement of laughter by sniggers, of tragedy with lamentation.

*

We are living through an implosion of Western ideologies, the generalisation of narcissism, the demographic suicide of Europe, and the dictatorship of **a meaningless world** speeding toward catastrophe.

Some see Islam as a remedy to nihilism. Islam, it's true, is anything but nihilistic. The problem here is that it entails exchanging one evil for another, given that Islam's aim is the destruction of European civilisation. **Only an explosion can cure Europe of her nihilism**. For when their physical and material survival is threatened by great crises, men, paradoxically, rediscover the transcendent in their lives. After a certain degree, regeneration entails tragedy.

(see **convergence of catastrophes; sacred; society, market**)

O

Order

Order is the basis of every creative civilisation, because it disciplines man's anarchistic animal nature through its political and cultural harmonies.

Order is unacceptable if it's not disciplinary, educative, selective — if it's purely repressive in service to a frozen elite. Any notion of order needs, though, to be treated with caution, for it can be stimulating or enervating, a source of vigour or of sclerosis. **There is no order without a project, without enthusiasm, without a movement.** Order is not simply repressive (the American syndrome), but a form of support, an attraction, **a disciplined constitution of a common ideal.**

An authentic order is found in the community of homogeneous, self-disciplined people, animated by the spirit of Aristotelian *philia*, friendship, and spontaneous solidarity. Order and harmony go together. In the European tradition, order isn't a static state, but the organisation of a shared becoming.

(see **discipline; liberty**)

P

Paganism

The philosophic and/or religious attitude, generally polytheistic and pantheistic, that is the antipode to the revealed salvation religions, to religious or secular monotheism, or to Western materialism.

For Christopher Gérard,[86] one of the principal contemporary practicing authorities on the subject: 'Paganism, as a coherent vision of the world ... is faithful to an ancestry, considered part of a very long memory, enrooted in multiple terrains, opened to the invisible ... an active participant in the world, a sought-after harmony between

---

86 Christopher Gérard (b. 1962) is a Belgian author and editor known for his advocacy of modern paganism. In 1992, he founded a new version of the journal *Antaios*, inspired by the original publication edited by Mircea Eliade and Ernst Jünger from 1959 to 1971. Gérard's *Antaics* focused on polytheistic traditions and was published until 2001. His novel *The Dream of Empedocles* (2003) has been translated into English.

microcosm and macrocosm. Paganism in essence is a natural religion, the most ancient of a world "born" with its birth — if the world were ever born. Rather than an eccentric fad — or the elegant nostalgia of literary refugees from some mythic Golden Age, I think paganism is on the way to becoming the first of the world's religions.'[87] He mentions 1.5 billion pagans on five continents, which would make it the world's largest religious group. Gérard adds, 'Without being narrowly moralistic ... a lived paganism seems to me incompatible with whatever makes man servile. As the exaltation of life — of the eternal *élan* — paganism refuses everything that debases man: drugs, dependencies, every kind of unhealthy life'. A lived paganism, in other words, is not destructuring, nor linked to the permissive, anti-vitalist mores of the present West (as certain prelates would have us believe). Gay Pride has nothing in common with the pagan bacchanalia! Paganism, moreover, is neither superstitious nor vacuously ritualistic, in contrast to Islam (this belief system which is most opposed to it), for Islam is all these things to the highest degree.

*

Pierre Vial has written that paganism is not *anti-Christian*, but *a-Christian* and *post-Christian*. 'To be pagan is to refuse the inversion of values that Nietzsche denounced in Christianity. It is to take the hero, not the martyr, as the model. Christian suffering has always repulsed me. To celebrate the redemptive value of suffering seems like a form of masochism'. (Today, modern European Christians practice their ethnomasochism and culpability on the immigrant colonisers; in every domain they practice the 'duty to repent'.) Vial continues, 'To exalt wretchedness, suffering, and sickness is unhealthy and I much prefer the Greek ideal of transcendence or the Stoicism of Marcus Aurelius.[88] Paganism ought not, though, to be confused with anti-

---

87 From Christopher Gérard, *Parcours païen* (Lausanne: L'Age d'Homme, 2000).

88 Marcus Aurelius (121–180) was a Stoic philosopher and Emperor of Rome. In his *Meditations*, he recommends that one's emotions and indulgence in sense

clericalism or atheism. Another point: a purely intellectual definition of paganism ... won't suffice. It's perhaps necessary, but it doesn't go far enough. For paganism to exist, it must be lived. Not simply in gestures, but in life's most ordinary expressions. Paganism is defined primarily in reference to the sacred ... It affirms the immanence of the sacred'.[89]

For both Gérard and Vial, paganism is the authentic 'religion', for it ties men of the same community together and ties them to a cosmos in which the divine is everywhere, where the gods are not separated from, but part of, the profane world.

*

Similarly, gnosticism, which inspires Freemasonry, has nothing to do with paganism. Paganism's constituting traits are: the presence of the sacred and the supernatural within nature; a cyclical or spherical conception of time; the refusal to consider nature the 'property' of the men who exploit and thus destroy it; the coming-and-going of sensuality and asceticism; the unqualified apology of the life-force (the 'yes to life' and 'the Great Health'[90] of Nietzsche's Zarathustra); the idea that the world is 'uncreated' and corresponds to a river of becoming, without beginning or end; the tragic sentiment of life refusing all nihilism; the cult of ancestors, of the line, of our people's biological and

---

gratification should be kept well under control in order to keep one's sense of judgement clear.

89 From *Une Terre, un people*.
90 'The great health.— Being new, nameless, hard to understand, we premature births of an as yet unproven future need for a new goal also a new means — namely, a new health, stronger, more seasoned, tougher, more audacious, and gayer than any previous health... Whoever has a soul that craves to have experienced the whole range of values and desiderata to date...needs one thing above everything else: the great health — that one does not merely have but also acquires continually, and must acquire because one gives it up again and again, and must give it up.' From Friedrich Nietzsche, *The Gay Science* (New York: Vintage Press, 1974), section 382.

cultural identity; the refusal of all revealed and universal Truths and thus the refusal of all fanaticism, dogmatism, and forced proselytism.

We need to beware, though, of certain so-called pagans who hold that paganism stands for 'absolute tolerance', in the name of 'social polytheism'. Such pagans, like the post-conciliar Church, support, for instance, immigration and Islam and refuse to struggle against the reigning social decadence. This pseudo-paganism of secular clerics gives the pagan spirit a Leftish slant. **It's a pseudo-paganism, in effect — purely negative and reactive, a hollow Judaeo-Christianity, an anti-Catholic fixation.**

It's not a philosophy of life, but an attitude of resentment. Besides, these pseudo-pagans, who lack true culture, have never been able to define nor positively live their assumed 'paganism'. In a totally absurd way, it's even led them to a pro-Islam position (whose *Qur'an* considers pagans 'idolaters' — and whose lot is that of the Eid al-Adha's slaughtered sheep[91]) — and to the egalitarianism of absolute toleration for every form of deviance, justified in the name of a purely casuistic 'social polytheism' (homophilia, anti-racism, ethnopluralism, tribalism, etc.). One doesn't even have to criticise the Church to assume the position of Monsignor Gaillot[92] and the post-conciliar humanitarians.

91　Eid al-Adha, meaning 'festival of sacrifice', is one of the major festivals of the Islamic calendar, commemorating Abraham's willingness to sacrifice his son Ishmael on Allah's order (an event which is described in the *Old Testament* as well as in the *Qur'an*). The festival also includes the sacrifice of an animal. Although it is true that the *Qur'an* enjoins Muslims to respect Jews and Christians as fellow 'People of the Book' (since they also derive from the Abrahamic tradition), and no similar injunction is given to extend respect to practitioners of pagan religions, historically Muslim rulers have generally extended the same rights to pagans under their control, such as to Hindus during the Mughal period in India. There are notable exceptions to this when Hindus who failed to convert were slaughtered outright.

92　The Most Reverend Dr. Jacques Gaillot (1935–2023) was a former French Catholic bishop nicknamed 'The Red Cleric' because of his extreme Leftist positions. He was removed from his position by the Vatican in 1995 for publicly opposing several of the Church's precepts.

Against this, we affirm that **paganism is in essence a partisan of social order — which it sees as reflecting the cosmic order;** it equally **opposes the fusion of peoples, random mixing, and thus a massifying individualism.** The pagan vision of the world is holistic and organic and views its people as a **hierarchical community of destiny.** Like ancient Greek paganism, **the notion of the City, inseparable from notions of patriotism and ethnic identity,** is fundamental to the pagan conception of the world. Similarly, Nietzsche's notion of the **will to power** perfectly accords with paganism (to the degree it respects the natural, cosmic order).

In Europe, paganism — her ancient religion, far older than Christianity — has taken several forms: first, there's a 'philosophical' paganism (or neo-paganism), with Hellenic, Roman, Germanic, Scandinavian, etc., components, all of which hold no belief in anthropocentric gods, but rather in a sacred, polytheistic, and pantheistic vision of the world, in which the divinities are eternal allegories representing the multiplicities of life and cosmos; this paganism knows numerous communal rituals linked to the different stages of human life and to the seasonal cycles; it's been evident in European art for centuries. There's also a 'wild' paganism that stretches from the (pseudo-pagan) New Age to European Buddhism. Another false paganism is intellectualist paganism, which is often just a form of anti-Catholic hatred; what Gérard calls 'salon paganism'. And finally, there's the latent or implicit paganism of traditional Catholicism and Orthodoxy, especially evident in their polytheistic cults.

There's no pagan 'Church'. Paganism isn't sociologically unified — one needs to speak of paganisms. The word itself is ambiguous, coined by Christians to designate the religion of peasants (*pagani*).

It might also be noted that **sects belong neither to paganism nor its philosophy, but to derivations of the mystic monotheistic salvation religions.**

*

Pagans today need to have the intelligence and wisdom not to — *a priori* — reject traditional Christians, and vice versa, for the struggle against the common enemy is what's most important. Not sectarianism, but a **historic compromise,** is needed here. **No reconciliation, by contrast, is possible with the Judaeo-Christianity of the post-conciliar Left.**

The main pagan reproach of Christianity (as made by Pierre Vial, Giorgio Locchi, and Louis Rougier[93]) is its roots in universalism and egalitarianism and its progressive view of history; totalitarian ideologies of salvation, such as globalist liberalism, with its end to history and its disarming humanitarianism, are simply **secularised forms of Christianity.** Universalism, for example, has been transformed into a secular cosmopolitanism, and Christian charity into a masochistic humanitarianism. Universal charity, as it comes from Judaeo-Christianity and clashes with the pagan world vision, has been central to Europe's moral disarmament, to its failure to resist the Third World's colonising invasion. Similarly, in situating God outside or above the universe and declaring the latter profane, Judaeo-Christianity opened the way to an atheistic materialism. Following Augustine[94] and Aquinas,[95] traditional Christianity claimed that the equality and universality of men before God is destined not for the City, but for the beyond, following the Last Judgement.

---

93   Louis Rougier (1889–1982) was an important French philosopher of his day. He was a vocal opponent of Catholicism throughout his career, and during the 1970s he began working with Alain de Benoist and GRECE, publishing works which were highly critical of Christianity, which he saw as being alien to the West. He was also one of the principal French expositors of neo-liberal socio-economic philosophy.

94   Saint Augustine (354–430) was an important bishop of the latter-day Roman Empire and was one of the Church Fathers. He outlines his idea of hierarchy in his *City of God*.

95   Thomas Aquinas (1125–1274) was a Dominican priest whose theological writings became important in both theological and philosophical debates, known as Thomism.

We need, henceforth, to recognise that the egalitarian, universalist, and anti-nationalist virus of the early Christians, neutralised by the Medieval Church and by chivalry, has returned in force with the modern post-conciliar Church.[96] Traditional Christianity, whether Catholic or Orthodox, incorporated important pagan elements, notably in the polytheism of the Holy Trinity, the cult of the saints and the Virgin Mary, etc. We might also mention Pelagius,[97] Teilhard de Chardin,[98] Giordano Bruno,[99] or other Churchmen who attempted a synthesis of European Christianity and paganism.

The most important thing today is to confront the common enemy, Islam — the most abstract, the most intolerant, the most dangerous of the monotheistic religions (founding model of totalitarianism, even more so than Communism), with which, unfortunately, the Catholic hierarchy and our pseudo-pagan 'ethnopluralist' intellectuals suicidally collaborate. In the course of the Twenty-first century, it's not unreasonable to expect that authentic pagans in Europe and India will be the ones manning the front line in the struggle against the desert's totalitarian religion — not Catholic clerics or republican 'secularists'.

---

96 The idea that Christianity was 'Europeanised' during the process of its assimilation in the West has been a subject of some debate. An important work on this subject is James C. Russell's *The Germanization of Early Medieval Christianity* (Oxford: Oxford University Press, 1994).

97 Pelagius (c. 354-c. 420) was an ascetic who was condemned as a heretic for denying the notion of original sin on the grounds that it was tantamount to denying free will. He certainly did not see himself as a pagan, however, since he accused Augustine of being under the influence of pagan Manicheanism.

98 Pierre Teilhard de Chardin (1881–1955) was a French Jesuit priest and paleontologist who wrote several books about the past and future evolution of consciousness. The Catholic Church believes that Teilhard de Chardin's ideas are in opposition to official doctrine, and in 1962 the Vatican issued a condemnation of his works.

99 Giordano Bruno (1543–1600) was a Dominican friar who held a number of controversial views, including pantheism and the idea that the stars in the sky are of the same nature as our own Sun. He was ultimately burned at the stake by the Church.

It would be vain to instrumentalise paganism as a 'political religion'. For paganism is above all an attitude, **a philosophical, spiritual positioning, a choice of values, and in no case does it have a vocation to institutionalise itself as a religion — as a 'new Church'.** European Catholicism — before it was desacralised by Vatican II — included important pagan elements, to such a degree that certain modern theologians accuse it of having been a 'pagano-Christianity' — the same reproach Luther and Calvin made of it. Slavic-Greek Orthodoxy still retains many pagan remnants.

The historic alliance of authentic pagan philosophers (inspired by the heritage of Greece, Rome, and India) to traditional European Christianity is a prerequisite to the merciless struggle that is to be waged against the Masonic gnosis, the obscurantism of the Muslim colonisers, and the virus of materialism.

(see **Judaeo-Christianity**)

People

An ethnic ensemble — biological, historical, cultural — with a territory, its fatherland, in which it is rooted.

'The people' — the very term is suspect to the cosmopolitan Left, which sees it as bordering on the politically incorrect — is not any statistical 'population'; it's an **organic community embracing a transcendent body made up of ancestors, the living, and their heirs.** Though marked with a certain spirituality, a people is diachronically rooted in the past and projects itself into the future — it's submerged in biological and genetic matter, but at the same time it's a historical, and spiritual, reality.

It's belonging to a specific people that distinguishes a man and makes him human. Though modern Western egalitarian doctrines reduce peoples to indifferent socioeconomic aggregates, peoples actually constitute the organic bases of the human race; similarly, such doctrines conceive of the ideal man as an individual 'emancipated' from his organic attachments — like an undifferentiated cell in a human magma.

It's necessary to recall, especially for certain Christians, that **a people's attachment is incompatible with Christianity's present cosmopolitanism.** The claim, for example, that 'I am closer to an African Catholic than I am to a non-Christian European' is a universalistic claim that relegates a people's nation to something of secondary significance. This is, indeed, the great drama of European Christianity, marked as it is by Pauline universalism. A Catholic attached to his people and conscious of the biological and cultural dangers threatening them might instead say, 'I respect all the Christians of the world, but *hic et nunc*[100] I fight for my people above all, whatever their religion'.

The Jesuit spirit might resolve the contradiction in reference to the *Old Testament*'s Hebraic tradition: 'Babel — the mélange of disparate peoples — is a punishment from God, Who wants His peoples to be separate and diverse — humanity is one in Heaven, but multiple on Earth'.

Arab Islam has no difficulty reconciling the notion of people (the 'Arab nation') with that of its universalism. The Jews, on their side, have similarly reconciled a ferocious defence of their ethnicity — their singularity — with their religion, however theoretically monotheistic and universalist it may be. At no moment have Judaism and Islam, unlike the Christian Churches today, engaged in doubting, guilt-stroking diatribes against 'xenophobia' and ethnocentrism. They are not masochistic...

*

Like every anthropological notion, 'people' lacks mathematical rigour. A people doesn't define itself as a homogeneous biocultural totality, but as a relationship. It's the product of an organic alchemy that brings

---

100 Latin: 'here and now'.

various 'sub-peoples' together. The Bretons, Catalans, Scots, etc., can be seen thus as the sub-peoples of a larger people — the Europeans.

*

We ought to highlight the ambiguity that touches the notion of the people. The universalist ideology of the French Revolution confused the idea of the people with that of an 'ensemble of inhabitants who jurisdictionally possess nationality', whatever their origin. **Given the facts of mass immigration and naturalisation, the notion of the French people has been greatly diluted** (as have the British or German peoples, for the same reason). This is why (without broaching the unresolvable issue of what constitutes a 'regional people' or a 'national people'), it's advisable to dialectically transcend semantic problems — and **affirm the historic legitimacy of a single, European people,** historically bound, whose different national families resemble one another in having, for thousands of years, the same ethnocultural and historical origins. Despite national, linguistic, or tribal differences, haven't African Blacks, even in Europe, been called on by Nelson Mandela or the Senegalese Mamadou Diop[101] to 'think like one people'? From Nasser[102] to al-Qadhafi, by way of Arafat, haven't Arabs been urged to see themselves as an Arab people? Why don't Europeans have the same right to see themselves as a people?

As for 'regional peoples', it's necessary to oppose Left-wing regionalists, self-professed anti-Jacobins and anti-globalists, who unhesitatingly accept the concept of French or American *jus soli* — who confuse citizens and residents, and who recognise as Bretons, Alsatians,

---

101 Mamadou Diop (1936–2018) was a prominent member of the central committee of the Socialist Party of Senegal. He served as the mayor of Dakar from 1984 until 2002 and held several ministerial positions, including in Public Works and Health, under Presidents Senghor and Diouf.

102 Gamal Abdel Nasser (1918–1970) was the leader of the Egyptian Revolution in 1952 and governed as president until his death. His pan-Arab ideology was highly influential in the region and continues to be influential in the present.

Corsicans, etc., *anyone* (even of non-European origin) who lives in these regions and chooses to accept such an identity.

*

In belonging to a people, its members are emotionally inclined to define themselves as such, which implies political affiliation. For this reason, we say that **a people exists at that point where biological, territorial, cultural, and political imperatives come together.** But in no case does mere cultural or linguistic attachment suffice in making a people, if they have no common biological roots. Alien immigrants from people X who are installed on the territory of people Y — even if they adopt cultural elements of their host people — are not a part of Y. As De Gaulle thought, there might be minor exceptions for small numbers of compatible (White) minorities, capable of being assimilated, but this could never be the case for, say, French West Indians.

Similarly, **in defining the notion of a people, territorial or geopolitical considerations must also be taken into account.** A people is not a diaspora: the Jews felt obliged to reconquer Palestine as their 'promised land' because, as Theodor Herzl[103] argued, 'without a promised land, the Jews are just a religious diaspora, a culture, a union, but not a people'.

There's a good deal of talk today, on the Left and the Right, about people being 'deterritorialised'. In reality, there's nothing of the kind. Every healthy people, even if they possess an important diaspora (Chinese, Arabs, Indians, etc.), maintains close relations with its fatherland.

*

Modernist gurus have long claimed that the future belongs not to peoples, but to humanity conceived as a single people. Again, there'll

---

103 Theodor Herzl (1860–1904) was a Jewish journalist from Austria-Hungary who is regarded as the founder of modern political Zionism.

be nothing of the kind. **Despite globalisation and in reaction to it, the Twenty-first century will more than ever be a century of distinct peoples.** Only Europeans, submerged in the illusions of their decadence, imagine that blood-based peoples will disappear, to be replaced by a miscegenated 'world citizen'. In reality what is at risk of disappearing are Europeans. Tomorrow will be no twilight of peoples.

On the other hand, the twilight of several peoples is already possible. One often forgets that Amerindians or Egyptians have disappeared — hollowed out internally and overrun. For history is a cemetery of peoples — of weak peoples — exhausted and resigned.

*

A caution is necessary here: Right and Left-wing theoreticians of 'ethnopluralism', opposed to humanity's homogenisation, speak of 'the cause of peoples', as if every people must be conserved. In reality, the *system that destroys peoples*[104] — the title of one of my books that was misunderstood by certain intellectuals — only threatens unfit peoples, i.e., present-day Europeans. It also threatens those *residu*[105] peoples, whose fate is of interest only to museum-keepers. It seems perfectly stupid and utopian to believe that every people can be conserved in history's formaldehyde. What a pacifistic egalitarian vision.

The main threat to the identity and existence of great peoples occurs, in contrast, through the conjunction of deculturation and the colonising invasion of alien peoples — which we're presently experiencing. The Western globalist 'system' will never threaten strong peoples. Are Arabs, Chinese, or Indians threatened? On the contrary. It reinforces their identity and their desire to conquer, by provoking their reaction to it.

The people in danger — largely because of its own failings — is our people, for reasons as much biological as cultural and strategic. That's

---

104 Faye is referring to his book *Le système à tuer les peuples* (Paris: Copernic, 1981).
105 French: 'residual'.

why **it's necessary to replace the egalitarian ideology of 'the cause of peoples' with the 'cause of our people'**.

*

There are three possible positions: first, peoples don't exist, or no longer exist — it's an obsolete category — only humanity counts (the thesis of universalistic egalitarianism); second, all peoples ought to exist and be conserved (the utopian — also egalitarian — ethnopluralist position — completely inapplicable to our age); and third, **only strong, wilful peoples can subsist for long historical periods — periods of selection in which only the most apt survive (the voluntarist, realist, inegalitarian thesis)**. We obviously support the third position.

What's essential is **reappropriating the term 'people' and progressively extending it to the entire Eurosiberian Continent.** The present understanding of 'European' by the reigning ideology at Brussels is inspired by French Jacobin ideology. This ideology makes no reference to an ethno-historical Great European people, only to a mass of disparate residents inhabiting European territory. This tendency needs to be radically replaced.

We propose that European peoples become **historical subjects** again and cease being **historical objects.** In the tragic century that's coming, it's especially crucial that Europeans become conscious of the common dangers they face and that, henceforth, they form a self-conscious **community of destiny**. This is well and truly a matter of forging a 'new alliance' that — through resurrection, metamorphosis, and historical transfiguration — will lead to a refounding of a Great European people and, in the midst of decline, succeed — not without pain, of course — in giving birth again to the phoenix.

(see **Eurosiberia; nation; populism; region**)

People, Long-Living; short-living people

A people that desires and knows how to preserve itself in history, ensure its biological line, and maintain the longevity of its civilisation.

This concept comes from the philosopher Raymond Ruyer.[106] The Arabs, Chinese, Jews, Indians, and others are typical examples of such long-living peoples. Numbed by Western civilisation, which they tragically created and which has turned against them, Europeans today no longer see themselves as a long-living people. For like **short-living people**, they are not concerned about their ancestors or their posterity — their lineage, cultural heritage, or future. They are devoted to the cult of the immediate present, in their pursuit of small individual pleasures and in the nervous preservation of their material acquisitions.

Small peoples are destroyed by their demographic, military, and technological disadvantages. Great peoples, on the other hand, who sink into the oblivion of time, die because of anaemia, of a lack of will — despite the apparent force of their actually fragile civilisation. This was the destiny of the Incas, the Aztecs, the Egyptians, and others. A long-living people is characterised by the following qualities: demographic vigour, collective ethnic consciousness, popular solidarity, and a common spiritual ideal. **A long-living people possesses deep biological roots, a memory and common history, an idea of the divine and a project.** This is everything that Western civilisation lacks,

---

106 Raymond Ruyer (1902–1987) was a French philosopher who explored the philosophical implications of modern scientific discoveries, particularly in biology, cybernetics, and information theory. He developed a unique metaphysical perspective, often described as a form of panpsychism, and presented his own version of gnosticism. Ruyer was critical of existentialism and the Leftist philosophical trends of his time. While his work was once overlooked, several of his books have been translated into English in recent years, including *Neofinalism* (2016), *The Genesis of Living Forms* (2019), and *Cybernetics and the Origin of Information* (2023). Guillaume Faye discusses Ruyer extensively in *Archeofuturism*.

since it can't even project itself five years into the future. All this is fit for reconstruction.

(see **history**)

Personality, Creative

The superior type of man who mobilises and leads his fellows, imbuing them with a goal and a project.

Humanity is divided into two types, as numerous psychologists have noted: the 'creative personalities' and the generic human. The latter imitate and reproduce social behaviours and are led only by disciplines external to themselves, by enthusiasms forged by others, by norms that are learned. The first type, the creative personality, is far rarer, imbued with superior capacities. They are their own master, they are self-disciplined and creative.

History is nothing but the fertilisation of peoples by their creative personalities — by their political leaders, poets, artists, spiritual masters, philosophers, inventors, warriors, or entrepreneurs. The very notion of a creative personality affronts the dominant egalitarianism. For it implies that human societies are not haphazard mechanisms, but force fields, dominated by wills and talents, whose advances always come from exceptional energies and intuitions.

Creative personalities exist at every level of the social organism, even the most modest. This notion has nothing to do with 'class' and even less with monetary wealth. In no case must the creative personality be confused with a 'bourgeois elite'. It can appear in the most unexpected realms. It doesn't expect success, for it's often disdained in its lifetime. It's the seed that fertilises the soil. Sometimes, it even reshapes history.

*

Present Western society is decadent because it tries to eliminate its creative personalities — for the sake of bureaucrats or ideological conformists. It's an old story, well known to Rome in its decline, but also a struggle lost in advance. No social system can abolish the power of fascination that the creative personality exerts over the generic human, the man at the base. Molière, Mozart, Baudelaire, Nietzsche, Van Gogh, or Céline are not forgettable. But the system tries to make us forget them — however in vain.

The creative personality is animated by what the Greeks called *poeisis,* poetry, the 'power to create'. Its dimensions are both political and aesthetic, though the two can be the same. The creative personality possesses both a force that comes from below — telluric, genetic, ancestral, Dionysian — and by a force that comes from on high — what the ancients called 'inspiration', that Apollonian energy of unknown origin. The creative personality can be defined by a single word: **enthusiasm** — which, etymologically, means 'divine possession'.
(see **aristocracy; born leader; elite**)

Philia
Aristotelian concept signifying 'friendship' — ethno-cultural consensus between members of the same City.

For Aristotle, democracy is possible only within homogeneous ethnic groups, while despots have always reigned over highly fragmented societies.

A multi-ethnic society is thus necessarily anti-democratic and chaotic, for it lacks *philia,* this profound, flesh-and-blood fraternity of citizens. Tyrants and despots divide and rule, they want the City divided by ethnic rivalries. The **indispensable condition for ensuring a people's sovereignty accordingly resides in its unity.** Ethnic chaos prevents all *philia* from developing. A citizenry is formed on the basis of proximity — or it is not formed at all. The abstract, integrationist doctrines of the French Revolution envisage man as simply a 'man', a resident, a consumer. Civic spirit, like public safety, social harmony, and solidarity, is based not on education or persuasion alone, but on cultural unanimity — on common values, lifestyles, and innate behaviours.

For more on this crucial notion, Yvan Blot's *L'héritage d'Athena*[107] ought to be consulted.

(see **democracy; fatherland**)

Politics, Grand Politics

An activity (the political) or a function (politics) whose object is the longevity and defence, in every domain, of a City (whose Greek etymological root is *polis*) — that is, of a human group constituting a community of origin and destiny — whose chief function is accordingly the exercise of sovereignty.

In contemporary political philosophy, sullied with economism, the essence of the political is 'the management of the nation', conceived as some sort of business. This transforms the political class into a caste of careerists, similar to the *apparatchiks* of the former Communist regimes. A **people's destiny** totally eludes the politician's political vision, as does every other **historical dimension** of political activity.

The political doesn't exist in day-to-day management or in the American pursuit of happiness. It's also not simply the **designation of the enemy,** as Carl Schmitt taught, however just and instructive this designation may be. The essence of the political is above all — fundamentally — the **designation of the friend** — i.e., the comrade, the one belonging to the same community and sharing the same values. In this sense, it is primarily the delineation of a field of belonging. Who is on our side? Who is who? Such is the central political question.

The essence of the political is aesthetic, poetic, and historical. According to the Greek verb *poeisis* — to create, to make. In effect, the ultimate vocation of the political is to create — to make — a people in history. It follows that the essence of the political is not solely about economics, justice, social equilibrium, civil peace, and international

---

107 *L'héritage d'Athena* (Ploufragan: Presses Bretonnes, 1996).

security, but also architecture, ecology, the fine arts, culture, demography, biopolitics, etc.

*

The political is the domain of will and sovereignty. It's not surprising that our age does everything to destroy the political for the sake of economics or individual interest. **Contemporary politicians have been depoliticised and Europe suffers from this abdication of the political, i.e., from the non-existence of the sovereign function.** These politicians are the subject of jokes and the false flatteries of money and the media, but their calculations are inevitably short-term and they lack a historical project; similarly, they have no real power, which resides entirely in the hands of the financial forces.

The state itself has ceased to possess either a monopoly of power or a political will. It has ceased being a political authority in order to be a techno-bureaucratic authority. In either Brussels or Paris, it's nothing but an administration, a corporation with short-term schedules. Functionaries or politicians — the two often being confused — act like salaried employees or corporate executives, but not like the people's servants. Without exception, European politicians are situated somewhere between the stars of show-business and the upper echelons of corporate management. Vanity and money, but no real power. For **real political power presupposes both a disinterested understanding of its exercise and a visionary spirit.**

*

Finally, we arrive at the notion of **Grand Politics**, a term fashioned by Nietzsche. It expresses the essence of the political: **to inscribe and maintain a people in history, as the autonomous creator and actor of its own destiny, preserving its identity and, if possible, spurring its ascension.** Grand Politics is inscribed thus in history's *longue durée*, which is the opposite of the politicians' 'petty politics' — which is basically presentist and non-historical. Grand Politics situates itself at that crossroad between the individual's welfare and the people's longevity, between pacification and power, between loyalty to tradition and ambitious innovation.

Grand Politics must henceforth take account of the following essential factors and objectives (the list is not exhaustive), which are totally ignored by French and European politicians today:

1. To confront the revival of Islam's ancestral struggle against European peoples.
2. To check the Continent's demographic decline and to reverse its colonisation by the Third World.
3. To ensure the economic protection of European territories.
4. To liberate Europeans from their subjugation to the Americans — to win their independence; to construct a real continental union of power with Russia and to have as their principal allies China and India.
5. To find an alternative to the present short-term, catastrophic direction of the global economy, especially in respect to ecology.

We are far from any of this. But the dramatic sanctions that will soon spring from our lack of foresight could well put things back in their rightful place.

*

The political never supercedes the spiritual. But the spiritual is nothing without the political. The notion of the political supposes **ideas of sovereignty and a transcendent sense of history.**
(see **history; sovereignty**)

Populism
The position which defends the people's interests before that of the political class — and advocates direct democracy.

This presently pejorative term must be made positive. The prevailing aversion to populism actually expresses a covert contempt for authentic democracy. Like its corollary anti-demagoguery, anti-populism is a semantic ruse of politicians and bourgeois intellectuals — to deflect the people's will, especially that of the modest social strata, reputedly dangerous, because they are the most nationalist.

The cosmopolitan bourgeoisie, whether of Left or Right, that presently holds power attacks 'populism' because it rejects direct democracy and because it's convinced that **the people is 'politically incorrect'**. On the subject of immigration, the death penalty, school discipline, fiscal policies — on numerous other subjects — it's well known that the people's deepest wishes (as evident in referendums and elsewhere) never, despite the incessant media propaganda, correspond to those of the government. It's logical, then, that those who have confiscated the 'popular will' tend to associate populism with despotism.

From this follows suspicions about Swiss-style cantonal democracy, or the EU's illegal sanctions against Austria for allowing the populist party, the FPÖ, into the government, though it had won the right at the polls. **In actuality, populism is the true face of democracy — in the Greek sense — and anti-populism that of the present, fundamentally anti-democratic elites.**

Anti-populism marks the final triumph of the isolated, pseudo-humanist, and privileged political-media classes — which have confiscated the democratic tradition for their own profit.

For some time now, the term 'people' has had bad press. One prefers to speak of the 'republic' — an equally fluid term which has been turned against its original meaning. For the intellectual-media class, 'people' means *petits blancs* — the mass of economically modest, non-privileged French Whites — who form that social category which is expected to pay its taxes, renounce all privilege, and above all keep quiet. **This is why massive naturalisations, jus soli, and the enfranchisement of foreigners in local elections have been introduced: to 'change the people'.**

The dominant ideology pursues a threefold strategy: first, to make ethnic Europeans 'correct' and, if possible, to restrain their reproduction; second, to leave all real power in the hands of international finance; and third, to assure the political class of ample financial rewards. This is the *soft*, modern form of oppression.

A situation like this is inherently fragile: one wonders if the anti-populist, anti-racist politicians ever suspect that once a certain numerical threshold is passed, their Muslim and alien charges will toss them into the rubbish chute of history?

(see **democracy**; **people**)

Preference, European; national preference, alien preference

A political notion inherited from Greek democracy, which accords superior rights to the City's natives — to 'citizens'.

It's an idea of good sense — practiced by all peoples on Earth, except by sick Western societies (France particularly) — the idea that **citizens in their own country ought to have an advantage of rights over foreign residents.** What else could the notion of 'citizenship' — which the Left evokes in every realm, but whose principles it thoughtlessly violates — possibly mean?

Being a native European has become a handicap in our ethnomasochistic societies. French (or European) preference, by an incredible ideological turn, is now considered 'racist'. In France and Belgium there's even discussion of opening the civil service to foreigners.

The notion of 'national preference' is the basis of international law and practiced in every country of the world. Only in Europe is it diabolised and, in a blatant denial of justice, condemned by the courts — constituting in effect a **usurpation of the principle of international reciprocity.** No country accords equal rights to Europeans (let alone superior rights), but Europeans are somehow obliged to grant equal or superior rights to their foreign residents.

*

The so-called 'anti-racist' laws, like massive social welfare programs, lead, objectively, to a situation in which foreigners (even illegal immigrants) are privileged, because once they were allegedly victims of xenophobic exclusion and hatred. **Official anti-racism in this way metamorphosises into an explicit anti-European racism.**

Official policy thus dictates that aliens are to be the beneficiaries of 'positive discrimination'. Protected by specialised associations, championed by the media, recipients of innumerable welfare services and payments, allegedly victimised, foreigners, objectively speaking, are **privileged,** in effect. And these privileges continue to grow along with the incessant arrival of new immigrants. Foreign preference is indeed now the rule — though justice and good sense would seem to dictate a situation of **European preference.** In Morocco, the rule is 'Moroccan preference' — in India, 'Indian preference' — everywhere this is the case, except in Europe.

The courts' condemnation of Catherine Mégret, the mayor of Vitrolles,[108] for allocating 5,000 francs to every newborn child of French or European parentage, reveals the degree to which the rule of ideology, fanaticism, and despotism afflicts all who follow the *natural law* of favouring one's own people.

The refusal of national preference inevitably culminates in foreign preference: another sign that egalitarian ideology has become crazy, that it has inverted the egalitarian principle to favour the

---

108 Catherine Mégret was elected mayor of Vitrolles in 1997 as a member of the National Front, France's largest nationalist party. In 1999, she followed her husband, Bruno Mégret, into the newly formed Mouvement National Républicain, a breakaway party created after his split with FN leader Jean-Marie Le Pen.

superiority of aliens. **Foreign preference is a collective pathology,** imposed by the reigning elites, though it won't last. Such an abnormal situation can only lead — and this will be for the better — to an extremely grave crisis. Social harmony and peace are possible only with the Aristotelian principle of 'every City its own privilege'.

(see **ethnomasochism; race, racism; xenophilia**)

Presentism

Cult of the present, of the moment, of fashion — a cult distinct to Western society — forgetful of the past and indifferent to the future.

Presentism is a form of blindness — it's the behaviour of 'those whose eyes are on the ground, not the sky, not on what's before or behind them' — in the expression of the Breton painter and identitarian Yann-Ber Tillenon.[109]

The long-term is never taken into account. Future generations don't count, the notion of lineage, like that of foresight, is absent. Only the 'present generation' counts. But when a fashion ceases to be fashionable, 'its *look*', as Olivier Carré[110] says, 'becomes tacky'.

Presentism fosters contempt for the survival of one's people. It's a consequence of a narcissistic individualism and the bourgeois spirit. It's become a way of **refusing a common future and a common past, memory and foresight, enrootment and collective ambition, identity and continuity.** Contemporary civilisation is smothered in presentism, which makes it extremely fragile, since it refuses to anticipate the crises that will inevitably befall it; for example, the threat of ethnic

---

109 Yann-Ber Tillenon was a member of GRECE but left in the mid-1980s alongside Guillaume Faye. He later co-founded the Breton group Ker Vreizh and remains active in regionalist and Right-wing circles.

110 Carré (1954–1994) was a painter who collaborated with Faye on the radio programme *Avant-Guerre*. In 1984, they co-produced a satirical audio piece titled *Scène de chasse en ciel d'Europe* (Hunting Scene in the Skies of Europe), which was later adapted into a comic book.

civil war, the inescapable clash with Islam, the dramatic economic consequences of an ageing population, the ecological effects of increased pollution and higher atmospheric temperatures, etc. Presentism affects the public spirit in general, as well as large economic groups, whose strategies are geared to short-term financial performance; it similarly limits political ambitions to the horizon of the next election and the international community fails to reduce the harmful emission of polluting gases. The fate of coming generations has become, in a word, the least of this civilisation's concerns.

Presentism is both the infantile demand for **everything right now** and the undivided reign of the **hic et nunc**.
(see **economism; modernity**)

Progress, progressivism
The belief that history is an ascending movement toward the constant improvement of the human condition.

The idea of progress has been in crisis for a long time (the famous 'disillusions of progress'), since progressivism insists that things are always getting better. The idea, however, is undermined from within by a generalised pessimism and the collapse of any confidence in the future, just as its achievements constantly fall short of expectation. The 'happiness of peoples', rhapsodised by Victor Hugo,[111] had no rendezvous in the Twentieth century — just the opposite. **What's particularly mind-boggling is that progressive ideology (like its modernist counterpart) continues to run in circles, even though the world it has created is heading, full speed, in a fog, toward disaster.**

*

---

[111] Victor Hugo (1802–1885) was one of the most prominent French writers of the Romantic period. He was active in liberal causes for much of his career.

The idea of progress — central to the 'modern' vision of the world since the Seventeenth century — is a secular and materialist offshoot of the religious doctrines of salvation. The Twenty-first century will not bring the end of history, nor the world prosperity of a universal state, but a terrible acceleration of history and a heightening of its tragic essence. Against progressivism, we would do well to substitute the metamorphic vision of history that Heraclitus[112] and Nietzsche inspired: nothing is immutable, nothing is linear. **Life is becoming and thus full of surprises.** Through a *dialectical contradiction* that frequently occurs in history, progressivism and ideologies of history's end have actually provoked a resurgence of history — because of the catastrophes they themselves are producing.

As for 'scientific progress', it possesses, let us repeat, nothing that is qualitative; it is purely quantitative and neutral; it even leads to disaster if not mastered (such as when it succumbs to purely market or profit motives) — or it can lead to significant benefits if thought out, planned, and ordered by the cold lucidity of a political will.

(see **convergence of catastrophes; history; modernity**)

Promethean
The central characteristic of the European's tragic mentality.

Prometheus gave man fire and for this the gods punished him. Chained to a distant, isolated rock, an eagle ate at his liver every day, which he grew back every night. European man possesses an inner fire that consumes him, destroys him, but at the same time elevates him. He is both suicidal and self-constructing. Heidegger, after the Greek *deïnotatos*, called him 'the most risky'.

Unlike the 'submission to God' advocated by the salvation religions, Prometheanism in European history is distinguished by a will to 'equal

---

112 Heraclitus (c. 535 BCE–c. 475 BCE) was a pre-Socratic Greek philosopher. Faye may be referring to his most famous statement, 'One cannot step into the same river twice.'

the divine'. **It combines the will to titanic power (in the Jüngerian**[113] **sense), hubris, rationality, and risk-taking.** Neither 'good' nor 'evil', neither beneficial nor detrimental, it is an inner force that must be ceaselessly mastered. It's to be found among entrepreneurs and among artists, scientists, and statesmen. The allegory of Goethe's Faust, like that of Don Juan, perfectly translates this Prometheanism, which overarches the European tradition. Prometheanism is both **force and feebleness.**

It's a force that produces a defiant, challenging mentality, it's a feebleness that risks succumbing to short-sightedness and self-destructiveness (as depicted in Wagner's *The Twilight of the Gods*).[114]

Prometheanism can be defined as an energy that comes from 'the contradiction of opposites'. Like a chariot harness, it is to be wilfully and forcefully used, for its energy is **order-creating.**

(see **personality, creative; tragedy**)

---

113 Ernst Jünger (1895–1998) was one of the most important German writers of the Twentieth century, and was the preeminent Conservative Revolutionary thinker of the Weimar era. In his book *Der Arbeiter* (*The Worker*), he discusses the idea of the Titanic forces as the heirs of Prometheus, a revolt against the gods which is today manifested particularly in war and technology.

114 *The Twilight of the Gods* is the final part of Richard Wagner's tetralogy of music-dramas, *The Ring of the Nibelung*. It is the story of the god Wotan as he pursues a magic ring which will give him absolute power over the universe. However, in pursuit of this goal, he makes many miscalculations and ends up sabotaging his own plans. At the end of the drama, he destroys himself and the world out of a sense of hopelessness.

R

Race, racism, anti-racism

A genetically distinct population.

The idea of a 'pure race' is obviously not a serious one. It's the **racial fact** that counts. A race can be the stabilised product of an ancient melange. Contemporary genetics, out of favour with the dominant ideology, has well and truly confirmed humanity's division into *genetically statistical populations*.

*

Races are not so much distinguished by phenotypic differences (skin colour, hair, height, etc.) as by genotypic variations affecting temperament and mental abilities — along with **innate physiological and biological differences.**

In reference to Henri Vallois'[115] work, Pierre Vial explains that, 'Identity rests, at root, on a biological reality — a reality that has been the subject of physical anthropology ... This biological belonging conditions numerous human characteristics, both at the individual and collective levels. The man on the street, still possessing a bit of common sense despite the media's ceaseless brainwashing, well knows that there's a difference between a Senegalese and someone from the Auvergne. Difference here doesn't necessarily imply inferiority or superiority'.[116]

The **ethnodifferentialism** Vial invokes differs significantly from the ambiguous concept of *ethnopluralism*. Ethnodifferentialism refuses all cohabitation with different peoples in the same territory, just as it

---

115 Henri Vallois (1889–1981) was a French anthropologist who wrote several books on the subject of race. Some of his works on other subjects have been translated, but his books on race have not.

116 From *Une Terre, un people*.

refuses racial colonisation or domination — while ethnopluralism potentially leads to disaster — supporting, as it does, the 'communitarian' cohabitation of different peoples within the same political territory — a cohabitation that has never succeeded in history and inevitably leads to racism and racial conflict. The notion of race doesn't exhaust that of ethnicity. Race is the biological constituent of ethnicity.

*

For strictly dogmatic reasons, the one-track thought (*la pensée unique*) of the dominant ideology denies even the existence of races (with the pseudo-argument that individual genetic differences are more important than differences between racial groups). It claims it wants to legally combat 'racism' — which is demonised in the way Victorians demonised libertinism. But how, one wonders, can something that supposedly doesn't exist be condemned? And how is it even possible to have 'racism' if races are fictitious?

Anti-racism, the indispensable viaticum of the self-righteous, is actually a form of xenophilia (the valorisation of the 'Other') and of race-phobia. Obsessed and terrified by the fact of race — a major problem with the advent of multi-racial society and the problems it brings — **Western ideology has succumbed to both race-phobia and, contradictorily, race-mania.** To declare oneself 'anti-racist' and to denounce racism are today an obligatory propriety for all ideologues, artists, politicians, and journalists, on the Left and the Right — an obligation as necessary as proclaiming oneself a 'good Muslim' in Saudi Arabia.

In Europe we've reached the absurd point where whoever affirms the 'inequality of races' or the 'superiority of the White race' (true or not, it doesn't matter) is accused of 'racial hatred', even if these affirmations are respectful of other races. Worse: 'to be racist' today (see the case of the Austrian leader of the FPÖ, Jörg Haider),[117] has nothing to

---

117 Jörg Haider (1950–2008) was the leader of Austria's Freedom Party (FPÖ) from 1986 to 2000. In 1999, he led the party to major electoral gains, resulting in a coalition government with the Austrian People's Party in 2000 — an event widely

do with seeing the 'Other' as inferior or with threatening this 'Other', but simply with defending one's own identity or defending oneself from the invasion. This suggests that European elites might have some sort of psychoanalytical problem with race — not unlike the one Victorians had with 'sex'. **Fixated on the question of race, anti-racists repress their own morbid instincts and concealed obsessions.** 'Race' for them is some sort of devilish spirit that needs to be exorcised. **Anti-racism, as such, becomes an ideological exorcism.**

Africans or Asians, in contrast, speak of race and the fact of race as if it were perfectly natural. Arabs and Africans have also recently published works (in France and Great Britain) asserting their intrinsic superiority over 'Whites': Muslim leaders have even affirmed the need 'of eradicating Whites from the planet'. They have never been prosecuted by French authorities. One might conclude from this that the elites don't consider 'anti-White' racism dangerous, since it's implicitly assumed that the White man will always defend himself and be dominant. This implies a certain contempt for other races — for it assumes that Whites will always dominate and that non-Whites are congenitally handicapped and in need of protection. In any case, it demonstrates the **repressed racism of the dominant anti-racist ideology.**

*

'Racial hatred' — an evidently absurd sentiment that reproaches other humans not for their acts but for their being — is an inevitable offshoot of multi-racial society. **All multi-racial societies are multi-racist.** None have ever functioned in harmony. They all generate discriminations.

On the subject of race, the dominant ideology has entangled itself in innumerable and insurmountable contradictions: affirmative action, quotas for Blacks, etc. One recognises the existence of races,

---

condemned abroad as legitimising the Right. In 2005, Haider and others left the FPÖ to form the Alliance for the Future of Austria. Known for his opposition to immigration, he was often accused of National Socialist sympathies. He died in a car accident.

though without recognising their legitimacy. The anti-racism of militants favouring racial quotas (for example, such as those demands for Blacks made by the Égalité collective)[118] is an expression of the most pronounced racism — and has the effect of **racialising society.**

Nothing, moreover, is ever said about 'anti-White racism', which is never repressed, though it's always present. Racism is seen in one way: the ethnic European alone is intrinsically guilty of this original sin.

*

At the end of the Nineteenth century, the neologism 'racism' had neither the same meaning nor the same present pejorative sense. It designated a doctrine that sought to explain differences between peoples and civilisations on the basis of their racial composition — what today we would call a 'genetic' explanation for a people's general character. And, it's everywhere ignored, the first self-proclaimed 'racists' — like Dr. Jules Soury,[119] René Martial,[120] or Jeremy Salmon — were partisans of miscegenation! For these racial pioneers, genetic crosses were the best way of achieving a 'race of aptitude' — wherever 'pure races' had failed because of their excessive specialisation. Like horses or dogs, they thought the human race was to practice selective cross-breeding in order to obtain the best results. **Originally, then, racism was a doctrine of miscegenation.** But thereafter it was added to every

---

118 The Collectif Égalité is an anti-racist organisation set up in France in 1998 by a Cameroonian academic, Calixthe Beyala. The Collectif asked citizens to refuse to pay their TV licenses until a quota for the appearance of Blacks in French television was established. Although no formal quota has ever been set, there has been an increase in the visibility of Blacks since her complaint.

119 Dr. Jules Soury (1842–1915) was a French neuropsychologist who posited a form of 'psychological heredity'.

120 René Martial (1852–1955) was a French anthropologist who supported eugenics and was a proponent of selective immigration by establishing biochemical criteria for anyone who would enter France from abroad. He felt that racial mixing was acceptable as long as immigrants met the necessary requirements. He also used his theories to support the anti-Semitic policies of the Vichy regime.

sauce — given that its powerful, emotional connotations no longer mean much anymore.

One is accused of 'racism' in the West on the basis of the most extravagant claim: whoever defends his identity and homeland from alien colonisers is deemed a 'racist'. Due to some magical quality, Europeans alone produce racist theories. One forgets, for example, the numerous racist and supremacist anti-White positions taken by the African disciples of the Senegalese sociologist Cheikh Anta Diop[121] — whose work the current leaders of the new South Africa or Zimbabwe never stop spreading — without offending anyone.

Racism today is confused with xenophobia. **It's not even a question of racism or anti-racism, but of affirming the importance of race in constituting humanity. Biological differences in this sense are a source of richness; they become sources of conflict only when racial barriers cease to exist.** As De Gaulle explained, France is obviously a country of the White race, and like every such country, it's perfectly able to welcome a small number of minorities (like Blacks from the French West Indies), but it certainly can't become a multiracial society without generating unmanageable conflicts. This is the case with every people. For those lacking a minimum of biological homogeneity are threatened in the long run with internal decomposition. **The racial fact is not everything, of course. But it's there.** To neglect it inevitably leads to catastrophe.

To make the notion of 'race' a taboo, to turn it into a quasi-religious prohibition, nullifies it — which has the added consequences of reversing its effects, for like every 'family secret', it becomes a time bomb. Its repercussions are easily imagined.

(see **chaos, ethnic; ethnomasochism; people; xenophilia**)

---

121 Cheikh Anta Diop (1923–1986) was primarily an anthropologist who is best known for postulating that the ancient Egyptians were Black Africans and thus the progenitors of civilisation. He also attempted to demonstrate the cultural and genetic unity of all African peoples, a unity which he believed would help to liberate Africa from colonial oppression.

Region, regionalism

A region is an ethno-geographic sub-grouping of a far larger bloc to which it belongs. Though not constituting a state or a people in itself, the region is a place of enrootment and a place of irreplaceable identity, especially in Europe.

Europe's regions are fundamental to the Continent. An entity of human scale, the region is heir to a long history that has fostered an identity, a sense of place and belonging, a community that is a counter-weight to an anonymous cosmopolitanism and a bureaucratic centralism.

The regions (beyond the geographic variations provoked by centuries of hazard) represent **Europe's constituent parts, her basic elements, which have made and unmade the various empires and nation-states marking her history.**

The region, as such, is the polycentric expression of the global unity of European peoples. It's an organic sub-group, an internal division, a reserve of ethnic memory—that helps avoid the fragile rigidity of national 'blocs'. An example of this can be seen in the fact that non-European aliens readily call themselves 'French' or 'Belgian', etc., on the basis of the catastrophic *jus soli*, but it's far more difficult to call themselves 'Scots', 'Burgundians', 'Sicilians', 'Bavarians', etc.

For ethnographic reasons, globalisation can never weaken the regional imperative. Only reinforce it.

*

Pierre Vial sums up the question in this way: 'Regional identities remain living and demand constant affirmation. This is obviously truer in some regions more than in others. To deny an Alsatian identity, a Breton identity, a Basque identity, or a Corsican identity is an absurdity, a non-starter … There's no need to confine ourselves to the present state of France, with its cold, rigid system … We favour a European confederation resting on a recognition and an affirmation of the Europe of the peoples. Europe of a hundred flags?[122] Perhaps even more. In any case, we favour a Europe with flesh and blood fatherlands (*patries charnelles*)'.[123] In endeavouring to organically (imperially) reconcile the ideas of regional enrootment, the historic nation, and Europe, Vial continues, **'It's not a matter of denigrating French identity, as bad-faith critics assert, but rather of giving this identity another chance of being realised** ... We need to affirm an identity that integrates two imperatives: to transcend the nation-state from on high, through Europe — and to transcend it from below, through the region'. Vial appeals to a **'Confederated French Republic'** (the Sixth Republic), conceived on the model of the German *Länder*,[124] but also on the basis of the Spanish experience, the Swiss canton, etc. He adds, 'It's within a regionalist framework that we'll be able to return to the political — that is, to being citizens who act directly on their own destiny. It will be a beautiful application of subsidiarity'. He concludes by affirming **the necessity of regrouping in the future all flesh and blood fatherlands (patries charnelles), all organic regional entities,** of Indo-European origin, **within a single continental Eurosiberian bloc,** imbued with a destiny of power obviously unrelated to the parody of Europe now represented by the European Union.

*

This vision of things — the sole realistic and ambitious strategy of European defence — rests on the following principles:

---

122 This term was coined by the Breton nationalist Yann Fouéré in his book *Towards a Federal Europe: Nations or States?* (Swansea: Christopher Davies, 1980).

123 From *Une Terre, un people*.

124 'States', which in present-day Germany includes Bavaria and Saxony. The German states are set up on a federalist model in which the various states retain a significant degree of autonomy from the national government, such as in retaining the right to sign treaties with foreign powers.

1. There exist regions with strong identities and ones with weaker identities. Identity nevertheless constructs itself. It's not simply a heritage, it's also a work. The organic, imperial principle is not mechanistic.

2. **The 'regionalism of the Left', this Trotskyite and globalist imposture, is no different from the cosmopolitan centralism of the Jacobins.** Such 'regionalists' are as supportive of the present colonising immigration as Parisian universalists.

3. Regional attachment is not secessionist. It's inscribed in a far larger ensemble, infused with power and sovereignty: 'The union makes us strong'. A central state (not a centralising state), imbued with a will and a project, is now more than ever necessary.

4. The 'French problem' won't be solved in an emotional manner, but constructively. **A regionalist re-enrootment, moreover, will do nothing to threaten French cultural identity**, just as it hasn't in Germany, Spain, Poland, Russia, etc.

5. In the long term, regions might replace the present *départements*,[125] heritage of the Revolution's abstract, identity-destroying rationalism.

6. It's necessary to denounce the ambiguities of certain regionalists: Savoyan autonomists, for example, who, in imitation of their Breton counterparts, accord their regional identity to all residents, even non-Europeans.

*

---

125 The present-day departments of France were set up in 1790 during the French Revolution. The departments were purposefully designed to break up the historical regions which had existed previously in an attempt to eliminate local identities in favour of a more universal, national identity.

The region is no panacea, no miraculous solution; it's a fluid but undeniable reality, marking a well-identified **territory**. Regionalisation will enable the central state to better govern and, paradoxically, to strengthen its political function by reducing its preoccupation with local administration. The efficacy of America's federal state system, for example, is partly due to the fact that it leaves interior administration to the states, which enables it to better defend the Union's federal power.
(see **enrootment; Europe; Eurosiberia; fatherland; nation**)

Resistance and Reconquest

Faced with their colonisation by peoples from the South and by Islam, Europeans, objectively speaking, are in a situation of resistance. Like Christian Spain between the Eighth and Fifteenth centuries, their project is one of reconquest.

These two notions of resistance and reconquest are intimately linked. Resistance today is called 'racism' or 'xenophobia', just as native resisters to colonial occupation were formerly characterised as 'terrorists'. This is a matter of diabolising and incapacitating those who, in good faith, become conscious of the tragic reality confronting their people and seek thus to resist their subjugation and extinction.

*

A semantic reversal is in order here: those—under the anti-racist banner of pseudo-humanitarianism—who favour the immigrant replacement population, whether they're politicians or self-proclaimed philosophers, ought, henceforth, to be called **'collaborators'**.

Reconquest will not become a conscious necessity until people feel their backs against the wall, not until tragedy knocks at the door and they sense its urgency.

Not until the state is visibly colonised by aliens and Muslims (which won't be long for reasons of demographics and enfranchisement) will there be revolt and resistance. For revolt and resistance arise only in the face of a power seen as alien and illegitimate. For the moment, civil society alone is affected and power still appears to be in native hands — thus no serious resistance is yet possible. But soon, in the course of things, aliens and Muslims will have their own municipalities, legislative deputies, and ministers. **It's of some urgency, then, that we start preparing and organising the resistance — by every means possible, politically and metapolitically — so as to ready ourselves for that moment when the alien colonisers start taking over the public powers.**

*

One of the principal bases of reconquest will evidently consist in **Europe's demographic redressing,** even though the situation is already far gone, since nothing at the moment will halt the massive influx of immigrants and naturalisations, as well as the influx coming from the maternity wards (a third of 'French' births!) — all of which, of course, threatens a veritable ethnic deluge. This has got to be one of central programmatic issues of every conscious political party.

Another key component of reconquest will obviously be that of **liberation. The repatriation of aliens can only be accomplished under the auspices of a revolutionary crisis.** Many of our false sages claim that it's already too late, that the aliens will never leave, that the best that can be expected is a more reasonable form of ethnic cohabitation. Hence, their tall tales of 'integration' and peaceful 'communitarianism'. This view, however, stems from a renunciation of hope, from an acceptance of Europe's death, from blindness and suicidal propensities — all in the name of a false intellectualist realism that consistently misjudges history.

Those fatalistically accepting the inescapable and growing presence of the alien masses actually do so on the basis not of reasoned analysis, but simply because they lack ethnic consciousness. What they see as the 'impossibility' of reconquest and repatriation comes, as such, from an indifference to their own people and destiny, not from any objective study of the matter.

*

On the contrary: nothing tells us what tomorrow will bring. **To attend to the imperatives of resistance and reconquest is the only veritable realism.** What seems improbable today will perhaps tomorrow appear certain, as the unthinkable becomes thinkable and the unrealisable realisable. Quite simply because the irruption of an emergency completely changes both what is given and what is valued.

*

Here are a few such examples: the Spanish *Reconquista,* the French abandonment of Algeria, the recovery of Alsace-Lorraine,[126] the Soviet collapse of 1991, Germany's defeat in 1945, its reunification in 1991, and, more immediately, Islam's transformation into France's main religion: all these examples were reputedly unthinkable according to 'analyses' made before their occurrence! There's no determined course to history — or rather its course is determined by the **idealism of the will** — in tandem with brutal changes brought on by crises or civil wars.

*

We cannot, of course, imagine exactly how the reconquest will occur. We think with the blinders of present-day reality. The essential, though, is to affirm the spirit of resistance, now and everywhere to come — summoning the idea-force of reconquest, even if we still don't know *how* it is to be realised. The Africanisation and Islamisation of Europe are simply unacceptable and must be seen as something entirely provisional. We also shouldn't forget that **resistance and**

---

126 Alsace-Lorraine was a territory created by the German Empire following its annexation of the regions from France in the Franco-Prussian War of 1870–71. This region was returned to France in the Treaty of Versailles that ended the First World War.

reconquest will need to be organised at the European level, and not merely nationally.
(see **colonisation; consciousness, ethnic; idea**)

Revolution
A violent reversal of the political situation, following the advent of a crisis and the intervention of an active minority.

Marxism's imposture has been in proclaiming itself revolutionary, while pursuing a revolution, like the French Revolution before it, that followed a pre-existing ideological and political system. A true revolution is *metamorphic,* that is, it's a radical transformation of values. The sole revolutionary of the modern era is Nietzsche, because he alone sought 'a revaluation of all values' — unlike Marx, who simply favoured a 'dialectical' evolution of bourgeois society. It's necessary for this reason to be extremely distrustful of the attraction certain intellectuals have for those tendencies associated with the German Conservative Revolution of the inter-war period,[127] which may have resisted modernity, but in the most reactionary way — since it implicitly advocated a return to the 'old world', to 'old values', and to a nostalgic resurrection of the 'past'.

'Revolution' (like 'people') is a term that horrifies the former revolutionaries of 1968, who now occupy important political and media positions and who have become (to use a Marxist term that they once used against their adversaries) the system's *watchdogs*.

*

---

127 The Conservative Revolution is a term first coined by Hugo von Hoffmansthal, which has come to designate a loose confederation of anti-liberal German thinkers who wrote during the Weimar Republic. There was a great diversity of views within the ranks of the Conservative Revolutionaries, but in general they opposed both democratic capitalism and Communism in favour of a synthesis of the German (and especially Prussian) aristocratic traditions with socialism.

For Europeans, revolution represents a radical abolition, a reversal, of the present system and the construction of a totally new political reality, based on the following principles:

1. An **ethnocentric Eurosiberia,** free of Islam and the Third World's colonising masses.
2. **Continental autarky**, in rupture with globalism's free-trade doctrines. This implies adopting the criteria of an organic economy — industrially and financially, as well as socially and ecologically.
3. A definitive **break with the present organisation of the European Union** — ungovernable, devoid of sovereignty and influence, lacking a credible system of defence, and indifferent to the peoples who compose it — a break for the sake of a radically different Europe.
4. A general recourse to an inegalitarian society that is disciplined, authentically democratic, aristocratic, and inspired by Greek humanism.

We are far from all this. This is why only a major crisis — the convergence of catastrophes — has the capacity to unblock the situation and to revive our sclerotic civilisation. **We have long since passed the point of no return,** the point where it's still possible to check the prevailing decadence through peaceful reform. In no case will the European Revolution be a 'velvet revolution'.
(see **autarky of great spaces; economy, organic**)

Right to Difference

The right of every people, ethnos, culture, nation, group, or community to live according to its own norms and traditions, irrespective of ideology or globalist homogenisation.

It's an ambiguous notion, like that of 'ethnopluralism'. Conceptually, the 'right to difference' refers back to the differentialist theory, which holds that every people, every ethnic group, is incompatible. It assumes, as such, the doctrine of 'each in his own home', the refusal to mix, and a critique of Western and American cultural homogenisation, with its assimilationist policies. Doctrinally, the 'right to difference' can also be used to oppose the economic myth of 'development' and the Westernisation of the Third World's traditional subsistence economy.

From this perspective, differentialism is positive. There are nevertheless numerous possible derivatives of it that are less than positive. First off, to what degree is 'difference' to be tolerated? Is it acceptable that agriculturalists in tropical countries destroy primal rainforests? How tolerable are harmful social practices carried out in the name of difference? The concept of difference seems truly ambiguous.

*

To demand the 'right to difference' for Europeans in Europe also seems a bit much, as if they were already a minority in need of protecting! This perversion of the 'right to difference' came initially from the multi-racialist ideologues of the *Nouvelle Droite*, who accept the presence of alien communities and, terrorised by accusations of racism and ethnocentrism, defend the 'right to difference' for both ethnic Europeans and aliens residing in Europe ... This ploy, however, didn't quite pay off, for despite their best effort, the good Monsieur Taguieff,[128] master of anti-racism, accused them of a 'differentialist racism'! In any case, **Europeans in Europe don't need to demand the right to difference, but rather the monopolistic right to exist according to their own model and their own civilisation,** with minorities allowed but a minimum right. To say this is to affirm the good sense practiced by every people. In the classical Greek humanist treatment of 'differences', foreigners were accorded certain civil rights, in exchange for their cooperation.

---

128 Pierre-André Taguieff (1946-) is a French sociologist whose work has focused particularly on the issue of racism. Some of his writings on the New Right have appeared in the American journal *Telos*.

The 'communitarian' adepts of the right to difference are now demanding that aliens be given the same rights as native citizens (especially the right to vote) and, at the same time, that they be allowed to conserve the customs of their community This is not the right to difference but the right to privilege. This is the contradictory position taken by the Greens, the Trotskyites of the PS,[129] and the 'modern' Right of Alain Madelin[130] and others — the first two out of ideological fanaticism, the third out of a cowardly opportunism.

Within a specific political entity and within a single people, the right to difference is never an absolute doctrine, tolerant of every difference, whatever it may be. The 'right to difference' risks becoming the 'right to tolerate everything'. As evident in every multi-racial, multicultural, multi-confessional society, **social harmony is impossible because differences remain too important.** Even overly diverse mores are inimical to a group's equilibrium. **Heterogeneity is tolerable only when subordinated to the organic principle of homogeneity.**

To speak, for example, of the 'homosexual community' constitutes a dangerous trend. Pushed further, this right to difference leads to **tribalism,** social dissolution, and thus to 'de-civilisation'.

In the case of Islam, integration-assimilation (the application of the right to difference) is simply impossible. Once it achieves a certain force in the state, Islam will no longer tolerate peaceful cohabitation with Christianity, Judaism, Buddhism, Hinduism, animism — not to mention paganism and atheism. It's absurd to demand the right to difference for those who would deny it to others.

The political and social harmony of a country supposes a minimum of ethnic and cultural unity. Said differently, **the right to difference is a concept valid at the geopolitical level (each in his own home,**

---

129 Parti Socialiste, the Socialist Party of France.

130 Alain Madelin (b. 1946) was a member of the National Assembly of France and the president of the Démocratie Libérale (Liberal Democracy) party. He was known for his pro-American and laissez-faire economic positions. He retired from politics in 2007.

each within his own boundaries), but invalid domestically, within a specific political unity. As partisans of the right to difference, who assume integration is possible without assimilation, communitarians ignore the lessons of history. They believe in the possibility (following the failure of the assimilationist *melting pot*) of an egalitarian society of juxtaposed castes.

These differentialist theories defended by the extreme Left, American liberals, French ultra-liberals, and certain Right-wing intellectuals are extremely dangerous: **they have passed from an egalitarianism of assimilation to an egalitarianism of juxtaposition,** which is one of the worst forms of egalitarian doctrine. As such, the 'right to difference', through a conceptual perversion, ideologically leads to a justification for homophilia (pro-homosexual favouritism), to legitimising 'positive discrimination'[131] (affirmative action) and racial quotas favouring alien populations, and to the most grotesque forms of feminism.

Diverted from its original objective (the right of every people to conserve its identity and homogeneity), the right to difference becomes a weapon in the war against Europe's ethnic cohesion and identity. **Starting out as pro-identitarian, the right to difference thus eventually becomes anti-identitarian.**

In its own land, a healthy people demands **an ethnocultural monopoly.** According to the Greeks, a harmonious ('organic') City presupposes the cohabitation of slight differences within the federating order of a larger community; differences, in a word, are subsumed to the Unity of the City, the latter being not some gray uniformity, but the gathering of natural differences — **within an organic totality, within a sole fasces.**

The symbolic image of the **pyramid,** as the Ancient Egyptians understood it, is extremely eloquent. A civilisation, like a building, is a living organism which must be protected from excessive uniformity, as

---

131 This term is equivalent to 'affirmative action' in the United States.

well as from excessive differentiations (social, ethnic, customary, etc.), for once *philia* (i.e., the 'convergence of sentiments' of which Aristotle spoke) ceases to exist, popular solidarity collapses. **The right to difference, like every right, must be limited, normalised, and counterbalanced by the duties of membership, which accompany it.**
(see **ethnocentrism; philia**)

S

Sacred

The quality of transcendent collective values that are capable, through ritual and symbol, of provoking a psychological mobilisation.

The sacred transcends the self, it appeals to a superior dimension, whatever the belief one holds. It may or may not be imbued with the 'divine' and it's attached to no single, particular religion.

Our present civilisation is desacralised, disenchanted; it has distorted and recuperated the sacred in the form of simulacra — and through a mix of New Age superstitions, whose inspirations are American in origin.

*

The drama of contemporary Europe — the cause of her present crisis and ethno-demographic decline — is in large part attributable to the absence of the sacred. In the face of a conquering Islam, one of whose motor forces is religious faith (however one might judge it), Europeans lack **an inner collective motivation;** their only recourses are immanent ones: the desire to maximise consumption, and to acquire signs of wealth. In themselves, these aspirations are perfectly natural (the quest for material opulence is an integral part of human psychology), but alone they cannot breathe life into a people or a culture.

Let's take the case of contemporary 'art': it's obvious degeneracy stems not just from the fact that artists lack 'talent' or aesthetic 'know-how', but from the fact that *they no longer want* these qualities, given that they no longer possess a sense of the sacred — that is, the inspiration, the interior flame that connects them to the invisible. This sacred deficit comes from the regnant *bourgeois spirit*, but it's also due to the abandonment of Christianity's sacred dimension (Protestant or post-conciliar), handed down by medieval Catholicism, itself the heir of paganism.

The essential elements of the sacred are the cult of the dead, of ancestors, and the various rites and rituals accompanying the different stages of human life (birth, death, etc.) — that is, **everything that makes the perpetuation of a people's lineage transcendent**. In this sense, the sacred is not some ethereal notion, radically separated from the 'profane', but rather a vertical link between life, biological reality, and what, *faute de mieux*,[132] is called the soul.

The sacred is inconceivable without a permanent bond between ancestors, from whom one receives heritage, and descendents, who are just as important as the present generation — something the contemporary mind finds totally absurd and incomprehensible.

(see **bourgeoisism; paganism**)

Selection

The collective process, based on competition, that eliminates the weakest and least competent, and that favours the most gifted and capable.

Selection concerns the natural evolution of the species, as well as the history of civilisations and the internal life of societies.

---

132 French: 'for want of something better'.

Natural selection privileges the survival of the fittest and thus the perpetuation of the species. This is the case in biology, as well as sociology. Every organisation, every system, that neglects selection is bound to disappear. Selection rarely assumes the form of a direct struggle. But it's truly the central principle of all life and of every civilisation. **The 'superiority' of a people, a species, or a civilisation rests, in the last instance, on its capacity for long-term survival, on its ability to overcome the snares thrown up by selection and to win the competition.** In this sense, a 'static racism' that judges one phylogenetic group superior to another is absurd.

Selective pressures touch everything: cultural forms, the circulation of elites, as well as the traditions filtered through history's sorting process. Selection is not an unjust form of discrimination, as egalitarian ideologues have it. Rather, it's the motor of life. **And though egalitarianism rejects the principle of selection, it cannot eliminate it. It instead replaces a socially organised selection with an unjust, primitive selection** based on nepotism, money, violence, etc.

*

In a healthy society, Nietzsche said, 'it's the strongest, most gifted who are aided'. This doesn't imply injustice for the least able. For the pinnacle of injustice, as evident today, comes from an anti-selection that leads to chaos and to a selection based on asocial criteria, which is a disaster for the entire community. The hatred of selection was a major theme of May '68, responsible for the present dilapidation of the national school system.

Contemporary society raises numerous obstacles to a just selection and thereby establishes a selection based on injustice and the law of the jungle.

There's nothing inequitable about selection, it's the acceptance of life, of the *natural hierarchy* of things — following Plato, Aristotle, and

Spencer's 'to each his own'.[133] In the European tradition, **the democratic principle is inseparable from the aristocratic principle — i.e., the selective principle.** A society without a real aristocracy, where the 'best' are not in charge, quickly turns to injustice and to the oppression of the weakest. Selection, in this sense, is no injustice to the weak, nor does it eliminate or exclude them, but instead guarantees their proper position within the social organism.

*

To claim, as egalitarian doctrines do, that everyone is as gifted as everyone else, and that hierarchical selection is contrary to the principles of humanity, is, as Pascal[134] saw, a 'monstrous lie' — something that can only dissolve society. An absolute egalitarianism refusing an open selection thus destroys all fraternity, all social order — for it allows dissimulated forms of selection to occur — based on preferential treatment, bought privileges, acquired advantages, etc. There is no greater injustice than to deny the most gifted and deserving their place — for the sake of according privileges to the incapable. The *égalité* and *fraternité* of the French Republic seem perfectly incompatible.
(see **aristocracy; egalitarianism; hierarchy; meritocracy**)

Society, Market

One of the appellations of present Western society — in which the market (or economic) function takes the place of the sovereign function and becomes the *ultima ratio*[135] — the ultimate and unique horizon against which all political decisions are made.

---

133 Herbert Spencer (1820–1903) was an English philosopher who first gave rise to the notion of 'social Darwinism'. He coined the phrase 'survival of the fittest' to describe Darwin's theories.

134 Blaise Pascal (1623–1662) was a French Catholic philosopher.

135 Latin: 'last resort'.

This term is preferable to that of 'capitalist society'. For it's not a matter of condemning the market economy, but rather of **deploring the market's dictatorship over every other consideration** (ecological, ethnic, aesthetic, social, etc.). The market can't be everything and material exchanges can't be the basis of social relations. In market society, everything has a price, but nothing is of value.

We need to be suspicious of the dogmatic criticisms Rightists (fascinated with the Marxist critique of capitalism) make of market society — as they proclaim their contempt for the market, the general economy, prosperity, and the imperatives of industrial power and techno-science. This is hypocritical, for the daily lives of these Rightists are, in practice, fully immersed in bourgeois consumerism. Imitating the extreme Left, they like to call themselves **'anti-utilitarians'** — a purely scholastic, disembodied posture, typical of Parisian intellectualism.

*

It's not a matter of rejecting the market, the productive-economic sphere, and techno-scientific power in the name of some anti-utilitarian utopia, but of **subordinating market functions to the sovereign function and thus putting them in service to the people, to its welfare, and to Grand Politics.**

It's no less necessary to denounce the imposture of bureaucratic socialism, which, in the name of combating market society and the 'dictatorship of capital', ends up creating social, economic, corporate, and parasitic feudalities not unlike those of market society.

Those who seek to abolish the market, like those who see it as the pinnacle of all things, are inclined to reductionism. **The market is nevertheless indispensable: it's a weapon in the hand of sovereignty — a means, not an end.**

At the global level, market society abandons the market to its own hazards — for these markets lack governance. Hence the fragility of a speculative economy prone to brutal, unforeseeable crises, as well as the impossibility of controlling the frontiers and, for Europe, of assuring its economic autonomy. Hence also the subjugation of states to economic conjunctures (the boom/bust cycles based on the market's temper), over which they now have no power. Like wine, the market is indispensable in controlled doses; once it becomes society's unique reference, society is turned into a drunken boat.

(see **autarky; economy, organic; liberalism; mercantilism**)

Sovereignty, the sovereign function, tri-functionality, bi-functionality

A people's controlling power, animated by authority, justice, and evenhandedness, capable of representing both its immediate interest and historical destiny.

The sovereign function cannot be simply an offshoot of 'democracy'. It has to have a sacral dimension if it is to assume and assure a people's longevity. There are several historical instances of sovereignty: the hereditary monarch, the acclaimed emperor, an elected president, etc. In any case, there are no ready-made forms of sovereignty. With it, it's necessary to reconcile the principle of popular authority and the sacred, sovereign function. The latter monopolises power for the sake of 'Grand Politics'. It organises society and economics without overwhelming them and causing them to spurn their responsibilities — it wages war — it decides a people's historical orientation, of which it takes charge. The essence of the sovereign function is imperial and organic, based on principles of subsidiarity: it's no substitute for other functions, but rather pursues a people's general interest, determining its fundamental orientation.

The drama of contemporary Europe resides in the **disappearance of every form of sovereignty**. The state no longer possesses sovereignty, since it no longer pursues historical goals nor does it have the power or will to act in the name of the collective destiny. The bureaucracies, the political class, and the economic forces manage a society without a head; the European Union is hardly sovereign.

In this respect, there's no need to instrumentalise Georges Duzmézil's theory of 'the three Indo-European functions' (the first: sovereign, sacred function; the second: warrior function; the third: productive or economic function).[136] As I see it, **only two principal functions can possibly coexist**, especially in the world that is coming: **a sovereign function and a socioeconomic function.** Within an imperial context, the sovereign function ought to subsume the military or 'warrior' function. The autonomy of the latter usually ends in disaster. **Bi-functionality seems more pertinent than the theory of the three functions.** The sovereign function embraces everything related to destiny and will, to the *longue durée* — the socioeconomic function addresses the management of everyday needs. More profoundly, the 'functions' pertain less to their activity than to the level of their importance. In the economy, for example, there are fundamental decisions that belong to politics and the sovereign function. As to questions of the people's 'defence', in all its applications and domains, it should never escape the sovereign function. **The theory of tri-functionality — overly abstract and intellectual — could thus replace the theory of bi-functionality, which is more concrete and better adapted to the world that is coming.**

The question of knowing if sovereignty ought to be 'republican' or 'monarchical', 'royal' or 'presidential' is badly posed. The kings of France, like the Roman emperors, utilised the word 'republic' to signify that the idea of sovereignty is a public service — a political 'thing'. In this sense, the position of Marx or Maurras,[137] of Rousseau or De Gaulle needs to be criticised, for in all their estimations institutions, in

---

136 Georges Dumézil (1898–1986) was a French philologist best known as a pioneer in mythography. He also studied the nature of sovereignty in ancient Indo-European civilisations, which led him to postulate the Trifunctional Hypothesis: namely, that Indo-European culture had developed along a tripartite structure of warriors, priests and farmers. He believed that this was the origin of both the Hindu caste system and the feudal system in medieval Europe.

137 Charles Maurras (1863–1952) was a French nationalist counter-revolutionary ideologue who was the founder of the Right-wing Action Française.

the formal sense, were the miraculous solution to the problem of good government. Everything, though, depends on the state of the soul, on the people's biological and spiritual state: **a healthy people always finds the sovereignty appropriate to it.**

*

In reality, there's no sovereignty that doesn't emanate from a people's soul, from its inner force, and its will to live — no sovereignty if there isn't a bond between a people's spiritual and historical nature, its ultimate source of legitimacy, and its principle of popular support. No monarch, no president, no commissioner, no general secretary, no emperor can 'institute' sovereignty if it doesn't already exist in a **people's identity and longevity.**

Sovereignty is *auctoritas* — that is, authority — that is, action.

There's no sovereignty if it doesn't aspire to perpetuate itself, if it isn't infused with a superior illumination, by a legitimacy that comes not just from below but from above, that is inspired and justified by a sacred spark. The entire question is a matter of redefining and regenerating the sacred.

(see **born leader; personality, creative; politics; sacred**)

State, nation-state, statism

The governing authority of a people or an instituted society as a political and territorial unit.

Whatever its form, the state — what the Romans called *Res publica*, that is, 'public and common institutions' — has always existed, except in tribal societies. The mandarins of the Chinese Empire, Roman administration, and that of the Greek cities or the Inca kings were states. Beginning in the Seventeenth century, with the advent of the modern era, the state started becoming tentacular. In contemporary democracies, nominal and functionary authorities (the 'public powers') are associated with elected authorities (government, municipal assemblies, regional authorities, etc.) Whether the national parliament ('the legislative power') is part of the state or part of civil society is still a matter of debate.

The **crisis of the modern state** has taken several forms in Europe. First off, it's been set up as a protected, privileged caste (an army made up of millions of functionaries), which lives at the expense of society's vital forces. Hence the question: does the state serve the people or do the people serve the state? Next: the state's pachydermatous weight has become another measure of political impotence. It overwhelms society without undertaking grand projects or movements. And then, it clashes with the competing powers of European technocracy and transnational business, doing so in ways that foster both a top-heavy state and, at the same time, deprives it of power. It's corrupted by the feudalities of the parties, devoid of an ideological project, and designed as a career-making machine. Actually, the state no longer governs. It no longer obeys its popular representatives. It no longer embodies a general will: it has lost all influence over the course of things. **It's no longer even a political authority and is not to be confused with the sovereign function it allegedly represents.** The paradox, in this era of free trade and collapsing social rights, is that we are witnessing an expansion of the state's parasitism. Given that it no longer performs its titulary tasks, it's rapidly losing its legitimacy.

Statism is the opposite of a strong state, it's merely a 'large' state. With statism, the state no longer exercises the sovereign function, but serves as a bureaucratic regime indifferent to the general interest: in this capacity, it acts in service to a caste, its enormous apparatus of functionaries. Everything happens as if the state's primary occupation is itself, that is, the privilege of its functionaries and its self-reproducing class of politicians. Paradoxically, we West Europeans are experiencing both **the increased prominence and decline of the state.** As its political force fades, its burdensome regulatory, sociological, and financial weight becomes increasingly insupportable.

*

Europe today is beset by **a global crisis of sovereignty,** resolvable neither by the impotent nation-states nor the European Union, both of which lack a political will and the necessary instruments of power. The sole solution would seem to entail doing away with all compromise and **constructing, in the course of the Twenty-first century, a grand-European state — federal, imperial, ethnocentric, and decentralised.** This would resume the former unifying efforts of the Roman and Carolingian Empires.
(see **Eurosiberia**)

State of Emergency[138]

An event whose unexpected convulsion disrupts the political situation and requires an immediate decision based on the rules of exception.

The state of emergency, as conceived by Carl Schmitt, is the stuff of history. It calls forth the great political figures and overturns established opinions. The 'state of emergency' is 'incorrect' and unthinkable within Western humanitarian and liberal political thought.

The liberal, bourgeois vision of politics and history approaches a state of emergency in terms of foreseeability, rationality, managerial normality, and peace, though it's actually a matter of risk, struggle, crisis, and ongoing emergency. In this respect, Robert Steuckers writes that it's necessary 'to pay constant attention to the *Ernstfall* (the state of emergency and the exception), to sudden irruptions (*das Plötzliche*), to the unexpected (*das Unerwartete*), as they are experienced, for they require an immediate decision (*eine Entscheidung*)'.

---

138 Carl Schmitt discusses the concept of *Ernstfall*, or the state of emergency, at length in his book *Political Theology* (Chicago: University of Chicago Press, 2005).

The outbreak of an ethnic civil war in Europe would constitute a distinct state of emergency, becoming a handmaiden of history, as it disrupts established mentalities and creates a situation in which the unthinkable and the impossible become thinkable and possible. Solely in states of emergency are real solutions found, true leaders brought to the fore, and peoples awakened. **For man, this short-sighted animal, only reacts when his back is against the wall. Crisis is the motor of history.**
(see **born leader**)

T

Techno-science
Technique derived from the scientific approach of the experimental method, which aims at enhancing the possibilities of action and domination.

A creation of European civilisation, techno-science is Promethean in essence. It's tragic and contradictory, the best of aspirations and the worst of dangers. For European peoples threatened by their demographic weakness, by devirilisation, by their submersion into the peoples of the South, bio-genetics can serve as a provisional recourse. Similarly, applied to armaments, techno-science is an indispensable shield, capable of compensating for Europe's lack of numbers.

But **techno-science is neutral.** It's a grave error, to which Habermas[139] and Heidegger have succumbed, to think that it can be, *sui generis*,[140] the bearer of some ideology. It's a weapon, a means, with which one can do what one wants. Techno-science is harmful if left

---

139 Jürgen Habermas (b 1929) is a German Marxist philosopher. He discusses the relationship between technology and ideology in his book *Technik und Wissenschaft als 'Ideologie'* (Frankfurt am Main: Suhrkamp, 1968).

140 Latin: 'of its own kind'.

solely at the mercy of the market's logic, positive if submitted to a sovereign will. It represents no opposition to tradition, but is an essential element of the European heritage — having first appeared with Pythagoras' school.[141] It's this force of alchemy, of which the medieval masters spoke. Techno-science is neither 'modern' nor 'materialist' in essence, but both traditional and futurist.

(see **archeofuturism; Promethean; will to power**)

Third Worldism

Doctrine, on the Left and Right, which claims the Third World has been 'exploited' — and that it's advisable to aid it, unceasingly, with financial and technological transfers, and to welcome its migrants.

Third Worldism is a snake that swallows its own tail: in claiming to aid poor countries, it deserts and divests itself of all actual responsibility for them. It imposes on these lands a Western economic model, destructive of local economies. One pities the Third World in terms of a self-culpabilising charity.

The proper attitude to the Third World is one of relative *indifference*, the opposite of the present 'right to intervene'. Europe has no obligation to peoples whose destiny is not their own. The endemic poverty, wars, and epidemics that ravage certain parts of Africa, Asia, and Latin America are not our concern. These populations are alone guilty of their incapacity to govern themselves. We are not 'responsible' for them. **To let the Third World take responsibility for its own fate requires that we refuse to assist it.** Besides, the Third World — this notion created in the 1960s by Alfred Sauvy[142] to designate those countries that belonged neither to the Western nor the Soviet spheres

---

141 Pythagoras (c. 570–c. 495 BCE) was a pre-Socratic philosopher who founded the Pythagorean Brotherhood, an esoteric body which made some of the earliest investigations into science and mathematics in Western history. Their ideas remained highly influential for thousands of years.

142 Alfred Sauvy coined the term in an article which appeared in L'Observateur on 14 August 1952. He initially intended it as a reference to the Third Estate in

and that were mainly former European colonies — has lost its former pertinence. What does a Mali, an Argentine, and a South Korean have in common? The notion of the Third World, though fluid, nevertheless retains an association with 'poor countries'. But why 'poor'? Third Worldists argue that the **countries of the North have exploited the Third World, while the reverse is true.** Europeans need to invert the charges and work on shedding whatever guilt they might feel toward it.

*

Third World parasitism takes the following forms:

1. Direct financial costs in the form of lost loans, European-financed exports, the annulment of debt, etc.

2. The cost of technical aid and cooperation, as well as technological transfers. Despite massive aid, no African or Arab country has ever attained even a modicum of economic balance.

3. The cost of exploiting raw materials in the Third World. For fifty years we've been told that we exploited the countries of the South. Their petroleum, raw materials, and their agriculture would, though, be of no use to Europe, if she thought geopolitically — in terms of a 'Eurosiberian space'. No Muslim oil exporter, for example, would be able to exploit the subsoil reserves of his country on his own. These reserves have been discovered and exploited by foreign companies, who pay an enormous rent for them. **Eurosiberia would have no need of Third World resources.**

4. The worst, the heaviest burden: dumping its excess population in Europe, which is equivalent to overwhelming her demographically and hamstringing her with an economic ball and chain.

France at the time of the French Revolution, which consisted of the majority of the population, yet had little in the way of political influence.

*

A certain number of legends also need to be resisted. Specifically the legend that European colonialism, in the form of exploitation and slavery, was a sin for which we must forever repent. This thesis of assigning blame is especially promoted by Algeria. European colonialism, though, was harmful to Europe, though it benefited the Third World, whose demography it vastly developed. This has boomeranged against Europe — an immense historical error. For **European colonialism was the starting point for the South's colonisation of Europe.**

It also needs emphasising that in the period of European colonisation, Third World populations, notably in the Maghreb, the Middle East, and Africa, lived under conditions of peace, liberty, public order, and prosperity far superior to whatever 'independence' brought. All Africans and Maghrebians of good faith who were born before independence today realise this.

*

Third Worldism, like anti-racism, is a pseudo-philanthropic doctrine that blames and paralyses Europeans. Unfortunately, this doctrine of Trotskyist origin has been relayed by certain Right-wing theoreticians, who favour Europe's cultural and geopolitical solidarity with the Third World (specifically the Arab-Muslim countries). Islamophilia and Third Worldism make in this way a cosy mélange for those Right publicists who know little of Islam and little of the Third World's socioeconomic realities — but who want to be politically fashionable (*bien pensant*), having still not recovered from their unavowed fascination with Marxism. It's exactly the opposite that needs to be defended: **far from being a potential ally, the Third World constitutes the worst possible danger to Europe.**

Now part of the dominant ideology, Third Worldism rests on the principle that industrialised countries once pillaged the Third World (as Leninist, Trotskyist, and Maoist schema explain), even though the

Third World now lives at the expense of European countries — which it financially exploits and colonises.
(see **autarky of great spaces; colonisation; economy, two-tier**)

Tradition, traditionalism

Tradition is the ensemble of a people's values and cultural structures, which are transmitted (*tradere* in Latin) from generation to generation — to form the scaffolding of its collective memory.

To destroy European traditions: this is the great enterprise of the regnant cosmopolitanism. It's as if European man were intrinsically guilty, tainted by original sin. Cultural Americanisation, Africanisation, or Arabisation, the effacement of the European's historical memory, Islamisation: Europe's deculturation is perpetuated by media onslaughts and by the public schools. This is why the struggle to maintain our traditions is integral to conserving our spiritual and genetic identity. **The essence of tradition is the ancestral heritage and its creative continuation.** Every heritage has to bear fruit.

At the same time it shouldn't be forgotten that **tradition is a translation.** To remain vital, tradition has to metamorphosise — changing its forms, while remaining true to its spirit. European culture — Faustian and Promethean — must balance its ancestral forms with the creation of new ones.

We need to defend tradition, as well as the notion of 'traditional society', but we refuse traditionalism. The latter appears whenever traditions die off, just as racism appears once a race declines. Traditionalism is the intellectualisation of tradition, as tradition ceases to be lived naturally or serve as an integral part of the living soul. It becomes folkloric, museological, a subject of scholarly study — in any case, something dead. Traditionalism is, paradoxically, foreign to the European tradition. The latter is metamorphic, always in the grip of innovation, always becoming, always in movement, appealing to what is greater.
(see **disinstallation; heritage; memory; people**)

Tragedy
The human condition is tragic because man alone, even when no danger threatens, remains conscious that he will eventually die.

'Nothing is ever acquired by man'. The tragic sensibility understands life as a hazardous, risk-filled journey, endlessly menaced by death, but at times illuminated by joy. The tragic shouldn't be confused with despair or pessimism. The man who kills himself is the victim of disappointed hope, that is, of a lie. The man of tragedy never kills himself from despair, his is a wilful death for the sake of something transcendent.

Salvation religions endeavour to conjure away death by a faith in the beyond and, against realism, cultivate the spirit of consolation. European civilisation has always been animated by the tragic spirit, because it never ceases taking risks, putting its life at peril in order to continue its historical unfolding. This attitude has been pushed too far, evident in the two World Wars — the two European civil wars — which initiated the Continent's effacement. The tragic spirit has been replaced with the presently dominant and senile 'spirit of indifference'.
(see **Promethean; sacred**)

U

Universalism
The belief that humanity forms a homogeneous ensemble, a single family, in which notions of people and identity are secondary.

An avatar of egalitarian ideology, universalism is a political monotheism, the parent of all totalitarianisms. The individual for it is but 'a citizen of the world'. All cultures are destined to fuse and no inequalities of nature or quality exist between them.

Universalism is the hypocritical weapon of the most diverse imperialisms, particularly those of Islam and Americanism, since it aims at imposing a single model — its model, supposedly, to federate all peoples — but actually in the interest of a single centre of power and interest. Humanity cannot conceive of itself — this will always be the case — except in terms of the organic juxtaposition of its particularisms — and not as a universalism encompassing and overarching (allegedly secondary) particularities.

(see **cosmopolitanism; globalisation, globalism**)

V

Values

Idea-forces and life rules that are translated into behaviours and transcend individual egoism, since they have no immediate utility, but constitute a long-term necessity for a community's survival.

Ideas have no legitimacy unless they correspond to values lived as practical engagements. Values depend not on fashions or technological progress or social avatars; they represent an unbreakable bond between generations — the basis for maintaining a people in history. **Many values translate the imperatives of biological survival into cultural terms.**

- Some of the fundamental values, for example, are:
- A refusal of massification, as well as a narcissistic individualism,
- An affirmation of the creative inequality of the human race,
- Concern for a people and its historical destiny,
- Loyalty to a lineage (ethnic consciousness),
- Individual freedom as self-discipline,

- The precedence of communal solidarity over egoism,
- Cult of the aesthetic,
- Respect for life's selectivity — and not 'all' life,
- The spirit of enterprise and creation…

There are values that concern the entirety of the human race, like global ecological responsibility in economic affairs. But we should be suspicious of 'values' expressed in abstract terms (altruism, love, respect for life, openness, etc.), for most of the time they hypocritically legitimise the very opposite.

The present dominant values (xenophilia, cosmopolitanism, narcissistic individualism, humanitarianism, bourgeois economism, hedonism, homophilia, permissiveness, etc.) are actually **anti-values** — values of a devirilising weakness, since they deplete a civilisation's vital energies and weaken its defensive or affirmative capacities. (see **tradition**)

W

West, Western civilisation

The planetary civilisation — prodigal son and bastard of Europe, today dominated by the American model — that aims at universalising the absolute primacy of market society and egalitarian individualism — one of whose consequences is to cause Europeans to forget their own destiny.

One ought not to confuse the West with Europe. **Western civilisation no longer retains any ethnic value, having become a cosmopolitan civilisation based on the American model.** Originating in Europe, Western civilisation has tragically turned against Europe, like a boomerang, imposing its universalism. It's thus necessary to **oppose European civilisation to Western civilisation.**

Western civilisation, which has become a world civilisation to the degree that it no longer occupies 'Western' territories, is characterised by **the absolute primacy it attributes to the economy** over every other consideration, as it speculatively pursues short-term profitability regardless of long-term ecological, ethnic, or social imperatives.

Such a civilisation is characteristically ignorant **of any notion of people or country.** It poses as a planetary 'society' that undermines and restricts every *sovereignty* and political will. Except one: the government of the American superpower, especially since the fall of Communism, endeavours to **pilot Western civilisation**, while Europe (despite her industrial and commercial power) is treated as a protectorate.

Western civilisation is the first civilisation in history not to be founded on some sort of spirituality — on transcendent, non-material values; even more than Communism, it has realised the dream of Marx and Trotsky in constructing a planetary cosmopolitan civilisation founded exclusively on materialistic and economic relations. In this sense, **the capitalism of Western civilisation, not Soviet Communism, most embodies the essence of Marxism.**

Situated between a hypocritical religion of human rights and a simulacra of 'democracy', Western civilisation neither supports principles of justice nor respects the existence of different peoples — instead, it strives to destroy their roots and equilibrium, and above all to give full reign to the forces of social barbarism.

*

It would be wrong to confuse Western civilisation with science and technology, as many traditionalists do. This civilisation instrumentalises techno-science, but the latter — let us repeat — is perfectly neutral and can serve any civilisational project.

Another error: to look sympathetically at Islam on the pretext that it opposes certain negative aspects of Western civilisation. To play this Islamic card against Western decadence — a frequent temptation inspired by the writings of René Guénon, Claudio Mutti,[143] and others — is to indulge the naïve illusions of scholars disconnected from all sense of the real, totally unable to see Islam's intrinsically totalitarian and globalist nature. It's only through their own values, though, that Europeans will regenerate themselves and get free from the maelstrom of Western civilisation — it won't occur by embracing **Islam, which since its birth has been Europe's avowed enemy.**

Today, at its height, Western civilisation is **ephemeral,** it won't make it to the Twenty-first century's end. It's like a Tower of Babel, internally corroded by its absolute materialism, its lack of critical spirit, and its ignorance of every long-term need.

(see **ideology: West; modernity; techno-science**)

Will to Power

The tendency of all healthy life to perpetuate itself — to assure its survival, its superiority, and its capacity for creation.

This Nietzschean concept has at times been misunderstood and abusively interpreted as 'a tyrannical desire for brutal domination'. Actually, it's a self-affirming will. The will to power is the vital urge to *become superior*, it's pride — the opposite of vanity or pretension — it's the acceptance of life as struggle, as an eternal combat for supremacy, it's the permanent incitement to self-perfection and self-improvement, it's the absolute refusal of all nihilism, it's the opposite of contemporary relativism.

---

143 Claudio Mutti (b. 1946) is an Italian writer and Evolian traditionalist. He is a convert to Islam (as Omar Amin) and was an early member of Giovane Europa (Young Europe), a nationalist group. In his work he has attempted to reconcile Evolian traditionalism, the Right, and Islam.

The will to power by no means implies crushing the weak, but rather protecting them. For it defies only the strong.

The will to power implies self-mastery and self-discipline, conditions necessary for an exterior affirmation. The danger of the will to power is in its very energy: it has to learn not to succumb to the stupor of its own hubris.

The will to power constitutes a spiritual horizon, because it accords with the essence of life itself. **It is the force of life and of history.** It's not simply about the struggle for domination, but also about survival and continuity. It's the core of the inegalitarian and imperial conception of the world. **A people or civilisation that abandons its will to power inevitably perishes, for what doesn't advance, retreats — what doesn't accept life as struggle hasn't long to live.**

X

Xenophilia

Etymologically: 'love of the stranger'.

A fascination with the 'Other' and a neglect of those who are 'Near' — xenophilia is one of the great collective psychopathologies of contemporary Europe. It comes from a perversion of the idea of charity, but it also comes from an absence of ethnic consciousness. It's evident in the contradictory ideology of 'anti-racism', which in fact is an inverted racial obsession. **What's called 'anti-racism' is but a pathological expression of xenophilia.**

Xenophilia systematically overestimates the value of the alien, which it sees as a victim, as it unconsciously devalues the 'Same'. It follows the principle that 'the stranger has everything to teach us' — it's avowedly contradictory since it associates differentialism and universalism, the identity of the Other and miscegenation, advocating everyone's 'right to difference', but at the same time the homogenisation of the human race. **Xenophilia is the counterpart of ethnomasochism.**

A rejection of xenophilia doesn't necessarily lead to xenophobia, which is just as paralysing, but also to an affirmation of one's self and one's people — that is, **ethnocentrism.**

(see **consciousness, ethnic; ethnocentrism; ethnomasochism**)

5

CONCLUSION

Why Are We Fighting?

Why are we fighting?
Before answering this central question, perhaps it's worth saying at first who this 'we' is. Perhaps it's 'you', despite the superficial labels identifying you with one of the various parties or sects that the present tragedy will not hesitate to sweep away? 'You' — despite the misunderstandings that divide us — who intuitively senses the mortal dangers threatening France and Europe? **'You' — coming from every horizon and having become conscious of the biological, ethical, political, and spiritual decline of European civilisation and the nations comprising it** — who has joined the resistance?

In this respect — and also in defining who 'we' are — it's necessary to repeat that agnostics, pagans, and authentic Catholic or Orthodox Christians must demote their secondary philosophical differences, carry out **a return to the real,** and learn how to align themselves against the common enemy, who everyone well knows.

Another preliminary question: for whom do we fight? It's not for a sect, a party, a denomination (except, if at all, in a provisional and temporary way) that we fight. It's not for petty personal ambitions or intellectual vanity. We're fighting not for the Right or the Left or the

Centre — not for socialism or liberalism. These are only instruments, they don't represent the essential.

We're no longer fighting for other peoples. Both because we lack the means to do so, but also because every people, in its history, faces its destiny alone — it doesn't need us to defend its identity.

* * *

We have to beware of false struggles. And here, there are two possible deviations:

The first is **intellectualist**: in the name of 'metapolitical and cultural struggle', one allies with purely abstract ideas for the sake of defending theoretical cliques and promoting the vanity of certain authors of limited audience, authors without links to the real and without any means of translating their ideas into a possible political or revolutionary project. This sort of deviation ends up, objectively speaking, rallying to the hegemonic ideology. Hence: the ensuing marginalisation, neutralisation, and collaboration.

The second deviation is that of the **politician** (a term to be distinguished, absolutely, from the term 'political'): under the pretext of struggling for a certain social project, one makes a career out of it, in the government or a party, just as one might make a career in business. Positions accordingly soften, short-term tactics impinge on long-term strategies, militants are duped, the ideological baggage gets lighter and finally disappears or is converted into electoral propaganda that is never expected to be applied. Don't think this means that political action is obsolete or useless. It's an indispensable offshoot of what needs doing. Political struggle, though, has to be founded both on an ideological formation (the means) and on a disinterested ideal (the goal). Whenever notions of money or social vanity intervene, the revolutionary will is inevitably overwhelmed by the system.

Simply put: one doesn't fight for a sect or an organisation — not for position or a career — but to establish a situation and carry out a tangible historical undertaking.

*

A similarly ambiguous and dangerous formula is to proclaim: 'I fight for my ideas'. No! **One doesn't fight for 'ideas', one fights for a people — ideas are only the struggle's instruments, not its goal.** A conception-of-the-world has to be incarnated in the real, as an expression of a historical will, and not as an exposition of a savant's 'ideas', which almost always remain dead letters. The profession of ideas is important, but under certain essential conditions:

1. These ideas may one day be realised in history, and thus as facts; they ought, then, to have the possibility of being realised and becoming a mobilising power.

2. These ideas ought not to be limited to critical descriptions of the actual state of things (this is the failing of 'hyper-criticism'), but extended to construct new doctrines and affirm a positive project. To struggle 'against' is necessary, but insufficient. What's necessary above all is struggle 'for' a new world. In an age of conformity and one-track thought, when there are no serious counter-propositions to the established order, **we must retain a monopoly on revolutionary ideas.**

3. One should never succumb to a 'petty realism' nor limit oneself to the politicians' lowest common denominator; it's necessary to go to the crux of the problem; and not because ideas unrealisable today will become so tomorrow. In this sense, historically-pregnant ideas demand an ambitious, visionary approach, indifferent to fashion and the apparent impossibility of their immediate application (see, for example, the notion of Reconquest).

4. It's important to extend the field of ideas to include 'non-theoretical ideas', that is, myths, artistic and aesthetic creations, everything that electrifies the imagination.

To sum up: **one doesn't fight for ideas, but, among other things, one fights with ideas.** Conversely: one well and truly fights the enemy's ideas. **One fights at the same time to maintain a certain number of key values in the people — values indispensable to its survival.**

* * *

We struggle not only 'against', but above all 'for'. Political, metapolitical, and cultural action — this antechamber of war — presupposes, to be sure, a designation of the enemy (of a hostile and negative energy), but it also presupposes a designation of the friend — *for whom and with whom* the struggle is waged. Similarly, it's not a matter of limiting oneself to negativism or being content with denouncing and criticising hostile ideas and values — it's just as necessary, as a counterpoint, to affirm positive ideas and values — understood as an alternative and a future.

We fight for Europe. We fight for a Europe infused with ideas of **identity** and **continuity**, of **independence** and **power** — this Europe that is an ensemble of ethnically related peoples. We fight, as well, not just for the Europeans of today, but also for those of tomorrow. We fight for the union and defensive mobilisation of all peoples of European origin, in our native lands, from the Atlantic to the Pacific — for the sake of an **ethnocentric Eurosiberia** — a bloc formed against the common enemy, which implies, of course, no rejection at all of French, German, Russian, Italian, Spanish, Flemish, etc., traditions.

We fight with a sense of urgency, to stop the invasion and to reverse Europe's biocultural destruction (in the form of Islamic colonisation and American domination). It's thus a matter of first putting out the fire. **Questions as to whether it will be a Europe of nations or a federal Europe of regions are secondary ones — to be resolved once the fire is extinguished, once the invaders have been thrown back.** The important thing to realise is that a Europe completely Islamised, Third-Worldised, and Americanised will be neither a federation nor an association of nations, it will no longer be anything European. We fight thus in knowing that the struggle of French or German or other nationalists — or regionalists — is irrelevant and suicidal, because from Brest to Vladivostok, we are, whether we like it or not, brother-peoples, and it's vital that we maintain the same solidarity between us that Muslim peoples maintain among themselves (despite their great internal differences). The enemy here provides, perhaps, an example to follow … The essential is not to struggle solely for isolated micro-nationalisms, each of which lacks the stature necessary to confront the tragic challenges of the coming century.

To criticise the immense failings, connivances, and corruptions of the present European Union is no cause to turn away from the European idea, away from the idea of Great Europe, the sole tangible, realisable ideal — the sole line of defence against an enemy who can assume multiple forms. That Europeans should remain internally divided: that's the strategy of the Pentagon and the Muslim states (which have already launched their countless masses in an assault against the Continent).

To fight for Europe's survival and regeneration will also entail refusing to cooperate with French 'sovereigntists' defending a cosmopolitan and Jacobin vision of France (in the universalist tradition of the Revolution) — just as it will entail refusing to cooperate with Left-wing regionalists rejecting the region's ethnic dimension.

Though European peoples are today besieged internationally and subverted domestically, nothing yet is lost — as long as there emerges — however haltingly, but powerfully — a **Great-European ethnic consciousness,** which could come about with the help of a few catastrophic storms to clear the way.

*

We fight for a vision of the world that is both traditional and Faustian, that allies enrootment and disinstallation, the citizen's freedom and imperial service to the community-as-a-people, passionate creativity and critical reason, an unshakable loyalty and an adventurous curiosity.

We fight for social justice, for the systematic establishment of European preferences in every domain, for Eurosiberian economic autarky, but also for free enterprise and for the conservation of the Continent's ecosystem.

We fight for the principle of *libre examen*[1] and for freedom of thought — for popular and aristocratic values of honour, virility, and power.

We fight not for ourselves alone, the living, or for our economic welfare, but above all for the **heritage of our ancestors and the future of our descendents**.

We fight for a cultural, spiritual rebirth, for a return to the real, to vitality. We fight to re-animate our ancestral virtues — we fight for Achilles,[2] Pericles,[3] and Romulus,[4] for Charles the Hammer and Francis of Assisi[5] — for the cathedral builders and the rocket scientists.

We fight for the continuity of that European civilisation (of which America is nothing but the prodigal child) that is tragic, because of its tendency to self-destruction and self-doubt, but at the same time because of its superiority over all the other civilisations in history. We fight thus in a spirit whose essence is *ethnocentric* — in a spirit that breaks with all that is presently leading Europe toward suicide.

As implied in all of the above, we fight to produce a shearing historical metamorphosis — to bring about the Fourth Age of European civilisation.

---

1   French: 'free inquiry'.
2   According to Greek mythology, Achilles was one of the Greek heroes of the Trojan War. The *Iliad* is largely about his exploits.
3   Pericles (c. 495–429 BCE) governed Athens during its 'Golden Age' between the Persian and Peloponnesian Wars, when Athens made many of its greatest achievements. He also introduced many democratic reforms.
4   Romulus and his brother Remus were the founders of Rome.
5   Saint Francis of Assisi (1181–1226) was the founder of the Franciscan Order of the Church.

*

And now: what is to be done? To respond, it's necessary to address a second key question: **how to fight?** It would be vain and pretentious to give a definitive answer — since history, by definition, is the field of the unforeseen. Only the general axes of our struggle are imaginable. First off, we need to reject those petty, presumptuous masters — whose professed convictions will never be paid for with their lives, their security, or their comfort, though they think they have the definitive answer to this most difficult question. The 'why', in any case, is always easier to formulate than the 'how'. The 'how', though, is crucial, for it presumes both a prescience of the history to come and a profound understanding of past errors and successes.

Let us start by answering the question in the spirit of that celebrated, laconic, and very pragmatic English proverb: 'That every man will do his duty'.

The first imperative is thus to think of oneself as being in **a state of dissidence — in resistance — against the entire system.** Hence, the necessity of seriously constructing a real counter-society, an embryo of the coming society. This is not to be done in a marginalising and extremist spirit (which only serves the enemy), but rather with efficacy and cunning, according to the precept of 'being in the world but not of it'.[6]

This struggle, moreover, is no desperate counter-current, since world events give us cause to believe that the situation is heading toward a great crisis — toward a chaos from which history will be reborn.

The second imperative is one of radical thought: to refuse to save an unsavable system, as conservatives vainly endeavour to do, and instead take a revolutionary stance oriented to the **post-chaos.**

---

6 This expression originates from *John* 17:15–16, where Jesus says 'My prayer is not that you take them out of the world but that you protect them from the evil one. They are not of the world, even as I am not of it.'

The third imperative is **to prefer a tactic of supple networks of solidarity to one of monolithic, faction-ridden sects.**

The essential thing is to act and to coordinate at a subterranean level. Everything is good, if it is well done and thought out. The circle, the party, the individual, the association, the enterprise, etc., have their place in this network — on the condition that they're organised at the Continental level and that personal or ideological differences don't undermine the common front against the enemy. **For it's never the system's censorship or repression that hinders the efficacy of a revolutionary movement, but rather the movement's internal dissensions and rivalries.** The main thing is knowing who is our friend and who is our enemy. In this sense, we might take Islam as a model, for from the beginning of its *jihad* against Europe it has known how to unite despite its grave internal divisions. Petty passions must give way to great passions.

The fourth imperative is not to abandon the political terrain, but to struggle, each in his own place, according to a **multi-form strategy** that addresses the different political, cultural, and metapolitical arenas of European life. There's no need to quit a political party if it's helpful to the cause, even if it's not one hundred percent in accord with our struggle. Even in the present situation, an objectively revolutionary, dissident party would have an agitprop (agitation-propaganda) capability independent of its electoral objectives and prospects. With such a polyvalent strategy, every combatant will have his speciality and his place; for certain militants it will be appropriate to adopt the maxim *larvatus prodeo* ('I go forth masked'), while others will openly advance toward the Great Day.

Fifth imperative: **in the long term, the birth of a revolutionary European-identitarian party is indispensable. It needs to be prepared.** Politics remains the indispensable horizon of action. And metapolitics, like all intellectual and cultural strategies, constitutes but one basis for what will be a political act — as long as politics here is not reduced to the activity of politicians, and metapolitical discourse doesn't deviate into a form of intellectual verbiage or pseudo-philosophical masturbation.

*

To sum up: **it's necessary that everyone does his duty and works in his place — devotes himself to constructing a body of fundamental values — against the common enemy — in a network of active, supple, interdependent, and confederated resistance — present on every front, at the level of Europe — with the aim of concentrating all the energies of the combatants.**

The latter are innumerable ... and more powerful than people realise. Many have yet to mobilise and regroup because they're still too closely tied to sectarian spirits and the defeatist logic of the ghetto. The system's present grave crisis, if properly used, can, however, multiply the vitalist forces in every recess of the European nation. For the future is full of both hope and tragedy. Hope because all the facts, and the general course of developments, are occurring in ways that validate our analysis and that, even if there's no reaction yet, more and more people share the analyses, values, and objectives presented here. It's tragic because we have to await the escalation of perils, persecutions — war.

*

Nothing is lost. It's completely inappropriate to see ourselves, in the nostalgia of despair, as a rearguard, a last outpost, that struggles with panache for a lost cause. No, we have to see ourselves as **the vanguard of the resistance,** whose lucid spirit exudes a certain optimism. But let there be no illusion. Victory won't be won through peaceful bourgeois reform or through the vaticinations of an aesthetic and 'literary' libertinism. We have to prepare ourselves for the coming tempest, to harden ourselves — for the sake of attacking, like a cobra, quickly and decisively, once the moment of opportunity strikes. In anticipating this moment, we need now to start arming ourselves — mentally and physically — we need to recruit, to proselytise, to educate, to organise in networks of solidarity and action. It's simple: let's model ourselves on our enemy.

*

And then, to speak symbolically and in a manner deliberately sibylline, what we strive to restore and re-animate will never come from the promises of middle class politicians, but will come instead from the spirit of the last Delphic prophecy,[7] which foresaw that, 'One day Apollo will return and it will be forever'.

---

7   The Oracle of Delphi, known as the Pythia, was the priestess at the Temple of Apollo in the city of Delphi in ancient Greece. The oracle made prophecies between the Eighth century BCE and 393 AD, when the Roman Emperor, in the wake of the Empire's conversion to Christianity, closed it along with all other pagan temples. The Oracle features in many ancient Greek and Roman texts.

INDEX

A

Aesthetics 14, 55–57, 103, 188–195
Alien vii–xv, 17, 57–64, 76–78, 92–103, 115, 128–143, 156–179, 202–238, 259
Americanism, anti-Americanism, philo-Americanism, the American-sphere, Americomorphosis 5, 58–60, 171, 255
Anti-Racism 14–19, 60–61, 79–85, 138–154, 178–187 200, 218–236, 252–259
Archeofuturism ix–xiii, 25, 61–62, 114–126, 152, 181–191, 210, 250
Aristocracy, new aristocracy ii, 62–76, 99–100, 116–117, 150, 184, 212, 242
Assimilation, assimilationism 15, 63–64, 79–80, 141, 203, 237–238
Autarky of Great Spaces 29, 64–66, 111–113, 125, 176, 235, 253

B

Belief in Miracles 40, 67–68, 165
Biopolitics 69, 109, 126, 176, 214
Born Leader 70–71, 100, 146, 212, 246–249
Bourgeoisism 72, 108, 153, 240

C

Chaos, Ethnic 73–91, 110–120, 157–170, 184–188, 212, 227, 241, 257
Chaos, post-Chaos 13, 73–74
Circulation of Elites 63, 75–76, 117, 148, 184, 241

Civil War, Ethnic 15, 50–51, 74–90, 220, 249
Colonisation ix–xv, 6–29, 45–58, 73–107, 124–138, 156–186, 215–234, 252–264
Communitarianism 15–19, 64–80, 232
Community, Community-of-a-people xv, xxvii, 12, 26–28, 65–82, 95, 117–132, 145, 166–167, 181–241, 255–265
Competition, struggle for life 23, 59–60, 75–83, 120–122, 141, 167–175, 240–241
Conception-of-the-World 55, 84, 163, 185, 263
Consciousness, Ethnic 14, 72, 85, 210, 232, 255, 259, 265
Consciousness, Historical 86, 196
Consumerism xiv–xxi, 12–14, 86–87, 123, 141, 179, 194–195, 243
Convergence of Catastrophes ix–xvii, 13, 25, 69–87, 109–110, 129, 188–196, 221, 235
Cosmopolitanism 14–26, 89–94, 120–124, 139, 157, 191–205, 228, 253–256
Cultural Struggle 91–92, 262
Culture, Civilisation xii–xxviii, 1–24, 48–106, 118–171, 185–214, 235–253

D

Decadence xxiii–xxv, 94–95, 114, 151–154, 170–208, 235, 258

Deculturation xxvi, 12–14, 27, 59, 94–96, 180, 194–195, 208, 253
Democracy, democratism, organic democracy xxi, 6, 21–22, 39, 62–100, 123–134, 156, 175–190, 212–217, 237–244, 257
Designation of the 'Enemy' and the 'Friend', 'enemy' and 'adversary' 100–102
Destiny, becoming xiii–xxv, 13–14, 26, 57, 70–103, 117–127, 140–152, 172–181, 201–214, 229–262
Devirilisation 1–14, 95–108, 154, 170, 249
Discipline 55, 75–81, 104–105, 117–118, 176–179, 191–197, 216, 255–259
Disinstallation 106, 121, 253, 265
Domestication 93, 106–108, 141, 153, 166, 194

E

Ecology, ecologism, ecological productivism 66, 108–110, 123, 176, 214–215
Economism 72, 86–87, 110–111, 153, 213–220, 256
Economy, Organic 111–113
Economy, Two-Tier 113–114
Egalitarianism 26, 75–81, 114–123, 146–185, 200–211, 238–242
Elite, elitism 23, 42, 63–72, 116–117, 150, 184–185, 197, 211–212
Empire, imperial federation 117–129
End of History xvii–xviii, 39, 119–120, 150–152, 221
Enrootment 96–106, 120–121, 134–144, 156–174, 219–231, 265
Ethnocentrism 19, 60, 92, 121–122, 161–163, 205, 236–239, 260
Ethnocracy xxix, 123–134
Ethnomasochism xxii, 2–12, 79–104, 123–124, 159, 172–183, 198, 219–227, 260
Ethnosphere, ethnic blocs 85, 124, 163, 188

Eugenics 69, 123–134, 226
Europe 127
Eurosiberia 29, 45–53, 66, 119–137, 160–174, 193, 209, 231–235, 248–251, 264

F

Fatherland, Great Fatherland, native land 2, 127–134, 163–174, 204–213, 231

G

Genopolitics xxix, 123–134
Geopolitics 34, 100, 135–136, 174
Germen xxviii, 11–17, 34, 69–73, 93–94, 137–154, 186
Globalisation, globalism vii, 5, 38–40, 65, 112–139, 163–174, 190, 208, 228, 255
Grand Politics 14, 57, 139–140, 185, 213–215, 243–244

H

Happiness, 'small pleasures' 110, 140, 164, 188–196, 213–220
Heredity 63, 93, 125, 141–144, 226
Heritage viii–xxvii, 14–18, 53, 80–92, 120, 138–144, 157–172, 204–210, 230–253, 266
Heroes 144–146, 266
Heterotelia 146–147
Hierarchy 115, 147–157, 178–186, 202–203, 241–242
History, conceptions of history vii–xxviii, 1–267
Homo Oeconomicus xxi, 134, 152–153
Homophilia 6–14, 103–104, 124, 153–154, 200, 238, 256
Humanism, superhumanism 14, 96, 156–158, 235
Humanitarianism xxii, 72, 93, 141–159, 194–202, 231, 256
Human Rights, human rightism xviii, 26, 93, 135, 154–172, 257

I

Idea, ideal, historic idealism xxiv, 4–82, 99–141, 157–265

Identity xi–xxvi, 2–34, 47–73, 85–103, 120–264
Ideology, hegemonic ideology, Western ideology, European ideology viii–x, 2–26, 55–70, 82–194, 206–235, 249–262
Immigration xxii, 15–47, 60–98, 133, 152, 165–183, 200–230
Individualism xxii, 12–14, 71–116, 141, 164–167, 180, 201, 219, 255–256
Inegalitarianism 75, 167–168
Interregnum xviii, 12, 74, 90, 168–169, 191
Involution 169–170, 194–195

J
Judaeo-Christianity 84, 114, 150, 170–171, 200–204

L
Land, territory 173–174
Legitimation (positive or negative) 174
Liberalism, managerial liberalism x–xix, 5, 22–23, 39–40, 66, 100–105, 159, 175–176, 202, 244, 262
Liberty, liberties 13–24, 147–179, 197, 252

M
Mass, massification xxii, 15–27, 42–43, 59–73, 86–98, 133–158, 175–216
Memory, collective memory ii, xxvii, 17, 73, 91–100, 120, 138–147, 161–181, 194–197, 210–228, 253
Mental AIDS 181–183
Mercantilism xxi, 123–134, 183–188, 244
Meritocracy 76, 99–100, 117, 148–150, 184, 242
Metapolitics xi–xii, 184–235, 268
Miscegenation xiv, xxvii, 91, 103, 143, 185–187, 226, 259
Modernity, modernism xiii, 7–12, 24–28, 58–61, 89–90, 150, 165–171, 188–192, 220–221, 234, 258
Museologicalisation 191

N
Nation, nationalism, new nationalism vii–ix, xxvii, 18–29, 47–57, 81, 99, 117–144, 181–193, 205–213, 228–248, 269
Neo-primitivism 14, 57, 92–96, 143, 169–180, 194
Nihilism 81, 194–199, 258

O
Order vii–xxvi, 1–11, 27–56, 74–112, 127–138, 150–156, 168–183, 196–201, 214–266

P
Paganism 7–9, 84, 145, 171–173, 189–204, 237–240
People, Long-Living; short-living people 210–211
Personality, Creative 211–212
Philia 73, 85, 197, 212, 239
Politics, Grand Politics xi–xii, 9–14, 32, 57–71, 101, 135–140, 152, 185, 213–215, 237–248, 268
Populism xii, 68, 100, 209–216
Preference, European; national preference, alien preference 103, 159, 217–219
Presentism 164, 180, 219–220
Progress, progressivism 188, 220–221
Promethean 106, 125, 158, 221, 249–254

R
Race, racism, anti-racism xxviii, 16–28, 108–161, 179–204, 219–227, 253–260
Region, regionalism 45, 111–121, 155, 193, 206–209, 228–233, 265
Resistance and Reconquest 2–4, 77–80, 160, 231–233
Revolution xvi–xvii, 17–38, 64–75, 121–155, 177–185, 206–212, 230–235, 250, 265
Right to Difference 235–239, 259

S
Sacred xi, 7, 72, 95, 171, 195–201, 239–254

Selection xxi, 63, 75–84, 99–100, 116–125, 143–150, 170–184, 209, 240–242
Society, Market xii–xxiii, 5, 20–196, 211–267
Sovereignty, the sovereign function, tri-functionality, bi-functionality x–xi, 9, 25–26, 51–58, 100, 117–139, 164, 212–215, 230–257
State, nation-state, statism xvi–xxi, 4, 17–28, 42–47, 71–82, 98–131, 157, 173–197, 214–249, 263–267
State of Emergency xvi, 4, 71–77, 157, 248–249

T

Techno-science 38, 61–69, 126, 158, 191, 243–258
Third Worldism 250–252
Tradition, traditionalism xi–xxiv, 47–55, 85–102, 121–128, 143–158, 171–222, 242–265
Tragedy 2–9, 30, 76–78, 133–140, 158–168, 196, 222–231, 254–269

U

Universalism xxi–xxii, 24–28, 85–91, 118–139, 161, 202–205, 254–259

V

Values xi–xxvii, 4–24, 43, 56–105, 121–129, 144, 156–167, 181–213, 234–239, 253–269

W

West, Western civilisation xviii, 12–28, 45–53, 82–94, 115, 130–139, 152–162, 198–207, 227, 247–258
Will to Power xxi, 4–17, 55, 102, 121, 152–159, 201, 250–259

X

Xenophilia xxii, 7–19, 61, 102–104, 124, 154–159, 177–183, 219–227, 256–260

OTHER BOOKS PUBLISHED BY ARKTOS

Virginia Abernethy	Born Abroad
Sri Dharma Pravartaka Acharya	The Dharma Manifesto
Joakim Andersen	Rising from the Ruins
Winston C. Banks	Excessive Immigration
Stephen Baskerville	Who Lost America?
Alfred Baeumler	Nietzsche: Philosopher and Politician
Alain de Benoist	Beyond Human Rights
	Carl Schmitt Today
	The Ideology of Sameness
	The Indo-Europeans
	Manifesto for a European Renaissance
	On the Brink of the Abyss
	The Problem of Democracy
	Runes and the Origins of Writing
	View from the Right (vol. 1–3)
Armand Berger	Tolkien, Europe, and Tradition
Arthur Moeller van den Bruck	Germany's Third Empire
Matt Battaglioli	The Consequences of Equality
Kerry Bolton	The Perversion of Normality
	Revolution from Above
	Yockey: A Fascist Odyssey
Isac Boman	Money Power
Charles William Dailey	The Serpent Symbol in Tradition
Ricardo Duchesne	Faustian Man in a Multicultural Age
Alexander Dugin	Ethnos and Society
	Ethnosociology
	Eurasian Mission
	The Fourth Political Theory
	The Great Awakening vs the Great Reset
	Last War of the World-Island
	Politica Aeterna
	Political Platonism
	Putin vs Putin
	The Rise of the Fourth Political Theory
	The Trump Revolution
	Templars of the Proletariat
	The Theory of a Multipolar World
Daria Dugina	A Theory of Europe
Edward Dutton	Race Differences in Ethnocentrism
Mark Dyal	Hated and Proud
Clare Ellis	The Blackening of Europe
Koenraad Elst	Return of the Swastika
Julius Evola	The Bow and the Club
	Fascism Viewed from the Right
	A Handbook for Right-Wing Youth
	Metaphysics of Power
	Metaphysics of War
	The Myth of the Blood

OTHER BOOKS PUBLISHED BY ARKTOS

	Notes on the Third Reich
	Pagan Imperialism
	Recognitions
	A Traditionalist Confronts Fascism
GUILLAUME FAYE	*Archeofuturism*
	Archeofuturism 2.0
	The Colonisation of Europe
	Convergence of Catastrophes
	Ethnic Apocalypse
	A Global Coup
	Prelude to War
	Sex and Deviance
	Understanding Islam
	Why We Fight
DANIEL S. FORREST	*Suprahumanism*
ANDREW FRASER	*Dissident Dispatches*
	Reinventing Aristocracy in the Age of Woke Capital
	The WASP Question
GÉNÉRATION IDENTITAIRE	*We are Generation Identity*
PETER GOODCHILD	*The Taxi Driver from Baghdad*
	The Western Path
PAUL GOTTFRIED	*War and Democracy*
PETR HAMPL	*Breached Enclosure*
PORUS HOMI HAVEWALA	*The Saga of the Aryan Race*
CONSTANTIN VON HOFFMEISTER	*Esoteric Trumpism*
	MULTIPOLARITY!
RICHARD HOUCK	*Liberalism Unmasked*
A. J. ILLINGWORTH	*Political Justice*
INSTITUT ILIADE	*For a European Awakening*
	Guardians of Heritage
ALEXANDER JACOB	*De Naturae Natura*
JASON REZA JORJANI	*Artemis Unveiled*
	Closer Encounters
	Erosophia
	Faustian Futurist
	Iranian Leviathan
	Lovers of Sophia
	Metapolemos
	Novel Folklore
	Philosophy of the Future
	Prometheism
	Promethean Pirate
	Prometheus and Atlas
	Psychotron
	Uber Man
	World State of Emergency
HENRIK JONASSON	*Sigmund*
EDGAR JULIUS JUNG	*The Significance of the German Revolution*

OTHER BOOKS PUBLISHED BY ARKTOS

Ruuben Kaalep & August Meister	Rebirth of Europe
Roderick Kaine	Smart and SeXy
James Kirkpatrick	Conservatism Inc.
Ludwig Klages	The Biocentric Worldview
	Cosmogonic Reflections
	The Science of Character
Andrew Korybko	Hybrid War
Pierre Krebs	Guillaume Faye: Truths & Tributes
	Fighting for the Essence
Julien Langella	Catholic and Identitarian
John Bruce Leonard	The New Prometheans
Diana Panchenko	The Inevitable
Stephen Pax Leonard	The Ideology of Failure
	Travels in Cultural Nihilism
William S. Lind	Reforging Excalibur
	Retroculture
Pentti Linkola	Can Life Prevail?
Giorgio Locchi	Definitions
H. P. Lovecraft	The Conservative
Norman Lowell	Imperium Europa
Richard Lynn	Sex Differences in Intelligence
	A Tribute to Helmut Nyborg (ed.)
John MacLugash	The Return of the Solar King
Charles Maurras	The Future of the Intelligentsia &
	For a French Awakening
John Harmon McElroy	Agitprop in America
Michael O'Meara	Guillaume Faye and the Battle of Europe
	New Culture, New Right
Michael Millerman	Beginning with Heidegger
Dmitry Moiseev	The Philosophy of Italian Fascism
Maurice Muret	The Greatness of Elites
Brian Anse Patrick	The NRA and the Media
	Rise of the Anti-Media
	The Ten Commandments of Propaganda
	Zombology
Tito Perdue	The Bent Pyramid
	Journey to a Location
	Lee
	Morning Crafts
	Philip
	The Sweet-Scented Manuscript
	William's House (vol. 1–4)
John K. Press	The True West vs the Zombie Apocalypse
Raido	A Handbook of Traditional Living (vol. 1–2)
P R Reddall	Towards Awakening
Claire Rae Randall	The War on Gender

OTHER BOOKS PUBLISHED BY ARKTOS

STEVEN J. ROSEN	*The Agni and the Ecstasy*
	The Jedi in the Lotus
NICHOLAS ROONEY	*Talking to the Wolf*
RICHARD RUDGLEY	*Barbarians*
	Essential Substances
	Wildest Dreams
ERNST VON SALOMON	*It Cannot Be Stormed*
	The Outlaws
WERNER SOMBART	*Traders and Heroes*
PIERO SAN GIORGIO	*Giuseppe*
	Survive the Economic Collapse
	Surviving the Next Catastrophe
SRI SRI RAVI SHANKAR	*Celebrating Silence*
	Know Your Child
	Management Mantras
	Patanjali Yoga Sutras
	Secrets of Relationships
GEORGE T. SHAW (ED.)	*A Fair Hearing*
FENEK SOLÈRE	*Kraal*
	Reconquista
OSWALD SPENGLER	*The Decline of the West*
	Man and Technics
RICHARD STOREY	*The Uniqueness of Western Law*
TOMISLAV SUNIC	*Against Democracy and Equality*
	Homo Americanus
	Postmortem Report
	Titans are in Town
ASKR SVARTE	*Gods in the Abyss*
HANS-JÜRGEN SYBERBERG	*On the Fortunes and Misfortunes of Art in Post-War Germany*
ABIR TAHA	*Defining Terrorism*
	The Epic of Arya (2nd ed.)
	Nietzsche is Coming God, or the Redemption of the Divine
	Verses of Light
JEAN THIRIART	*Europe: An Empire of 400 Million*
BAL GANGADHAR TILAK	*The Arctic Home in the Vedas*
DOMINIQUE VENNER	*Ernst Jünger: A Different European Destiny*
	For a Positive Critique
	The Shock of History
HANS VOGEL	*How Europe Became American*
MARKUS WILLINGER	*A Europe of Nations*
	Generation Identity
ALEXANDER WOLFHEZE	*Alba Rosa*
	Globus Horribilis
	Rupes Nigra

www.ingramcontent.com/pod-product-compliance
Lightning Source LLC
Chambersburg PA
CBHW032018230426
43671CB00005B/132